ECONOMICS IN THE LONG VIEW

Volume 1 Models and Methodology

Other volumes of this work

Volume 2 Applications and Cases, Part I
Volume 3 Applications and Cases, Part II

ECONOMICS IN THE LONG VIEW

Essays in Honour of W. W. Rostow

Volume 1 MODELS AND METHODOLOGY

Edited by
Charles P. Kindleberger
and
Guido di Tella

New York University Press · New York *and* London · 1982

First published in the United States 1982 by
New York University Press
Washington Square
New York, NY 10003

Library of Congress Cataloging in Publication Data

Main entry under title:

Economics in the long view.

Bibliography: v. 3, p.
Includes index.
Contents: v. 1. Models and methodology—v. 2–3. Applications and cases.
1. Economic history—Addresses, essays, lectures. 2. Economic development—Addresses, essays, lectures. 3. Rostow, W. W. (Walt Whitman), 1916– . I. Rostow, W. W. (Walt Whitman), 1916– . II. Kindleberger, Charles Poor, 1910– . III. Di Tella, Guido, 1931–
HC51.E27 1982 330 81-22440
ISBN 0-8147-4579-2 (v. 1)
0-8147-4580-6 (v. 2)
0-8147-4581-4 (v. 3)
0-8147-4582-2 (set) AACR2

Printed in Hong Kong

Contents

VOLUME 1 MODELS AND METHODOLOGY

VOLUME 2 APPLICATIONS AND CASES, PART I

VOLUME 3 APPLICATIONS AND CASES, PART II

Note on the Editors

Charles P. Kindleberger taught at the Massachusetts Institute of Technology from 1948 to 1980, retiring as Ford International Professor of Economics Emeritus; Fellow at the Center for Advanced Study in Behavioral Sciences at Stanford, California. His latest book is *International Money*.

Guido di Tella, Associate Fellow, St Antony's College, Oxford; Professor of Economics, Catholic University, Buenos Aires. Author of, among other books, *Etapas del Desarrollo Económico Argentino* and *Argentina under Perón, 1973–76*.

List of the Contributors

T. C. Barker, Professor of Economic History, University of London.

Sir Alec Cairncross, formerly Master of St Peter's College, University of Oxford.

R. Cameron, William Rand Kenan University Professor of Economics, Emory University.

S. G. Checkland, Professor of Economic History, University of Glasgow; Visiting Fellow, Australian National University, Canberra.

R. Cortés Conde, Senior Research Fellow, Centre for Economic Research, and President of the Instituto Torcuato di Tella, Buenos Aires.

F. Crouzet, Professor of History, University of Paris–Sorbonne.

E. Dahmén, Professor of Economics and Economic and Social History, Stockholm School of Economics.

C. H. Feinstein, Professor of Economic and Social History, University of York.

R. Findlay, Ragnar Nurkse Professor of Economics, Columbia University, New York.

W. P. Glade, Director, Institute of Latin American Studies and Professor of Economics, University of Texas at Austin.

R. Hall (Lord Roberthall), formerly Economic Adviser to HM Government, United Kingdom.

R. M. Hartwell, Fellow of Nuffield College, University of Oxford.

D. Kendrick, Professor of Economics, University of Texas at Austin.

D. S. Landes, Robert Walton Goelet Professor of French History, Harvard University.

W. A. Lewis, James Madison Professor of Political Economy, Princeton University.

J. Marczewski, Honorary Professor, University of Paris I Panthéon-Sorbonne.

R. M. Marshall, Professor of Economics, University of Texas at Austin, and Secretary of Labour, US Government, 1976–81.

E. S. Mason, University Professor, Emeritus, Harvard University.

R. C. O. Matthews, Master of Clare College and Professor of Political Economy, University of Cambridge.

D. C. North, Professor of Economics, University of Washington.

J. C. Odling-Smee, Senior Economist, International Monetary Fund.

R. de Oliveira Campos, Ambassador of Brazil in the United Kingdom.

W. N. Parker, Professor of Economics, Yale University.

Sir Michael Postan, sometime Professor of Economic History, University of Cambridge.

C. W. Reynolds, Professor of Economics, Food Research Institute, Stanford University.

Sir Austin Robinson, Professor of Economics, Emeritus, University of Cambridge.

S. B. Saul, Vice-Chancellor, University of York.

P. Temin, Professor of Economics, Massachusetts Institute of Technology.

G. N. von Tunzelmann, Lecturer in Economic History, University of Cambridge and Fellow of St John's College, Cambridge.

Preface

This collection of essays in economic history is intended to honour W. W. Rostow for his outstanding contribution to this discipline over more than forty years. The editors are a former colleague in the Office of Strategic Services, the Department of State, the Massachusetts Institute of Technology and, for one term, at the University of Texas at Austin: Charles P. Kindleberger; and Guido di Tella, a former student of Rostow's at MIT who wrote his first book under his aegis.

Most leading economic historians have come across Rostow's imaginative ideas and opinions, and quite significantly have considered it necessary to come into the discussion, either to support, complement or contradict them. Few have been able to ignore them. As the chapters in the three volumes will show, the contributors from all over the world do not necessarily agree with Professor Rostow's views on economic history, or for that matter on anything else, as they pay tribute to his originality, significance and productivity which have stimulated enormously the historiography on business cycles, economic growth and long-term trends.

This compilation is divided, roughly and arbitrarily, into a first volume on Models and Methodology, and another two on Applications and Cases. A chronological order has been attempted in dividing Volume 2 (pre-First World War) and Volume 3 (post-First World War).

The editors were distressed to learn of Sir Michael Postan's death in December 1981 as the proofs of Volume 1 were being read; they feel a special debt of gratitude to him for his contribution of an appreciation of Rostow's intellectual background and personal development, as well as an evaluation of his main and most important production as an economic historian. From this essay we get a clear picture of Rostow the man and of Rostow the economic historian and social scientist: a personal and indeed welcome introduction to this *Festschrift*, based on information supplied by Dean Elspeth Rostow.

The next three chapters in Volume 1 are by D. C. North,

R. Cameron and S. G. Checkland. They point out the need for economic historians to make use of a broader set of theoretical tools beyond those provided by neo-classical economics. D. C. North stresses the significance of current research in demography, ideology, technological and institutional change, and the way it is transforming economic history, shifting it away from the biases built in the previously narrower approach. This new approach carries over from cliometrics the quantitative method and the rigorous use and testing of hypothesis: by broadening the framework it makes economic history more congenial to the traditional historian, and offers the potential of explaining a vast range of historical observations that could not be accounted for within the compass of neo-classical theory.

In the same vein R. Cameron emphasises the need to expand the scope of our analysis if we are to understand the inter-relationship of population, resources and technology in the process of economic growth, stressing the fact that the economy is conditioned by social institutions, embodying values and attitudes. In the past institutional innovation has been at least as responsible as technological change for the economic transformation of Europe, and can still – hopefully – face the challenges posed by the present demographic upsurge in the world and by the energy shortage.

S. G. Checkland's essay is an attempt to analyse the role of the state in the long-term theory of growth, a subject that brings him to delve in the intimate but not necessarily direct relationship between the state and the stage of growth attained. Three different levels of analysis are explored: universalism based upon the nation-state, an insistence on the degree of national uniqueness, and finally a view rising above the nation-states to some kind of structure of world interaction. If brought together in a new synthesis these can throw light on the intricate problem of the role of the state in the process of growth.

While economic historians may benefit from an extended approach, P. Temin underlines the changes that have taken place within the realm of economic analysis. The economic depression in the first place, the post-World War expansion in the second instance and, more recently, the worldwide inflationary process (accounting for the revival of the more orthodox monetary theories) have had a tremendous bearing on economic theory. While this is generally acknowledged, a different strand is pointed out, of a less orthodox flavour, stemming from some of Keynes's psychological insights and from the behaviourist assumptions of Duesenberry and Simon which throw light on some peculiar but relevant aspects of human conduct. The *homo economicus*, free of restrictions, may not, after all, be the best and most relevant paradigm.

R. M. Hartwell, W. A. Lewis, E. S. Mason and R. de Oliveira Campos move on to the problem that has concerned many economic historians, W. W. Rostow in particular, i.e. the nature, constraints and characteristics of the long-term process of growth. R. M. Hartwell discusses parallelism and divergence in 'historical perspective', by which he means the very long run. For some economic historians the long run is the twenty years of the Kuznets cycle, for others the fifty years of the Kondratieff cycle. Hartwell seeks to push beyond these limits to explore the rise, fall, and occasional failures to move of civilisation, which give the result progress and dissimilarity.

W. A. Lewis in turn analyses the major constraints to growth in mature economies, questioning some of the standard answers (the low savings ratio, the inelasticities in the supply of labour, the lack of natural resources or the scarcity of foreign exchange, entrepreneurship and technology) forcefully arguing that the ultimate constraint is the ability of the institutional system to absorb change in an orderly fashion.

Most fittingly, E. S. Mason and R. de Oliveira Campos deal with the stages approach. Mason stresses the insights into the process of growth contributed by Rostow, both in his *Stages of Economic Growth* and in *The World Economy*, but questions whether the historical examples in the latter provide enough evidence to support the sharp demarcations suggested in the first book, and reveals a more continuous, persistent and cumulative process of growth than the stages theory would lead us to believe.

R. de Oliveira Campos's essay appraises the take-off approach from the point of view of the developing countries, for which purpose he deems it necessary to study the interaction between economics and politics. Rapid growth increases social mobilisation, increasing political demands, thus putting strains on the political system. Instead of being rectilinear, the process appears as an adventure threatened by deadlocks. This author's views are a remarkable example of the new wave of scepticism about growth promoting in a straightforward manner democracy and political stability, at least during the course of the crucial transformation from a developing to a fully developed society.

The chapter by Sir Austin Robinson reflects in turn the increasing scepticism regarding the benefits of rapid industrialisation programmes for new countries, while it puts forward the alternative of an agriculture-led strategy. This alternative is not problem-free, mainly because of the danger of accumulating food surpluses, the risk of benefits failing to filter down and a possible increase in the rate of population growth. Such a strategy, being the more decentralised, is prone to greater administrative problems than the more centralised industrial alternative. Still, in Robinson's view it is an appealing path that many new countries may find worth while exploring.

The first volume is closed by chapters by R. Findlay, C. W. Reynolds, and Guido di Tella, all former students of Rostow. They deal with the connection between trade, rents and growth. Findlay's analysis of the trade – growth nexus in the formative period of the Industrial Revolution points out that the causal arrow must run from growth – in the form of technological change in the manufacturing sector – to trade, rather than the other way round assumed by most of the literature on the subject. But even if the 'manna from heaven' nature of technological progress has to be supplemented, the least that can be said is that trade and growth are inextricably intertwined during the first take-off process known to the world.

Reynolds recalls the Prebisch–Singer terms of trade argument of the 1950s, and remarks the drastic change brought about by the post-1973 rises in the price of oil which resulted in an equally drastic change in the pattern and allocation of the world's economic rent. An attempt is made to measure not only the natural resources-based rent but the other two as well, i.e. the one emerging from market imperfections, source of 'protection' rents, and the one stemming from entrepreneurship, source of the so-called 'innovation' rent. Di Tella ends the first volume with an analysis of the impact of the discovery of new resources on the expansion of the world economy, particularly in the nineteenth century. He distinguishes two different kinds of economic frontier expansions, a less dynamic, equilibrium version, and a more dynamic, more equilibrium version, allegedly more relevant to the cases in question. As in the previous contributions, these resources-based rents are put into a more ample perspective, where accumulation and growth are consequences of the strive for non-normal profits by Schumpeterian-styled entrepreneurs.

The second volume deals mainly with specific cases and applications, embracing several centuries and diverse countries in different continents, mostly ordered in a chronological sequence up to the First World War. The volume is relevantly opened by W. N. Parker's views on the European process of development from the standpoint of what he calls a millennial perspective. He selects three different, stylised relationships: the traditional, near subsistence, Malthusian society; the commercial, trade-oriented, expansive Smithian society, free from the limits imposed by the national market on the division of labour; and the capitalist, Schumpeterian society, engaged in a process of creative destruction. The three dominate four particular stages, but are present throughout, their interaction throwing light on the process of growth.

W. P. Glade digs into the roots of the industrialisation process in Latin America, going back to colonial times. Despite the emphasis placed on trade, there is no doubt that the bulk of the goods consumed in the American colonies were produced on the west of the Atlantic. He traces the spread and original organisation of colonial industry, analysing the various reasons which impeded their becoming the springboard to nineteenth-century industrialisation, i.e. the effective insulation from competition and foreign technical knowledge, an insulation that took them further and further away from the European type of evolution.

F. Crouzet's essay explores some aspects of the triangular relationship between the United States, Britain and France between 1793 and 1814, pointing out how, as a consequence of the European War, the United States, a relatively small and new country – by European standards – found itself propelled as a sea-trading power to be reckoned with. This new role was reversed after 1814 when the United States turned away from high-sea ventures and towards 'internal improvements', something not too different from what took place in some European cases: France, Prussia and Belgium. Its power was still to be reckoned with, but its international role receded at least until the middle of the century.

D. S. Landes's detailed account of the French liberation loan of 1871 illuminates the financial conditions prevailing in Europe at the time, showing the limitations that even triumphant powers have in exacting compensation from the vanquished, an experience repeated to some extent the other way round after the First World War. It also shows how the business and financial sectors of both countries vied to take advantage of the loan that had to be issued, with a substantially independent attitude from their respective governments.

S. B. Saul explores in his chapter the peculiarities of a group of small European countries in the nineteenth century. Some special traits are found among such apparently diverse countries as Belgium, Denmark, the Netherlands, Norway, Sweden and Switzerland. They exhibited a greater homogeneity which allowed them to make more easily the necessary social adjustments to take advantage of the new technologies and the changing patterns of trade. Fewer interests had to be reconciled and a more rational economic policy resulted out of this. They were forced, because of their small home markets, to specialise and explore the foreign ones, where they did not find much resistance because of their small significance. These countries had indeed many limitations which are the ones usually pointed out, but in being small they had as well many advantages: as Saul says, 'the importance of being unimportant'.

R. Cortés Conde's analysis of Italian migration from 1880 to 1913 notes the economic determinants of this very intense process and finds a high correlation between the higher level of income in the new American countries, north and south, the result of their higher productivity. The lagged total and average level of remittances are taken as an effective measure of the immigrant's capacity to earn, save and remit. Economic reasons were not the only ones behind these human waves, but they certainly played a crucial and quantifiable role.

T. C. Barker deals with a subject quite in line with Rostow's chief preoccupations, i.e. the role of the new methods of transportation during the nineteenth and early twentieth centuries. While many historians have written extensively about railways, surprisingly few have done so on the spread of motor vehicles, arguably a process which has had an even greater impact not only in transportation, but also in the way of living. The chapter by Barker fills this void, focusing especially on the situation attained before the First World War, more significant than at times is conceded.

The chapter by C. H. Feinstein, R. C. O. Matthews and J. C. Odling-Smee, which closes the second volume, deals with a subject already studied by Rostow in *The British Economy in the Nineteenth Century*. The authors make a new and up-to-date appraisal of the available figures for the 1873–1914 period, both in global and in sectoral terms, which tend to indicate that the alleged retardation of the British economy did not start around 1873, but that it took place only after 1899. An analysis of the productivities of the various factors and sectors is made, where labour and capital productivity can be seen to move in such a way as not to affect total factor productivity, while agriculture and mining can be seen as the main factors influencing the fall in total productivity, joined by manufacturing after 1899.

G. N. von Tunzelmann opens the third volume, which deals with applications and cases for the post-First World War period, with an analysis of the structural change and the role of leading sectors in British manufacturing from 1907 to 1968, questioning the reasons given for the sluggishness of the British inter-war performance, attributed by Rostow to the delay to move from steel, chemicals, and electricity to the typical mass consumption industries: automobiles, plastics, electronics and aeronautics. Von Tunzelmann concludes that the 'shift effect' of resource allocation among sectors was much less important in explaining productivity growth than the internal effect within sectors. Moreover the belief that a structural shift towards the new industries explains the coexistence of high, economy-wide growth rates and high unemployment in the 1930s does not seem to be substantiated.

E. Dahmén's analysis of Sweden's recent industrial development crisis endeavours to merge the conventional macro approach with historical research, utilising a conceptual frame of reference of a neo-Schumpeterian and Austrian type. A sketch of the general economic developments is made, including an account of what most analysts made of macromodelling with broad aggregates, and what this leads them to believe. This kind of analysis disguised some of the major changes that took place particularly in the mid-1960s, a crucial break in the development process, something which would have been detected through a more detailed and disaggregated analysis and a more adequate and broader frame of reference.

D. Kendrick studies the shift in emphasis which is occurring in the macroeconomic paradigm in the US: a shift from the demand to the supply side. This shift is causing a change from aggregative economics, to analysis of the problems in certain sectors and certain regions. This shift calls for a new organisation of the data for the US economy as the ones presently available are organised in aggregative terms for similarly organised econometric models. Insufficient attention is paid to sectors, to the location of economic activity, and to the relationships between economic data. The main purpose of the paper is to explore a new method of organising US economic data, the so-called 'relational database approach'.

R. M. Marshall's concerns refer to the slowing down in productivity growth already detected in the US economy during the 1970s. While recent studies have attempted to find the reasons for this evolution – the shift towards a service economy, the demographic changes in the labour force, the slower growth of investment, the sharp rise in energy prices, the increase in government regulations, and the reduced spending on research – much remains unexplained. One reason is that conventional quantitative techniques fail to capture important behavioural and dynamic forces underlying the productivity process, i.e. individual and national values, relations between workers and management, systems within which workers and enterprises function, and institutional and governmental behaviour. An understanding of these factors must be integrated with traditional resource availability analysis to explain changes in productivity, a statement quite in line with some of the statements made in the first chapters of Volume 1.

We have made one exception in our chronological ordering with Charles P. Kindleberger's contribution, since his subject is very much akin to the one studied by Sir Alec Cairncross. Kindleberger's paper comparing the resumption of gold payments in Britain in 1819 with the restoration of the pound to par in 1925 follows in his tradition of comparative economic history, and is addressed especially to Professor Rostow's expressed view that monetary questions, and the level of sophistication in dealing with them, were less significant before the First World War than after it.

The last three contributions by Sir Alec Cairncross, Lord Roberthall and J. Marczewski deal with shorter-term problems in relatively recent times. Cairncross analyses the traumatic devaluation of sterling in 1949, indeed a turning-point in British economic policy. A detailed narrative of events is made, so as to help the understanding of the conditions and expectations prevailing at the time. This squarely leads to the issue of whether the pressures that led to devaluation were ephemeral, reversible and resistible, or how far they were enduring and likely to be cumulative. An appraisal of the effects of devaluation is obscured by the outbreak of the Korean war, which set the world economy out of balance. However, the wisdom of the decision has to be measured not just in terms of its effectiveness, but also in terms of its appropriateness given the circumstances, and how correctly these were appreciated.

In his chapter Lord Roberthall analyses the British economic performance since the Second World War. The high hopes of overcoming the depression and unemployment in the pre-war years were reasonably successful until the early 1970s, despite an increasing and ominous pressure on the price level. Since 1973, developments in the world and in the UK have been quite different: the outside world has been less benign and the ability of the British economy to adapt has indeed been diminished, while the power and the willingness of the trades unions to exercise it has augmented. The consequences have been felt in increases in the rate of inflation and in the rate of unemployment, reaching figures comparable to all but the worst years of the Depression.

J. Marczewski's paper closes Volume 3, making a comparative analysis of stagflation in France and Germany over the last decade: 1971–9. The analysis is made in quantitative terms starting with the inflationary gap in total resources, followed by that of the structure and evolution of the inflationary gap of costs in France and Germany, which shows a striking similarity. Labour costs, income from property and entrepreneurship, taxes on production (less subsidies), and imports are assessed as contributing to the inflationary gap in costs. A similar analysis is made of the inflationary gap on expenditures, household's consumption and capital formation, enterprises' capital formation, public expenditures and exports. These analyses allow an evaluation of the causes which lie behind the stagflation of these countries and of the world at large.

Volume 3 ends with a bibliography of W. W. Rostow's major works, which unfortunately had to leave aside the long list of articles and addresses, some of them extracurricular, extremely indicative of the evolution of Rostow's thinking.

The editors would like to thank the contributors for their warm response and for their patience in face of the insistence in meeting deadlines. They would also like to thank Lois Nivens for her help in the compilation of the bibliography, and Celia Szusterman for her help in the editing of the three volumes.

1981 C. P. K.
G. di T.

1 Walt Rostow: a Personal Appreciation*

M. M. POSTAN

I

The subject of this essay is Walt Rostow himself: or more precisely Rostow's development and achievements as an economic historian. A bio-bibliographical essay like this is bound to be highly personal: personal to the writer as well as to the subject. An attempt to put down on paper the story of Walt's life and of his academic activities, while he himself is still alive and as active as ever, would daunt any writer. It should be all the more daunting to a writer linked to Walt, as I have been, by many years of companionship and friendship. What, nevertheless, justifies my enterprise and has eased some of its difficulties is my belief that our personal and academic proximity may have enabled me to evaluate Walt as an economic historian with an understanding better than one I could have gained from further afar.

Our proximity does not, of course, go beyond the late 1930s, when our paths first crossed; but what I know of Walt's early years merely goes to show that in his case not only was the child the father of the man but was also the son of his father. He was born in October 1916 to a family which was Russo-Jewish immigrant on his father's side. His parentage was not, however, as typical as bare facts might suggest. The bulk of Jewish immigrants to the United States came from the lower ranks of the Jewish settlement pale in Poland and Russia: poor, deeply rooted in Yiddish culture and detached from the Russian or Polish milieu to which they geographically belonged.

* All of W. W. Rostow's books and articles referred to in this essay but not accompanied by an endnote can be identified in the bibliography of his writings included in Volume 3.

In this respect Walt's father, Victor Rostow, was *sui generis*. He apparently came from somewhat higher levels of Russian Jewry: better educated and more Russified both in language and cultural affiliation. Victor Rostow was able to continue in America the education he had received in Russia and to graduate from the Pratt Institute in New York as an industrial chemist: a qualification which eventually enabled him to establish himself. Yet, for all his lifestyle of a middle-class American, he preserved and transmitted to his family many of the essentials of his Russian heritage. The heritage was, needless to say, liberal–socialist of a kind characteristic of Russian middle-class intellectuals of the time. Like most Russian liberal–socialists he was exhilarated by the Russian Revolution of 1917 when it came, but repelled by it when it culminated in a Leninist dictatorship. This outlook also determined his American choices and preferences. Like all educated Russians viewing America across the Atlantic, he chose as personifications of America men like Ralph Emerson, Walt Whitman and Eugene Debs and such lesser radicals popular in Russia as Jack London and Upton Sinclair. It was symbolic of his outlook that he should have called his sons Walt Whitman, Eugene Victor and Ralph Emerson.

However, more important than the choice of names was Victor Rostow's choice of residence. Very early in his career he moved his family from New Jersey to New Haven, Connecticut, largely because he envisaged a Yale-oriented education for his boys. Yale offered scholarships to a few New Haven boys, and Victor Rostow assumed, as it turned out rightly, that his sons would win them. The other important decision which Victor Rostow made on behalf of Walt was to discourage him from taking up a scholarship at a private school (Hopkins Grammar) and to insist that he should continue in public school where he could mix with boys from different backgrounds. In all other respects and in all subsequent decisions Victor did nothing to interfere with his sons' preferences and rightly relied upon their good sense and ability to take them far.

Their abilities were, of course, there in super-abundance. Not only did Walt and his brothers inherit their father's intellectual interests, but they could also draw on what appears to have been the formidable resource of their mother's ability and character. Lilian Rostow, though not herself a certificated intellectual, shared her husband's and sons' scale of values, and held 'progressive' views which were bound to strengthen the liberal ambience of the Rostow household. However, her main contribution to her sons' future came from the energy and vitality which she brought to bear on her sons' careers and the store she set by their academic ambitions.

In 1932, having won at the age of 15 a scholarship to Yale, Walt entered an uninterruptedly ascending path. His chosen subjects at Yale were economics and history: a choice from which he was not to diverge throughout his career. At that time the senior ranks of the Yale faculty could boast of several distinguished economists and historians, at least two of whom were able to influence Walt's academic preferences. David Owen, a specialist in the English history of the nineteenth century, attracted Walt to that field of historical studies, while James Harvey Rogers, one of the most distinguished American economists of the time, introduced Walt to the kind of economics which Walt's later work exemplifies. The economics was 'institutional' in the sense of being grounded in statistical and historical evidence and fitted into the social and political environment; yet also 'theoretical' in its use of economic concepts and theorems.

However, Walt's intellectual development and his orientation as an economist owed much more to some of his contemporaries or near-contemporaries at Yale, more particularly to Richard M. Bissell, who had just returned from his studies at LSE well primed with the economic theories then current in England. His seminars became the main centre of high-level discussion of economic doctrine which made a great contribution to Walt's incipient progress as an economist. The seminars were also a meeting point for a number of young men of promise, among them Max Millikan who was to play an important part in some later stages of Walt's career.

The economic and political views then formed found their earliest vehicle in the *Harkness Hoot*, a magazine long since defunct, for which Walt and his elder brother Eugene wrote while at Yale. The Rostow articles for the *Hoot* bear witness to the liberal and largely Keynesian outlook of their circle at Yale.

The next stage in Walt's academic career was his Rhodes scholarship to Oxford. He won it in December 1935 and resided in Balliol from October 1936 to June 1938. In Balliol he found himself working under the sympathetic guidance of Humphrey Sumner, a great teacher and humanist, and rubbing shoulders with a number of intellectually and politically active contemporaries; Edward Heath and Denis Healey among them. It was while in Oxford, and while discussing his subjects with Sumner, that Walt finally confirmed the intellectual choice he had made at Yale. He was going to be neither an economist, pure and arid, nor an historian, hard and dry, but a student of contemporary economic problems capable of fitting them into their historical perspective and explaining them with the aid of economic theory. He accordingly picked his first subject of research from a field in which his kind of economic history could be most profitably cultivated and which happened to bridge the two periods of English history on which he had concentrated in his undergraduate studies. The field was that of England's economic record in the second half of the nineteenth century.

These studies culminated in a seminal article on *Investment and the Great Depression*. He submitted the article to me for publication in the *Economic History Review* and came up from Oxford to stay with Eileen Power and me at Heytesbury. This was the first occasion on which we met. It was in every respect 'non-editorial', since most of our discussions centred on Walt's methods of study and exposition. Though I needed no converting, Walt preached forcibly the virtues of economic history written round economic problems and employing the tools of economics. Other meetings and protracted discussions of proper ways of doing economic history were to follow and have not yet ceased.

On his return to the United States in 1938 Walt, after a year occupied largely by the final stages of his doctorate thesis, spent another year (1939–40) as a Social Science Research Council Fellow doing his part of the Gayer–Rostow book on the British economy. In 1940 he took up an academic appointment at Columbia which he held until 1941. The two years at Columbia were to a large extent a period of gestation. During that period he was engaged on the final stages of the Gayer–Rostow enterprise. He also taught economics to undergraduates and, in doing so, apparently grounded himself more firmly than ever in the subject. Above all, he added to his erudition. Always a fast and voracious reader he was able, while at Columbia, to read more widely and deeply than ever.

These largely formative activities appeared to be interrupted, yet in some way also stimulated, by his wartime experiences. From 1941 to 1945 he served as a major in the US army attached to the Office of Strategic Services in London where he found himself involved not only in the choice of bombing targets in Germany but in the whole range of problems concerned with the use of air force, its relation to the general strategy and to the German war economy. The service in the army earned him an Hon. OBE and the Legion of Merit; but presumably it was the reputation he acquired at OSS that commended him for a post in the State Department, where for a year he served as assistant chief of the Division of German–Austrian Economic Affairs.

This was, as it was intended to be, a temporary diversion from an academic career. Early in 1946 Walt accepted a professorship in Economic History at Harvard. When, shortly afterwards, Oxford University offered him a visiting Harmsworth Professorship of American History, he took a one-year leave to go to Oxford. At the end of that year Gunnar Myrdal sought him to join the newly-organised Economic Commission for Europe in Geneva where he became assistant to the Executive Secretary, a post he held until 1949. The decision to go to Geneva was not easy: it not only meant resigning a permanent position at Harvard, but also compelling Elspeth Rostow, whom he had just married, to give up her positions at Barnard and Sarah Lawrence. He felt however that a call to the Commission in Geneva was one of duty: all the more so for the part he had played in initiating it.

Walt's work and activities in the Commission were important, even though they did not leave much visible testimony. The Commission was set up in Geneva as one of the European instruments of UN designed to further the rehabilitation of war-ravaged Europe with regular economic assessments and projections. Its membership was highly prestigious. With Myrdal at its head, Kaldor as one of its members, and a gifted band of other economists and political scientists (who were at a later stage joined by Eugene Rostow), it promised very well. If not all its initial promise was eventually fulfilled, the fault was not that of its members, certainly not that of Walt who, during his membership of that organisation, penned several forceful papers (not intended for publication) on the problems of the postwar world.

His residence in Geneva was moreover marked by a happy change in his personal circumstances. As I have just mentioned, shortly before taking up his post in Geneva, Walt married Elspeth Davies, a gifted young historian whose company and support he has enjoyed ever since. The support has been not only moral or emotional but also in many ways professional. Elspeth has not shared all Walt's interests as an economist and has not been drawn into current affairs at Walt's level. However, herself an historian of American politics and culture she was able to contribute, however obliquely and invisibly, to Walt's general views of American polity. Her contribution was most direct and most visible in Walt's teaching activities at Austin, where the two Rostows have for seven years conducted a joint seminar in American history.

In 1949 he detached himself from the Commission and accepted the visiting Pitt Professorship in American History in Cambridge. In the year following his tenure of the Cambridge chair he was appointed to the Professorship of Economic History at the Massachusetts Institute of Technology which he was to hold until 1961.

His years in MIT were both formative and productive. They were what he himself, for all his dislike of the term, could have described as years of increasing 'relevance'. In the Department of Economics at MIT he found himself amid a group of highly distinguished, perhaps the most distinguished, American economists of the time. His contacts included mathematical economists and econometricians as eminent and as stimulating as Paul Samuelson and Robert Solow, international economists like Paul Rosenstein-Rodan, sociologically oriented institutional economists, like Everett Hagen, and such historian–economists as Charles Kindleberger. These contacts widened and deepened his own conceptions of economic theory, while the high quality of his research students at the Institute fed his appetite for high-level teaching. His penchant for study bearing directly on policy was served best by the most important of all his MIT contacts, that with Max Millikan, an old friend and contemporary at Yale, who had come to MIT to head the Center for International Studies. The Center was a 'think tank' intended to analyse fundamental problems of international policy. Walt, with his interests in the contemporary world, with his qualifications as an historian, his wide reading as an economist and his burning interest in international problems was an obvious recruit for the Center. There he took charge of major research projects, two of which were concerned with Russia and China and gave birth to full-scale books on the position and prospects of the two countries.

In the autumn of 1958 a year's leave of absence from MIT enabled him to spend another year in Cambridge. Brief as the term of his residence was, it enabled Walt to re-establish his personal contact with Cambridge Keynesians and, in doing so, to transcend their current interests. In the course of that year he lectured and eventually wrote about a subject which Keynes and his followers had neglected – that of economic development. His lectures on the 'process of industrialisation', the thought and reading that went into them, and the discussions which followed them, led directly and almost immediately to the writing of the best-known of his books, that of *Stages of Economic Growth*.

On his return to MIT Walt continued to occupy himself with historical problems relating to the economic and political situation in America and the world at large. These occupations went with growing involvement with current affairs. He was drawn into various policy oriented gatherings and into repeated encounters with policy makers of every kind. Most of the writings instigated by these activities were of course well outside Walt's purely academic interests. Yet, taken as a whole, they faithfully reflected Walt's point of view in economics and history, and in this respect exemplified his belief in the contemporaneity of all historical study. This belief he was to make explicit in a more recent University paper addressed to a student readership.[1]

From the point of view of his subsequent career, the most important of his non-academic contacts were those which he, in the company of other younger professors at Harvard and MIT, established with John Kennedy. Quite early in these contacts Walt formed a rapport with Kennedy which, on the latter's election to the Presidency, led to Walt's recruitment to Kennedy's entourage. The succession of government posts Walt was to hold between 1961 and 1969 began with that of Deputy Special Assistant to the President for National Security Affairs, and included that of Counsellor and Chairman of the Policy Planning Council (PPC) at the Department of State and Special Assistant to the Presidents in the White House. These were all highly important and influential positions. As they lay well outside Walt's academic progress they could not be discussed here except as an interval in his career as an economic historian. They were however invariably inspired and infused with Walt's outlooks as a student of history and economics and could not therefore be wholly detached from the story of his development as a thinker and a writer. This is even true of the part he played in advising the President during the traumatic years of the Vietnam war. Like the activities of most government advisers whose advice is shrouded by the rules of official confidentiality, the policies Walt advocated and principles they embodied have been concealed from view and almost inevitably misunderstood and misjudged. But nobody who had an opportunity of discussing the subjects with him at the time, or seeing some of the memoranda he wrote, could fail to observe how closely did his attitudes fit into the corpus of ideas he made his own in the course of his progress as an economic historian: profoundly liberal in inspiration and invariably cast on the historical, i.e. long-term, scale.

Walt's political and administrative activities ceased with the ending of Lyndon B. Johnson's term of office in 1969. At the end of his Washington stint Walt received and accepted an invitation to the Professorship of Economics and History at the University of Texas at Austin, a position which he still holds. For all its remoteness from the main centres of American politics and academic life, his residence in Austin has turned out to be exceedingly fruitful. It has enabled him to spawn a large number of papers, at least six books, of which one – on the world economy – is a true *magnum opus*: a compendium of historical and economic facts and ideas summarising the fruits of lifelong reading, research and cogitation.

II

With the possible exception of some of his reports and memoranda wholly devoted to current political issues, Walt's sequence of publications is more continuous and cumulative than the repeated changes of posts and geographical locations would indicate. Nothing reveals this continuity more faithfully than the recurrence in all his later work of the embryonic ideas he promulgated in the first essay he published, that on Britain's economy in the late nineteenth century. That essay must, therefore, be taken as the starting point in all attempts to view Walt's scholarly output in the aggregate.

Some of that essay's propositions – the notion that the British investments abroad after 1866 depleted resources available for investment at home – and some of the economic landmarks postulated in it, may not have survived the test of later researches, including Rostow's own. Its abiding contribution, however, lies in the distinction it draws between economic fluctuations of different duration, in its discovery of movements of 'medium range', i.e. thus longer than the short-term business crisis and shorter secular trends. Even more abiding, and almost equally novel, was its emphasis on specific characteristics, i.e. the quality and the direction as well as the volume, of investments, and on the different behaviour of individual sectors of the economy.

Each of these anticipatory ideas were to be elaborated and supported by Rostow's output in a number of subsequent studies that eventually assembled in his *Essays on the British Economy*, published in 1948. Support on a most massive scale came, of course, from the collection of data which Walt, in co-operation with A. D. Gayer and Anna Schwartz, published in 1953. The collection became standard books of reference and offer the best testimony to the consistency and durability of the propositions Walt first put forward in 1938.

The next stage in Walt's work, roughly coinciding with his visiting professorships in England and his activities in MIT, reflects a change in the interests of most postwar economists. Whereas before 1939 economists and economic historians dealing with the contemporary or near-contemporary Europe were preoccupied with economic fluctuations, their attention now shifted to the problems of long-term development and economic growth. In Walt's case the shift was neither abrupt nor unheralded. His earlier studies, though predominantly English, bear witness not only to his preoccupation with the time-scale of economic processes but also to his awareness of their world-wide dimension. The awareness became more acute and ostensible after 1945. His researches and publications from now onwards were to embrace, more than ever before, the history and economics of the modern world in its entirety.

A number of studies and, above all, two books he wrote at that time bear witness to Walt's preoccupation with growth and with international economics. I refer here to two books advisedly. So famous became the second of the two books, *The Stages of Economic Growth*, that it overshadowed the intellectual import of the earlier book, *The Process of Economic Growth*, published in 1953. The latter's purpose and achievement were largely methodological. It was apparently conceived and should have been used as a guide to historians and economists intending to cross the frontiers between history and economics in search of a theory of economic growth. It formulated and listed the problems of growth, which historians should and could study. In the past historians had complained of the inability of economists to fashion hooks on which historical data could be hung; they were now offered an assortment of hooks firmly embedded in the body of economic doctrine, and, at the same time, fashioned to support historical fact. To this extent the book was an invitation to historians and economists to organise their studies of economic development more pertinently and more systematically than they had so far done, an invitation which, I am sorry to say, was not generally taken up in the years immediately following the publication of the book.

In the second of the two books, that on *The Stages of Economic Growth*, published in 1960, the mustering of historical facts and their hanging on the appropriate hooks were done by Rostow himself. The book, however, went much further than that. While providing historical, or near-historical, answers to his theoretical questions the book transcended the limits which historians responding to his earlier questions might have gone. It offered a generalised scheme of economic growth applicable to most societies and perhaps even to most periods of history. What emerged was not so much a historical account (abounding as it is in historical events) but an evolutionary model. In this respect a comparison with Marx's *Kapital*, which some critics thought extravagant, was quite justifiable. Rostow in his book, like Marx in his, transformed a mere chronological sequence of past experiences into an evolutionary progression of related social situations.

It is in this transformation from chronology to evolution, (a transformation which some of Walt's critics could not swallow) that the book's true originality and importance will be found. It matters not to a benevolent critic, like the present one, that in the historical experiences of England or other Western countries the actual turning-points from stage to stage did not always occur at the points or in the sequential order postulated by Rostow. Nor does it matter much that the relevant quantities – capital accumulation, trade balances, national incomes, etc. – did not always move at the rate or even in the direction which Rostow's scheme postulated.

Criticisms of this order might justifiably apply to a book concerned with pure history, but not to a treatise on the morphology of economic development. Morphological studies are classificatory in both form and function. Their function is to identify complex situations by ordering individual facts within them into significant groups. The significance of such groupings depends on their ability to reveal how individual facts cohered in the past, and how the coherences were, and are, apt to recur. A good morphological scheme would also serve the purposes of identification by capping its groupings with appropriate titles. From this point of view, to draw attention to the 'purely semantic' nature of Rostow's treatise is to commend it, not to condemn it. How good and revealing Rostow's semantic inventions are is shown by the case and speed with which they have been adopted. The 'take off', 'the preconditions of the take off', 'self-sustained growth', mass consumption', have now been incorporated into the accepted terminology of development studies. It always amuses me to count the number of times Rostow's semantics are invoked by the very men who, to begin with, cited them only to disparage the value of his scheme.

Yet novel as the book was and still is, and much as it transcends the chronological and the theoretical range of Rostow's purely historical works, it still stands in recognisable succession to his precursory products of prewar vintage. A number of his earlier ideas recur in it in a more generalised way. Its emphasis on such extra-economic determinants as applied science and technology; its constant reference to leading sectors, its concern with fluctuations longer than the short ones – all these are abiding ideas of all Rostow's work.

The same ideas continued to be served more fully in Walt's latest and most voluminous treatise, that on the world economy, as well as in his group of essays published in 1980 under a collective title of *Why the Poor get Richer and the Rich slow down*. The title may at first sight restrict the book to the most fashionable of current issues; yet most of its themes and arguments amplify the economic and historical ideas which have engaged Rostow throughout his academic career. More particularly, in his two opening essays he delves again into the problem of 'long-run' movements, especially that of the 'Kondratieff' cycles. His approach to the subject is characteristically catholic. It is catholic not only in that he accepts a great deal of what was written on the subject by his predecessors, above all Schumpeter and Kuznets, but also that it is time-oriented, i.e. historical, and multi-factoral. The multi-factoral analysis is eclectic in the best and highly commendable sense of the word for it invokes nearly all the parameters of economic analysis – intellectual technological, demographic and physical.

In Rostow's own showing, the historical and multi-factoral approach is dictated by the very nature of the problem. In his introduction to the volume he harks back to the distinction which Marshall drew between methodologies appropriate to the study of economic changes of different duration. Whereas the study of short-term changes can be conducted on the assumption that their non-economic environment ('parameters') remains sufficiently static to be safely neglected, the study of long-term movements must shift the *onus inquiriendi* to long-term changes in the parameters themselves. This is of course what Rostow has always tried to practise and what preserves the historical essence of his later-day writings, even when they happen to be ostensibly concerned with current issues.

III

The survey of Walt's publications attempted here is by necessity too brief to embrace the entire corpus of his publications; or even that of publications directly related to economic and historical subjects. A number of articles and addresses have been left out, more particularly the several minor works clarifying or supplementing his ideas on stages of growth or presaging some of the propositions of his forthcoming study of the world economy. Of these publications, the one deserving separate mention is his book discussing the initial stages of the Industrial Revolution in the light of his earlier theories of the 'pre-conditions' and the 'take off' of economic growth.[2]

However, most of the items in the bibliography of Walt's writings not so far mentioned here are, so to speak, 'extra-curricular'. Judged by their titles most of them lie well outside the field of economic history or indeed outside Walt's other academic interests. Yet some of them, in spite of their titles and even in spite of their real themes, must be considered here, if only because they are highly characteristic of Walt as a student, and exhibit his attitude to academic study and to intellectual activity in general.

Most deserving of such consideration are the two books on China and Russia, produced by him with the assistance of teams of collaborators under the aegis of the International Center at MIT.[3] Both of them are obviously the work of an historian, but were not conceived as histories and were not addressed to students of history. Their object was more general and more pragmatic. They set out to analyse and to put into a historical perspective the economic and political systems of the two countries so as to help the members of the public and the politicians seeking to understand the two countries and to forecast their future. Here again it matters not that the emphasis Rostow and his collaborators placed upon the different aspects of Russian and Chinese politics, society and economies diverge from that placed by some academic China hands or Kremlinologists. In my own, admittedly not expert, opinion few of the historical or statistical facts cited in these volumes could be faulted; but even if they were, the books would still stand by virtue of their bearing on the immediate problems of policy. In this sense both volumes are not books of reference, but studies in pertinence.

Even further away from the field conventionally assigned to economic history, but very close to Walt's preoccupation with economic growth, is his book on political development corresponding to the stages of economic growth.[4] By its very intention this book is a pioneering enterprise and by its very nature a very difficult one. It sets out to lay bare the correspondence between economic changes and their political counterparts. To assume a counterpartial relation between economy and politics without at the same time sharing Marxist economic determinism is philosophically and conceptually a very delicate exercise. The delicacy of the exercise may partially explain why its challenge has not yet (though may still be) taken up.

Less experimental and well within Walt's purely academic record are his other recent publications devoted to the current problems of the modern world: more particularly in two books – *Getting from Here to There* and *Why the Poor get Richer and the Rich slow down*. Judged superficially by their titles and by their themes these publications may give the impression of being solely concerned with day-to-day issues. That they in fact exemplify Walt's theoretical position as a student of history and economics has already been argued here. Yet it can also be shown that even their purely practical and even political propositions link, however indirectly, with Walt as an historian and economist. The practical prescriptions they offer are those of positive government action to enforce economic growth, of income policies and of greater and better planned action on behalf of the Third World. These are all ideas shared by a large number of progressive or 'liberal' publicists. But a reader familiar with Rostow's corpus of ideas will not fail to note the links between the policies he recommends and the points of view he has developed in his academic studies. Thus, in emphasising the need of promoting and directing investments, he sounds over and over again one of the *leitmotif* of his earlier work, that of difference between individual sectors and the importance of the leading ones. In this way his latter-day publications have taken their place in the continuous stream of Rostow's intellectual activity. Above all, they demonstrate how, in spite of his many and various excursions away from the narrowly academic path, the course he followed for over forty years has been one of unbroken sequence.

These brief references to Walt's publications and activities outside the field of economic history must be supplemented with what we know of Walt's unpublished activities within the field. His oral contributions to the public discussion of economic and historical problems have been too scantily reported to be recorded in any *bibliographie raisonné*. What however deserves recording is his activity as a teacher. Throughout his university career and more particularly in its latest phases, in both MIT and at Austin, Walt has conducted postgraduate seminars on topics ranging over the entire breadth of his interests. One of the seminars, that on recent American history, which he has run at Austin jointly with Elspeth Rostow, has, according to all accounts, been infused by the same innovative ambition and has had the same stimulating effect as the ambition and the effects of his entire career as an economic historian.

NOTES AND REFERENCES

1. 'The Irrelevance of the Relevant', *Addendum*, vol. I, no. 1 (University of Texas at Austin, 1970).
2. W. W. Rostow, *How it all Began* (New York: McGraw Hill, 1975).
3. W. W. Rostow, *The Prospects for Communist China* (New York: Technology Press MIT, 1954); *The Dynamics of Soviet Society* (New York: W. W. Norton, 1967).
4. W. W. Rostow, *Politics and the Stages of Growth* (Cambridge University Press, 1971).

2 The Theoretical Tools of the Economic Historian

D. C. NORTH

The economic history we write is no better than the tools that we employ. There are only three alternative sets of theoretical tools available to the economic historian: classical, neoclassical, and Marxian. How blunt are they?

Walt Rostow's pioneering study *The British Economy in the Nineteenth Century* (1948) was a major influence in directing economic history toward the explicit use of neoclassical theory which eventually produced the cliometric revolution of the 1960s. In the ensuing twenty years neoclassical theory has come to be the dominant tool of the economic historian in the United States and increasingly in other countries as well. In this essay I propose to explore the promise and limitations of those neoclassical tools and briefly compare them with the alternative tools of classical and Marxian theory as approaches to improving our understanding of long run economic change.

I

The neoclassical model,[1] with the behavioural assumption of wealth maximisation, holds for any kind of economic system (capitalist, socialist, etc.). The output of society is a function of the capital stock which in turn consists of the stock of technology (past innovation), the stock of knowledge (which together with the inventors's skills expands the stock of technology), the stock of human capital (skills embodied in humans to produce output), the stock of physical capital (machines, buildings, etc.), and finally the stock of natural resources. Assuming a linear and homogeneous production function, output (Y) can be expressed as follows:

$$Y = F(N, T, R, P, H)$$

where *N* is the stock of knowledge, *T* the stock of technology, *R* the stock of natural resources, and *P* and *H* the stock of physical and human capital respectively. Labour is embodied in human capital in this formulation. All returns are equated at the margin so that any alteration in the relative rates of return to one part of the capital stock will lead to a reallocation of investment. Moreover, since the stock of resources is relative to the stock of knowledge and technology and there are no diminishing returns to increments to the stock of knowledge, a rise in the rate of return to resources (as in the classical model) will lead to investment reallocation to knowledge and technology, which in turn will expand the resource stock.

Under these conditions the growth of output and the growth of output per capita will be determined by the fraction of income saved (i.e. the rate of investment in expanding the capital stock) and the rate of growth of population. A higher rate of growth of savings than of population will lead to growing per capita income.

The important logical implications for the economic historian are (1) diminishing returns to the stock of land and resources do not exist because new knowledge (which can be converted into expanded resources) can be developed at constant cost; (2) changes occur as a result of changes in relative prices at the margin; (3) transactions costs are zero which is another way of saying that institutions don't exist. Let me explore each of these in turn.

II

The most dramatic feature of the neoclassical model is that the capital stock and therefore output can be expanded at constant cost. The fixed factor of land and resources and hence diminishing returns does not exist and the result is an optimistic model consistent with the idea, promise, and realisation of human progress. It can be no accident that the neoclassical model was a nineteenth-century creation. The underlying assumption that makes possible this result is that new knowledge can be created and transformed into resources at constant cost. The wedding of science and technology which made possible this result was a major feature of Walt Rostow's vision of the Industrial Revolution. But whether this marriage occurred at that early date is a matter of some controversy amongst economic historians. Rostow, in the company of some English economic historians, sees the symbiotic ties between science and technology as the essential feature of that watershed, while others (myself included) date the marriage vows a century later.[2] Yet the indisputable fact is that it did occur and that for at least a century the Western World has enjoyed unparalleled economic growth in per capita income at the same time that population growth has occurred at an unprecedented rate. This is surely the most remarkable single phenomenon of all economic history. The tension between population and resources has been the most fundamental building block in exploring secular economic change. It simply is not a basic building block in exploring modern Western experience, however – precisely for the reasons that the neoclassical model highlights, hence the power of this model for the modern economic historian.

III

The crucial role of relative price changes as a force inducing change is another major contribution of neoclassical theory to understanding long-run economic change, but that role is also subject to significant limitation. In effect any parameter shift will lead to an adjustment process which produces a new equilibrium in which returns are again equated at the margin. Thus an exogenous expansion in population will in the short run lead to a rise in the price of food and raw materials since the short-run supply curve is inelastic. Real wages fall and rents rise. Since the potential profitability of owning land rises at the margin the price of land is bid up. The ratio of capital to land rises because it becomes more profitable to get more output from a given amount of land by using more capital (i.e. better drainage, more irrigation, etc.). The exact amount of substitution depends on production functions (the state of technology). By this process even over an intermediate period the supply curve of foodstuffs becomes more elastic. However a still further consequence is to raise the profitability of altering the production function by devising new technologies of food production (i.e. to develop new fertilisers and seeds, or breed more productive plants and animals), resulting in an elastic supply curve and a fall in the price of food and raw materials. The real wage of the worker rises, the price of land falls, and a new equilibrium is established.

This scenario does indeed reflect the influence of relative price changes in factor and product markets. The adjustment process occurs as a result of the 'signals' provided by changing relative prices which redirect the factors of production. But now let us go over the same scenario in a real-world context. The initial shift in the demand curve to the right as a result of population expansion does lead to a rise in the price of foodstuffs and raw materials, but the initial speed of the adjustment process depends upon the costs of information. The 'thinner' the market, the more primitive the technology of information, the longer it will take the adjustment process to take place. But that is just the beginning. The worker (and particularly the urban worker in history) who has enjoyed a customary living standard may protest the rising food costs with riots and appeal to government to impose price ceilings. The potential value of land will rise but if there have been customary land agreements (or a prohibition on the alienation of land) the adjustment is uncertain. In the absence of exclusive ownership rights over land a farmer may not be able to capture the increased benefits of more capital-intensive use of the land. Farmers may petition the state to alter property rights so that they will be able to obtain the exclusive benefits of land ownership but individuals who have had customary access to land will oppose such an alteration in property rights. Finally the development of new knowledge and new technology will be forthcoming only if there is some private capturability of the returns to new knowledge and new techniques.

The difference between the two scenarios is a result of the assumption of zero transaction costs and of a behavioural function that is too narrowly construed to account for a significant fraction of human behaviour that affects secular stability and change.

IV

It is certainly incorrect to state that neoclassical economists have ignored transactions costs: they have become the open sesame to account for every residual that exists when pure neoclassical models fail to produce the Walrasian general-equilibrium result that they suggest. Aside from the fact that much of the transactions-cost literature is imprecise and untestable, the plain fact is that the implications of positive transactions costs are just beginning to become an integral part of the neoclassical models. We are now well aware of the fact that the state exists, that it grants property rights, that property rights are imperfectly specified, that the gainers seldom compensate the losers – in short, that political and economic institutions and organisations exist – *and that they matter*. We have made the concept of Pareto efficiency meaningless since whatever the performance of an economy, it is efficient by definition because there were real transactions costs that produced that result. But how and why the performances of economies differ at a moment of time and over time is still a mystery. A theory of the state, a theory of property rights, and a theory of ideology are necessary to resolve these problems. The first two deal with transactions costs; the third is necessary to resolve the narrow construction of the behavioural function in the neoclassical world.

V

There is a fundamental contradiction built into the behavioural assumption of neoclassical models which makes it impossible for the economic historian to account for much of the stability of economic and political organisation on the one hand, or to account for a great deal of the change in institutions on the other. It arises from the dilemma posed by the free-rider problem first elucidated in Mancur Olson's *The Logic of Collective Action* (1965). Olson extended the logic of neoclassical theory to explain the existence of groups in society. Large groups would exist only when the benefits of group action could be limited to the membership (such as with the American Medical Association or trade unions with a union shop) and the private benefits of membership exceeded the private costs. If the benefits were not exclusive such groups would tend to be unstable and disintegrate because individuals need not incur the costs of group organisation to receive the benefits (hence the term 'free rider'). The dilemma does indeed explain a great deal of economic behaviour from the failure of individuals to bother to vote to the fact that most of us most of the time do not bother to protest policies of which we disapprove. But unexplained is a crucial and significant residual – from individual actions such as voting or the anonymous donation of free blood, to large-group protest movements which throughout history have altered its course. For example, in the illustration developed in Section III above, it would not have paid the individual urban worker to incur the danger to life and limb by protesting rising food prices nor for the farmer to organise to lobby for altered property rights. It would have paid the individual to stay home, look at television and let someone else do the protesting. Quite simply, an enormous amount of change in history has occurred as a result of large-group action in which there were not exclusive benefits to the participants.

The obverse side of the coin is equally perplexing. Individuals do obey the rules of a society even when an individualistic calculus of costs and benefits should dictate different action. It is true that individuals do cheat, shirk, steal, litter, murder and generally engage in opportunistic behaviour when the benefits exceed the costs. Hence the power of the neoclassical model in explaining the economics of crime and modern industrial organisation theory explaining shirking and opportunistic behaviour. But if the only constraint on individual behaviour were the narrowly-construed maximising assumption of neoclassical theory then no society would be viable since the cost of enforcement of any body of rules would be, if not infinite, certainly enormous.

The plain fact is that individuals engage in large-group protest movements on occasion when they believe the rules to be unjust and equally obey the rules disregarding opportunity cost (in narrowly-construed terms) at times when they believe the rules to be just. This would not be a significant problem for the economist or economic historian if this behaviour were stable (i.e. unchanging tastes), but in fact the degree of alienation which spurs protest movements and the conviction of the legitimacy of institutions which induces individuals to obey rules even when they could gain by doing otherwise vary radically. It is essential to have a theory of ideology to be able to discriminate between when individuals will act as free riders and when they won't. Without an explicit theory of ideology or more generally of the sociology of knowledge we not only cannot resolve the free-rider dilemma but we also cannot:

1. explain the enormous investment that every society makes in legitimation. This investment includes much of the educational system that can in no way be accounted for as either human capital investment or a consumption good. It can only be explained as a process of socialisation by which the standards and values of a society are inculcated into successive generations;
2. predict the voting behaviour of legislators where a large residual remains after incorporating interest-group explanations;
3. account for the decisions and 'doctrinal changes' of the independent, tenured, judiciary not subject to standard interest-group pressures. The frequency with which these decisions run counter to the major interest groups in the society results in a large void in the social scientists's ability to explain changes in resource allocation outside the market place. The changes in

interpretation of the American Constitution in the past two centuries by the Supreme Court are a part of that puzzle;
4. explain the proclivity (and even the boast) of historians to rewrite history each generation. Such rewriting does not happen because historians typically discover new evidence which clearly refutes existing hypotheses but because different weights are assigned to the existing evidential material to provide different explanations consistent with current ideology. I do not mean to imply that historians do not find new evidence; obviously they do, and to the degree that such evidence does provide tests of previous hypotheses there is an advance in the state of historical knowledge. But changing historical interpretation of the past cannot be explained solely or even largely in terms of the development of new evidence;
5. account for the charged emotional content of many historical debates such as the standard of living of the worker during the Industrial Revolution or the nature of slavery in America.

VI

How useful are the tools of classical and Marxian theory in remedying the deficiencies of neoclassical theory?

Certainly before the nineteenth century the classical model[3] is a more useful framework of analysis than the neoclassical model since the persistent tension between population and resources did indeed produce recurrent crises. But one would need to add an important caveat. Sometimes these crises were resolved by physiological reduction in the population (a Malthusian result) but sometimes, as Ester Boserup (1965) stressed, population pressure induced technological (and I would add, institutional) change which overcame these crises.

The Marxian model is a powerful model of secular change precisely because it incorporates all of the elements left out of the traditional neoclassical framework: institutions, property rights, the state, and ideology. It is difficult to pin down, however, because there appears to be almost as many interpretations of Marx as there are Marxian theorists. Marx regarded technological change and not population growth as the primary engine of change. Technological change led to production techniques whose potential could not be realised within the existing economic organisation. The consequence was to energise a new class to overthrow the existing system and establish a body of property rights which would allow the realisation of the production potential of the new technology. Just as the heart of the classical model is a continuing tension between population and resources, the heart of the Marxian model is the tension between the productive potential of a technology and the existing economic organisation. Neoclassical theory has only recently rediscovered the important role of property rights in determining the efficiency of an economy. Marx's insight on the subject is a major contribution to explaining secular change.

However if technology is the primary engine of change, the change itself takes place through the action of classes rather than individuals. Here the neoclassical model is surely a better starting point than the Marxian model since aggregation in the former takes place through commonality of interest; such interest frequently points to fundamental divisions within classes which account for a great deal of economic history. While Marx's informal analysis frequently recognised divisions within the bourgeoisie and proletariat it is not a part of the formal theory and amounts to ad-hoc reasoning. Writing economic history as a struggle between classes (as defined by Marx) omits a vast amount of the subject from scrutiny.

Marx made a number of early and important contributions to the sociology of knowledge but did not resolve the free-rider dilemma. Marx simply made the leap of faith that individuals will participate as classes; yet Lenin and subsequent Marxist activists provide convincing evidence that they recognise the dilemma since much of their literature is aimed at convincing the proletariat to act like a class and not remain free-riders.

For the economic historian the crucial issue concerning the state is to account for the kind of property rights the state adopts and in particular to account for the ubiquitous tendency of states throughout history to adopt property rights that did not promote economic growth, and for the inherent instability of states. While political scientists gave up large-scale generalisations about the state a long time ago, both Marxists and recently neoclassical economists have provided some insight into these issues.

I know of no authoritative statement of a Marxian theory of the state. Both Marx and Engels had the elements of (several) theories of the state and Marx's followers have written voluminously on the subject although they concentrate their attention on a theory of the capitalist state. When stripped of all the rhetoric such theories have some similarity to a neoclassical approach to the state (although with the significant difference that the neoclassical approach is not confined to capitalist states).[4] However anything so elegant as a theory of the modern pluralist state is still a long way from appearance.

VII

Whether this brief survey of the theoretical tools of the economic historian leaves the reader with the conviction that they are blunt or sharp I do not know. But one can say with conviction that they are being sharpened. Recent work in economic history is beginning to tackle the intractable problems that are examined in the foregoing pages. We still don't have a theory of demographic change, but a good deal of promising work is going on in England (the Cambridge group), in France (the *Annales* School) and in the United States (see the excellent survey contained in the book *Historical Studies of Changing Fertility* edited by Charles Tilly, 1978). We do not have a theory of technological change, but recent work by Nathan Rosenberg (1976) and Paul David (1976) has highlighted many of the issues and a study by Stephen Cheung (forthcoming) explores technological change within a transactions-cost framework. We are a long way from a theory of the sociology of knowledge that would allow us to account for the free-rider problem, but growing research on non-market decision-making is forcing economists to explore issues of ideology.[5]

The most promising developments are in transaction-cost analysis which offers the promise of a framework for analysing institutions and change in institutions. The direction this research is taking is to conceive of political and economic institutions as a set of rules, compliance procedures, and codes of behaviour devised to exploit the gains from trade as a result of specialisation (including a comparative advantage in violence). The rules and regulations define the terms of exchange, whether between principals (i.e. between ruler and constituents in political organisation or market exchange in economic organisation) or between principals and agents in hierarchical political and economic organisations (between rulers and bureaucrats, owners and managers, managers and workers). Constitutions, the legal framework, the specification of property rights, the by-laws of organisations, trade-union contracts embody these constraints on behaviour.

Compliance procedures are concerned with detecting deviations from the rules, regulations, or stipulated contract agreements and with instituting and enacting punishment (or rewards). If one could costlessly measure the characteristics of goods and services in exchange or the performance of agents, then the problem of detecting deviations from the rules would not be important. Measurement constitutes the formalised description of a good or service and therefore without some form of measurement property rights cannot be established nor exchange take place. Compliance costs in addition consist of the cost of enacting penalties for non-performance. Because measurement and enforcement are costly it pays parties to an exchange to maximise with respect to deviations from the agreement. If either party to a contract can with impunity receive the benefits of the exchange without fulfilling his or her part of the bargain, then it is to his or her advantage to do so. Tax evasion, cheating, shirking, opportunism, problems of agency (and the resources devoted to monitoring and metering) are at base issues that arise because of the costliness of compliance procedures. Therefore both the set on constraints of behaviour in the form of rules and the procedures designed to detect deviations and enforce compliance with the rules are devised to maximise the revenue of principals subject to these transaction-cost constraints.

There is substantial literature dealing with the organisational implications of maximisation subject to the constraint of technology; but these constraints must be melded with the transactions constraints arising from compliance costs in order to develop a theory of political and economic institutions.

However, the argument is still incomplete. Compliance is so costly that the enforcement of any body of rules in the absence of some degree of individual restraint from maximising behaviour would render the political or economic institution non-viable: hence the enormous investment that is made to convince individuals of the legitimacy of these institutions. A theory of institutional change would be incomplete without incorporating ideological considerations.[6]

VIII

Taken together the current research in demography, ideology, technological change, and institutional change is transforming economic history away from the biases that are built into a strictly neoclassical approach to economic history. These research developments will enable economic history to directly confront issues of the structure of economies that underlie performance as well as to explore the factors that make for secular change in the structure of economies.

For historians these developments carry over from cliometrics the quantitative methods and the rigorous use and testing of hypotheses that have made the new economic history an important step forward in scholarly research. Broadening the framework to set history within the political and economic institutions offers a framework congenial to the traditional historian, explicitly incorporating ideology into the framework offers the potential of explaining a vast range of historical observations that simply could not be accounted for within the compass of neoclassical theory.

I do not mean to imply that a theory of history is emerging. It is not, and I do not believe that developing a theory of history is a useful exercise. Rather, what we are seeing is a way of approaching historical problems that possesses an underlying consistency and at the same time possesses the flexibility to explore a broad range of historical issues.

Business history has always been plagued by a lack of theoretical underpinnings. Most of it has been ad-hoc implicit theory in the form of superficial description of the development of a business enterprise. The transactions-cost approach to economic organisation offers the beginning of a theoretical framework which can make business history an analytical discipline and a complementary field of scholarly research to theory dealing with economic (and political) organisation.

For economists the approach is in the tradition of Adam Smith, Karl Marx, Alfred Marshall, and Joseph Schumpeter. They regarded economic history as important: it provided a dimension of time to the static world of the economist, it attempted to put together the pieces of an economic system rather than examine isolated bits of the jigsaw puzzle, it incorporated an awareness of the interdependence of economic organisation with the political and social aspects of society. In brief, it attempted to theorise about the changing constraints that the economic theorist held constant.

NOTES

1. This exposition of the neoclassical model draws from an unpublished study by John Floyd (1969).
2. For a discussion of the role of science in the Industrial Revolution see A. E. Musson (1972).
3. And presumably the Marxian model, since Samuelson (1978) maintains that when one adds the limitations of land and resources to Marx's model one arrives at the same classical model as Ricardo and Malthus.
4. See my 'A Framework for Analyzing the State in Economic History' (1979).
5. For a summary of the literature see J. B. Kau and P. Rubin (1979).
6. For a review of the growing literature and elaboration of this argument see the book by the author, *Structure and Change in Economic History*.

REFERENCES

Boserup, Ester, *The Conditions of Agricultural Growth: The Economics of Agrarian Change Under Population Pressure* (Chicago: Aldine Press, 1965).

Cheung, Stephen, 'Property Rights and Invention' (forthcoming).

David, Paul, *Technological Choice, Innovation and Economic Growth* (Cambridge University Press, 1976).

Floyd, John, 'Preferences, Institutions and the Theory of Economic Growth' (University of Washington discussion paper, 1969).

Kau, James B., and Rubin, Paul, 'Self Interest, Ideology and Log rolling', *Journal of Law and Economics* (October, 1979).

Musson, A. E. (ed.), *Science, Technology, and Economic Growth in the 18th Century* (London: Macmillan, 1972).

North, Douglass, 'A Framework for Analyzing the State in Economic History', *Explorations in Economic History*, (July, 1979).

North, Douglass, *Structure and Change in Economic History* (New York: W. W. Norton, 1981).

Olson, Mancur, *The Logic of Collective Action* (Cambridge: Harvard University Press, 1965).

Rosenberg, Nathan, *Perspectives on Technology* (Cambridge University Press, 1976).

Rostow, Walt, *The British Economy in the Nineteenth Century* (Oxford University Press, 1948).

Samuelson, Paul, 'The Canonical Classical Model of Political Economy', *Journal of Economic Literature* (December, 1978).

Tilly, Charles (ed.), *Historical Studies of Changing Fertility* (Princeton University Press, 1978).

3 Technology, Institutions and Long-Term Economic Change

R. CAMERON*

ADVERTISEMENT

Rostow informs us that as an undergraduate at Yale in the 1930s he decided 'to work professionally on two problems: the relatively narrow problem of bringing modern economic theory to bear on economic history; and the broader problem of relating economic to social and political forces, in the workings of whole societies.'[1] Throughout his long, varied, and distinguished career as a teacher, scholar, and public servant he has with remarkable single-mindedness adhered to that youthful decision. Readers may therefore find it surprising that in an essay devoted precisely to those two problems, and in a volume honouring Rostow, I should have referred only in passing to a small portion of the large corpus of his scholarly writing. The omission is deliberate. In the first place, I have already commented in print on two of his most celebrated works.[2] More importantly, I have thought it useful to demonstrate another, independent approach to the problems that have preoccupied him. If that be *Hamlet* without the prince, I can only say *mea culpa*.

* The author would like to express his appreciation to members of the History Seminar at Emory University and to Professor Robert W. Fogel and the members of the Workshop in Economic History at Harvard for constructive discussion and suggestions in verbal presentations on this topic.

If we are going to bring history into the analysis, we must consider the effects of technical change. This is the question that we have neglected to discuss for twenty-five years.

Joan Robinson[3]

What's that you say, Mrs Robinson?

Paul Simon[4]

I

The concern of the classical economists with the distribution of income led them to formulate the famous tripartite classification of the factors of production: land, labour, and capital.[5] This was amended somewhat by J. B. Say and John Stuart Mill with the addition of a fourth factor, entrepreneurship;[6] but the basic principle remained satisfied: this classification could account for the distribution of the total product of the economy, which was their primary concern.

Another concern of the classical economists, and of most of their successors in the neoclassical tradition, was the concept of equilibrium, the notion that there is some natural relationship among the elements of an economic system to which they will automatically return if for any reason that relationship is disturbed. Regardless whether that concern emerged because of the influence of Newtonian mechanics or because of some more subtle, deep-seated fear for the stability of society, the fact remains that the concept of equilibrium – in households, in firms, in markets, in the economy as a whole – played a major role in the development of economic theory.[7]

These two devices, the factors of production and the concept of equilibrium, along with all the other paraphernalia of classical and neoclassical economics, account for the remarkable success that economics achieved, both as an intellectual discipline and as a policy science, even before the development of modern macroeconomics. Yet for all its accomplishments, classical and neoclassical economics had very little to say about long-term change. Within the classical paradigm of the factors of production, given that the quantity of land was fixed by nature, the only independent variables susceptible to change were capital and labour. The logical implications of this state of affairs were not very pleasant: the Malthusian population dilemma, on the one hand,

and the Marxian polarisation of classes (and eventual revolution) as a result of the indefinite accumulation of capital, on the other. There was a third alternative which many nineteenth-century economists seized upon – the notion of the 'stationary state' – but that required even more restrictive assumptions, including the concept of equilibrium.

Of course, most economists were too practical and had too much common sense to be literally bound by their restrictive assumptions. They recognised the facts of technological and even institutional change, although their theories could not account for them. To be sure, Adam Smith attributed 'the invention of all those machines by which labour is so much facilitated and abridged' to the division of labour;[8] but he also admitted the contributions of 'those who are called philosophers or men of speculation, whose trade it is not to do any thing, but to observe every thing; and who, upon that account, are often capable of combining together the powers of the most distant and dissimilar objects'.[9] The concept of the entrepreneur, as the agent who combined the other factors of production, might have been used as well as an agent of technological change by creating 'new combinations' or new production functions; but nothing much seems to have been done along that line until Schumpeter's *Theory of Economic Development*.[10] In short, neither classical nor neoclassical economics had a workable endogenous theory of technological or institutional change – nor of any other long-term change, for that matter. As Rostow put it, 'The most vital and fully articulated bodies of modern economic thought have been developed within Marshallian short-period assumptions; that is, the social and political framework of the economy, the state of the arts, and the levels of fixed capacity are assumed to be given and, usually, fixed.'[11]

Economists outside the classical/neoclassical tradition did attempt to account for long-term economic change. Indeed, that was the main objective of the German historical school(s), from which the formal discipline of economic history emerged. But in so doing they almost totally neglected – scorned might be a better word – markets and market-related behaviour and phenomena, which formed the essence of classical and neoclassical economics. And they never developed an operational theory of institutional, let alone technological, change.

Another offshoot of the German tradition (besides economic history) was the so-called American institutional 'school(s)'. Its members, as its name suggests, were interested primarily in institutions, both economic and non-economic; but at least one of its leading figures, Thorstein Veblen, also evinced considerable interest in technology, without, however, developing a theory of either institutional or technological change.[12] Indeed, one critic has charged him with 'continually hinting that a description is a theory, or, worse, that the more penetrating is the description, the better is the theory'.[13] A latter-day saint of the institutionalist school, C.E. Ayres, provided one of the most intriguing accounts of the historical interaction of technology and institutions;[14] but, like Veblen's, his 'theory' is really description, and flawed description at that.[15] According to Ayres, technology is a dynamic, 'progressive' force – impersonal, automatic, self-propelled – whereas institutions are uniformly resistant to change. In Ayres' view, economic development – indeed, history itself – was the outcome of a permanent tension or struggle between progressive technology and conservative (or reactionary) institutions. However fascinating for undergraduate readers, Ayres's 'theory' shared the faults of his predecessors' in the institutionalist and historical schools, as well as their neglect of and contempt for market processes.[16]

A hint of better things to come from orthodox economics appeared in the 1950s and 1960s with empirical investigations of the 'sources of growth' economists.[17] These showed that only a fraction, generally less than one half, of the increases in measurable output of advanced industrial economies could be attributed to measured increases in the conventional inputs of land, labour, and capital. The 'residual' increases in output were deemed to have resulted from technical change, organisational improvements, and other nonconventional factors, although in proportions that are not yet agreed upon. At about the same time T. W. Schultz and his followers in the 'human capital' school showed how investment in education, on-the-job training, and such could foster increases in productivity.[18] Soon thereafter a number of economists began treating expenditures on research, invention, and other aspects of technical change as endogenous to the price system.[19] Meanwhile some economic historians drawing on the theory of public goods and related literature attempted to deal with certain aspects of institutional change, especially those concerned with property rights, by employing the tools of neoclassical economics.[20]

These developments are most welcome, because they greatly extend the range of usefulness of conventional theory. They do not, however, in and of themselves solve 'the broader problem of relating economic to social and political forces, in the workings of whole societies', the problem to which Walt Rostow has devoted the greater part of his scholarly efforts.[21] That is because these developments are still restricted to cases involving economic incentives, and thus cannot account for the role of non-economic factors in economic change; and the models employed still incorporate restrictive assumptions of the *ceteris paribus* type. But it is obvious to all that historical change involves non-economic as well as economic motives and factors, and that in the long run *everything*, even the natural environment, is subject to change. Moreover, economic development, which is one kind of long-run economic change, consists by definition of changes in technology, economic organisation, and other structural features. In other words, in the long run the parameters themselves are variable. There are no fixed points other than historical benchmarks. What is needed, therefore, as a first step toward solving the 'broader problem' is a more comprehensive classification of the classical factors of production or, as I prefer to call them, the determinants of economic change.[22]

II

The classification that I propose envisages the total output of an economy at any point in time, the composition of the output, and its rate of change through time as functions of the 'mix' of population, resources, technology, and social institutions.[23] For heuristic (not analytical) purposes, the relationships can be formulated as follows:

$$Y = f(P, R, T, X)$$

where Y represents total income or output, P, R, and T stand for population, resources, and technology, respectively, and X, the 'great unknown,' represents social institutions or 'the socio-cultural context' of economic activity. The framework is comprehensive in principle because, by definition, any relevant variable that does not pertain to the first three determinants is included in X. By analogy, the rate of change of the economy in time is the time derivative of the function: $dY/dt = df/dt$.

There are at least three reasons why the equation cannot at this time be applied directly for analytical purposes. In the first place, each of the determinants is not a single variable, but rather a cluster of related variables. Secondly, not all of the variables within the clusters have been quantified, and some of them probably are not quantifiable. Finally, the determinants are not 'given', but result from complex mutual interactions. In principle – again, for heuristic purposes – it might be possible to set up a system of simultaneous equations in which the number of equations equalled the number of unknowns. Unfortunately, in the present state of our knowledge we have very few good ideas about the form of the equations, or even how to identify the dependent and independent variables. Nevertheless, as I hope to demonstrate, the equation is useful in its present simple form as a framework for the analysis of long-term economic change. But first a few words about each of the determinants.

Population is the most easily quantifiable of the determinants. It is analogous to 'labour' in the classical schema, except that it enters into the equations on the side of demand as well as that of supply. Moreover, it is not sufficient to think solely in terms of total population and its rate of change as the only meaningful variables. Age and sex distribution, the biological characteristics of the members (size, strength, health, and so on), the level of acquired skills or human capital, and the rate of labour force participation, among other things, are features of a population that have a bearing on its economic performance.

Resources is the 'land' of classical economics writ large. The term embraces not merely the amount of land, the fertility of the soil, and conventional natural resources, but also climate, topography, location, the availability of water, and other features of the natural environment.

With a static technology and a given set of social institutions – the situation implicitly assumed by the classical economists and approximated in reality for long stretches of human history – the resources available to a society set the effective limits to both the size of its population and its per capita income. Such was the setting that elicited the Malthusian principle of population. Technological change or innovation, however, allows those limits to be expanded, both through the discovery and utilisation of new resources and through more efficient utilisation of existing resources, including labour. The continental United States today supports a population in excess of 220 million at one of the highest material standards of living ever achieved. Prior to the arrival of Europeans the same area, whose inhabitants employed a stone age technology, could support at a near-subsistence standard only a few million. Medieval

Europe, with a far more advanced technology than that of the pre-Columbian Americans, grew to a maximum of perhaps 60 million inhabitants at the beginning of the fourteenth century before declining to 40 million or fewer as the result of a demographic crisis. Four hundred years later, after a long period of steady but not dramatic technological and organisational change, the population had grown to approximately 150 million. Today, after roughly two centuries of economic growth based on modern technology, the population of Europe (exclusive of the Soviet Union) exceeds 500 million, and its members are more affluent than their ancestors of the fourteenth or even the nineteenth century could have imagined.

The interrelationship of population, resources, and technology in the economy is conditioned by social institutions (or the 'socio-cultural context' or the 'institutional matrix' of economic activity), including values and attitudes. At the level of national economies and other similar aggregates the most frequently relevant institutions are such things as the social structure (number, relative size, economic basis, and fluidity of social classes), the nature of the state or other political regime, and the religious or ideological proclivities of the dominant groups or classes and (if different) of the masses as well. In addition, there are a host of lesser institutions that may need to be taken into account in considering any given problem, such as voluntary associations (business firms, labour unions, and so on), the educational system, even family structure and other value-forming agencies. One social function which such institutions perform is to provide elements of continuity and stability, without which society would disintegrate; but in performing this function they may serve as barriers to economic development by fettering human labour, withholding resources from rational exploitation, or inhibiting innovation and the diffusion of technology. Ayres, as noted above, pitted institutions against technology as the black hat against the white. But institutional innovation is also a possibility, with consequences not unlike those of technological innovation, permitting a more efficient or intensive use of both material resources and human energy and ingenuity. North and Thomas have argued, in fact, that institutional innovation was more responsible than technological change for the economic and population growth of Europe between the fourteenth and eighteenth centuries.[24] Without entering here into that particular discussion, it should be clear that institutional innovation has occurred and that some of its consequences have been favourable to economic development.

It may be objected that such a broad classification, while it satisfies an aesthetic desire for comprehensiveness, sacrifices explanatory power to gain generality. I do not, of course, any more than Rostow, propose to dispense with the conventional tools of analysis, only to supplement them with a new way of looking at long-term economic change. The advantages are, broadly speaking, twofold: we gain a better understanding of the dynamics of historical change, and thereby a better perspective on current problems, which may enrich our contribution toward their solution. I share wholeheartedly Rostow's view that economic history, correctly understood and interpreted, may and should assist in solving contemporary problems. A couple of (greatly abridged) case studies will illustrate the point.

III

Two of the most urgent world problems today for which economic history has some relevance are those of population pressure and the 'energy shortage'. (Others could be adduced; for example, pollution, even the problem of world peace, or, more specifically, the possibility of nuclear war, has its economic dimensions.) Let us begin with population.

The population of the world some ten thousand years ago has been plausibly estimated at between five and ten million inhabitants.[25] Resources were at least as plentiful as today but, given the technology of the times, mostly could not be utilised. We have a fair idea of the technology from artifacts, but can only guess at institutional structures, which in any case can be described as primitive. In material terms life was, in the classic phrase of Hobbes, 'nasty, brutish, and short'. From skeletal remains it has been estimated that the average length of life was not more than about twenty years; infant and childhood mortality were extremely high, with perhaps no more than 50 per cent of children born surviving until age ten; survivors beyond the age of fifty were extremely rare. Given the nature of their economy, stone age populations were subject to recurrent rounds of feast and famine, depending upon the movement of the game and the luck of the hunt. In periods of famine, all but the strongest perished; in prolonged famines entire communities succumbed.

The invention of settled agriculture – which was no doubt a social invention rather than an individual achievement, and very likely the work of women – substantially increased the volume and, perhaps more importantly, the regularity of food supplies. This permitted a significant increase in the size and densities of populations, and eventually led to institutional changes that completely altered the way of life of the affected peoples. Permanent settlements grew, some eventually to become cities as the surplus production (above that required for the subsistence of the cultivators) allowed the formation of a ruling – non-producing – class. In this way the earliest civilisations, those of Mesopotamia and Egypt, took shape, eventually spreading throughout the Near and Middle East and the Mediterranean basin.

By the beginning of the Christian era world population had increased to perhaps 300 million.[26] Determining the extent to which the average standard of living improved concurrently with demographic growth is a more difficult problem. Undoubtedly there was some improvement, which both encouraged and permitted the growth of population. C. Clark estimated that the real earnings of a typical free artisan in Rome in the first century A.D. were approximately equivalent to those of a typical British factory worker in 1850 and to those of an Italian worker in 1928.[27] By extrapolation, that would imply that Roman artisans were substantially better off economically than millions of peasants and urban dwellers in Asia, Africa, and Latin America today. Such comparisons, however, contain difficult conceptual problems as well as statistical pitfalls.

Another possible measure of material well-being is average length of life. Here, again, one must be wary of incomplete and inconclusive statistics, especially since they say little about the relative incidence of disease and other causes of death among different social classes. In general, however, it appears that the average length of life in the best years of the Roman Empire was about 30 years, which represents a slight improvement over earlier societies, but is still considerably less than in all but the very poorest societies in recent times.

Since the fall of Rome Europe has experienced at least three well defined periods of population growth, which I have elsewhere termed 'logistics,' interspersed with intervals of decline or stagnation.[28] Some scholars believe the surges were worldwide, although the evidence they present is not very persuasive.[29] In any event, the first European logistic occurred between the ninth or tenth and the beginning of the fourteenth century; the second from the latter part of the fifteenth to the beginning or middle of the seventeenth; and the third from the middle of the eighteenth to the second quarter of the twentieth. A fourth surge, which is truly worldwide, began after the Second World War and is the principal reason for concern about overpopulation.

How can we account for these fluctuations? In all three historical cases the advent of population growth was associated with improvements in food supply as a result of either technological or institutional changes, or both. Oversimplifying somewhat, the medieval surge resulted primarily from the introduction of the heavy wheeled plow and a host of auxiliary innovations, which also entailed a major organisational (institutional) change, namely, the three-course rotation with open fields and nucleated villages. Evidence for the sources of the early modern surge is much spottier. No major, widespread agricultural innovation comparable to the heavy plow occurred, although significant productivity-enhancing improvements took place in the Low Countries, changes which gradually diffused to England and elsewhere. North and Thomas have argued that institutional changes involving larger markets, economies of scale, reductions in transactions costs, and greater specialisation were primarily responsible.[30] To the extent that this is so those changes should be related to technological improvements in maritime shipping (the hinged sternpost rudder, better rigging, larger ships, and so on). Finally, the population surge of the third logistic, which was also intimately associated with the concurrent processes of industrialisation and urbanisation, can basically be traced to a series of technological and institutional changes in agriculture that are commonly lumped together in the phrase 'agricultural revolution'.

The deceleration and eventual reversal of the first two surges came about primarily as a result of the phenomenon of diminishing returns, as the increase in numbers outpaced the increases in production. The drastic fall in population in the mid-fourteenth century is directly traceable to the infamous bubonic plague and possibly other infectious diseases; and the lesser, more localised declines that occurred in the seventeenth century probably also owed much to epidemics and the endemic warfare of the period. In both cases, however, the population had become more susceptible to disease as a result of the decline in the standard of living and of increasing malnutrition.[31] The European population did not actually decline at the end of the third logistic, although the rate of increase did so, but the most striking aspect of the demographic history of the last two centuries has been an apparently permanent alteration in human behaviour. The dramatic fall in mortality in industrial nations in the last century or so, followed after a lag by a similar fall in fertility, marks a fundamental turning point in human social development.

What bearing does this brief survey of world demographic history have on the present concern with overpopulation? Does the framework of analysis that I have outlined permit us to make any informed judgments on the problem? Taking the very long-run view, we can say that from the invention of agriculture until the eighteenth century world population doubled every thousand years, approximately. In the 150 years from the mid-eighteenth to the beginning of the twentieth century it doubled again, and once more in the first two-thirds of the twentieth century. Just a few years ago demographers were projecting yet another doubling by the end of the present century, but those projections have now been revised downward. It would appear that the inflection point on the logistic curve of population growth has been passed, and that for the foreseeable future growth will occur at a decreasing rate. Technology, which in the past successively raised the limits imposed by resources on human population growth, now makes it possible for mankind to limit its numbers voluntarily. A significant proportion of the human race has already undergone the change in values and behaviour necessary to achieve a stable world population, and it appears that the remainder may do so as well.

IV

The energy problem is of a fundamentally different nature. The potential supply of energy is far more abundant in relation to demand than is that of food, and the real cost of energy is much lower than in any previous century. Insofar as there is a critical shortage, it results from two causes, both temporary. One is the excessive dependence of the world on petroleum as a fuel for both transportation and power production, induced in large part by the extremely low real cost of petroleum during the first three quarters of the present century. The other is the action of the international cartel of petroleum producers to take advantage of that excessive dependence, a cartel facilitated by the fortuitous geographical location of a large part of the world's current petroleum production in a group of nations most of which were already united, after a fashion, by religious and ideological zeal. But the causes of the current alleged shortage are temporary. Even if the cartel does not break up as a result of internal dissension, the discovery of new deposits elsewhere in the world will eventually erode its power.

More importantly, petroleum is not the only potential source of energy. As I have just pointed out, the main reason for our excessive dependence on it has been its relative abundance and low real cost. Petroleum replaced coal for many purposes simply because it was cheaper and more convenient, but the coal is still available. At present or projected rates of utilisation of energy, existing known supplies of coal will suffice for hundreds if not thousands of years. Moreover, oil shale is available in abundance, and we already have available the technology for producing liquid hydrocarbons from it. It is merely a matter of cost; when the price of liquid petroleum rises high enough, petroleum from shale will come to the market. Nuclear power is also available, although in smaller quantities than was predicted in the 1950s. To be sure, there are environmental hazards associated with the production and consumption of all three of these substitutes for petroleum. (Petroleum itself, and its derivatives, are not free of environmental dangers, for that matter.) That is one reason why those substitutes are not already more widely used. But 'environmental hazard' is really another aspect of cost. The recent concern with ecological problems associated with the use of fossil and atomic fuels results from the belated public awareness that the social costs of their utilisation exceed the private costs of production. The fumbling, frequently misguided attempts to prevent or restrict their use can be regarded as a desire to equalise social and private costs, but there are more effective ways of doing so than through restrictive legislation or administrative regulation. The most effective is obviously taxation that makes the market price reflect the true social costs.

Neither energy shortages nor environmental problems of this sort are new. It was the 'shortage' and consequent high price of wood for fuel that induced Londoners to substitute the foul-smelling but cheaper 'sea coales' in their hearths in the late Middle Ages. Numerous ordinances to prevent or restrict the burning of coal were issued from the thirteenth to the seventeenth centuries, but its use continued to spread.[32] The strong economic inducements in its favour forced authorities and consumers alike to accept the environmental hazards and inconveniences as a part of the price. Interestingly, when cheaper, more efficient centrally generated electricity replaced coal as a domestic fuel in the twentieth century, many Britons insisted on disguising their new electric heaters as old-fashioned coal grates.

This faintly amusing, seemingly trivial example actually has, by implication, a profound significance not only for the subject of energy sources and their substitutes, but also for our understanding of the nature of long-term economic change. The characteristic features of the modern industrial era are (1) the extensive use of machinery as substitute for or supplement to human skill and strength and (2) an extensive reliance on mineral sources – first coal, then petroleum – for fuel and power. Both of these features emerged first in England, and well before the conventional dates of the 'industrial revolution'. In addition to using coal for domestic heating, cooking, and laundry-work, Englishmen began employing it in a variety of industrial processes as early as the sixteenth century. By the opening decades of the seventeenth century it was widely employed as a fuel for salt refining and the manufacture of glass, bricks, and tile; subsequently it was taken up by dyers, hat makers, alum producers, sugar refiners, and brewers, and by the end of the century it was used in reverberatory furnaces to smelt lead, tin, and copper.[33]

Attempts had been made early in the seventeenth century to smelt iron ore with coal, but impurities (mainly sulphur) in the raw coal rendered it unusable for the purpose. Finally, in 1709, Abraham Darby, a Quaker ironmaster in Coalbrookdale (Shropshire), successfully used coal in the blast furnace by first converting it into coke; even then, however, it was almost half a century before the process was widely adopted, even though Darby did not take out a patent. Not until the 1780s, when the puddling process and Cort's rolling mill were introduced for refining pig iron, did coke-smelting completely drive out the older charcoal process. It used to be thought, even by such an eminent authority as T. S. Ashton, that the delay in adopting coke-smelting after Darby's innovation was due either to imperfections in the product or to irrational prejudices on the part of ironmasters or their customers. C. K. Hyde has recently demonstrated, however, that the substitution of coke for charcoal depended upon discriminating estimates of cost.[34] Similar considerations, rather than any psychological or cultural differences in the character of entrepreneurs, account for the 'delays' in the adoption of coke-smelting on the Continent and in the United States.[35]

England's precocity in the use of mineral fuel derived not only from the growing shortage and rising relative price of timber, but also from the fortuitous presence in England of widespread, easily accessible veins of coal. In the beginning these veins were worked from the surface, and subsequently in shallow pits. As the demand for coal increased, however, it became necessary to dig deeper and deeper until stopped by the water table. Drainage thus became a major problem (which was also encountered in other mining industries, notably the tin mines of Cornwall). Various devices, such as adits and horse-powered pumps were employed, but it eventually became evident that more powerful pumps would be necessary. Several experiments with steam pumps were made in the seventeenth century, and in 1698 Thomas Savery patented a 'fire engine' specifically for use in the Cornish tin mines. But Savery's engine was unreliable, and so it was not until Thomas Newcomen erected an atmospheric steam engine in a Staffordshire coal mine in 1712 that a tolerably satisfactory solution was found to the problem of mine drainage. Subsequently many improvements on Newcomen's engine were made, of which the most celebrated are those of James Watt, and it was applied to a variety of industrial tasks in addition to mining.

Meanwhile the growth of the coal industry exerted demands of its own for improvements in transport. The collier fleets from Newcastle had already become famous in the seventeenth century, but the more crucial problems developed in inland transport. These were solved by the introduction of first plank, then iron rails on which carriages were propelled by human, horse, and gravity power. By the time that the steam engine was first successfully employed in locomotives in the early nineteenth century, England already had several hundred miles of iron 'railways'. Similarly, the first major canal for the transport of bulk merchandise, the famous Bridgewater canal from Worsley to Manchester, completed in 1761, owed its existence to the demand for coal.

Thus the 'energy shortage' of early modern times produced creative responses on the part of literally thousands of individuals that led in time to the modern industrial order. Is it too much to expect that, as the age of fossil fuels draws to a close, mankind will be able to devise newer, even cheaper and more reliable sources of energy?

NOTES AND REFERENCES

1. Preface to the first edition of W. W. Rostow, *The Stages of Economic Growth: A Non-Communist Manifesto* (Cambridge, 1960), 2nd edn (Cambridge, 1971) p. xvii.
2. R. Cameron, 'Comparative Economic Progress: A Review Article' (devoted in large part to *Stages*) in *Comparative Studies in Society and History*, 3(Jan 1961) 231–9; and R. Cameron, a review of *The World Economy: History and Prospect, American Historical Review*, 84 (Apr 1979) pp. 414–5.
3. Joan Robinson, 'Misunderstandings in the Theory of Production', *Greek Economic Review*, 1 (Aug 1979) p. 6.
4. Paul Simon, *Mrs Robinson*, song from the motion picture *The Graduate*, © 1967.
5. Adam Smith, *An Inquiry into the Nature and Causes of the Wealth of Nations*, Glasgow edn, R. H. Campbell, A. S. Skinner, and W. B. Todd(eds) (Oxford, 1976) I, 69: 'Wages, profit, and rent, are the three original sources of all revenue as well as of all exchangeable value.' (Note his omission of interest, and the inclusion of profit as the return on capital.) David Ricardo, *The Principles of Political Economy and Taxation* (London, 1911) p. 1: 'The produce of the earth . . . is divided among three classes of the community . . . the proportions . . . which will be allotted to each of these classes, under the names of rent, profit, and wages, will be essentially different . . . To determine the laws which regulate this distribution is the principal problem of Political Economy.' Cf. Joseph A. Schumpeter, *History of Economic Analysis* (New York, 1954) pp. 309, 568–9.
6. Ibid., pp. 554–7.
7. Ibid., pp. 918–20, 963–71.
8. Adam Smith, *Wealth of Nations* (Glasgow edn), I, 20.
9. Ibid., I, 21.
10. Schumpeter, *History*, pp. 556–7, 893–8; Joseph A. Schumpeter, *The Theory of Economic Development* (Cambridge, Mass., 1934; first German edn, 1912).
11. W. W. Rostow, *The Process of Economic Growth*, 1st edn (New York, 1952) p. 3. The more astute and conscientious textbook writers even made this explicit, although the majority did not.
12. See, e.g. Thorstein Veblen, *The Instinct of Workmanship* (New York, 1914) and Thorstein Veblen, *The Engineers and the Price System* (New York, 1921); for a historical application, Thorstein Veblen, *Imperial Germany and the Industrial Revolution* (New York, 1919).
13. Mark Blaug, *Economic Theory in Retrospect*, 3rd edn (Cambridge and New York, 1978) p. 712.
14. C. E. Ayres, *The Theory of Economic Progress* (New York, 1944) (2nd edn, New York, 1962).
15. Cf. R. M. Hartwell, 'C. E. Ayres on the Industrial Revolution', in William Breit and William P. Culbertson, Jr. (eds), *Science and Ceremony: The Institutional Economics of C. E. Ayres* (Austin, Texas, 1976) pp. 49–62.
16. I hoped, in vain, to find a corrective for the latter defect in Rostow's contribution to the Ayres *Festschrift*, 'Technology and the Price System', ibid., pp. 75–113.
17. Moses Abramovitz, 'Resource and Output Trends in the United States since

1870', *American Economic Review*, 64 (May 1956) 5–23; Robert M. Solow, 'Technical Change and the Aggregate Production Function', *Review of Economics and Statistics*, 39 (Aug 1957) 312–20, and other writings; Edward F. Denison, *The Sources of Economic Growth in the United States and the Alternatives before Us* (New York, 1962); Edward F. Denison, *Why Growth Rates Differ: Postwar Experience in Nine Western Countries* (Washington, 1967); Angus Maddison, *Economic Growth in the West: Comparative Experience in Europe and North America* (New York, 1964).

18. T. W. Schultz, 'Capital Formation by Education', *Journal of Political Economy*, 68 (Dec 1960) 571–83; T. W. Schultz, 'Investment in Human Capital', *American Economic Review*, 51 (Jan 1961) 1–17; G. S. Becker, *Human Capital: A Theoretical and Empirical Analysis, With Special Reference to Education* (New York, 1964). There is now a large literature on human capital.
19. Jacob Schmookler, *Invention and Economic Growth* (Cambridge, Mass., 1966); Nathan Rosenberg, *Perspectives on Technology* (Cambridge and New York, 1976); Nathan Rosenberg (ed.), *The Economics of Technological Change* (Harmondsworth, 1971) is a collection of articles by various authors; Arnold Heertje, *Economics and Technical Change* (London, 1977) is a good, reasonably up-to-date survey.
20. Lance E. Davis and Douglass C. North, *Institutional Change and American Economic Growth* (Cambridge and New York, 1971); Douglass C. North and Robert Paul Thomas, *The Rise of the Western World: A New Economic History* (Cambridge and New York, 1973). Davis, in his presidential address to the Economic History Association, 'It's a Long, Long Road to Tipperary, or Reflections on Organised Violence, Protection Rates, and Related Topics: The New Political History', *Journal of Economic History*, 40 (Mar 1980) 1–16, explicitly mentions the priority of Frederic C. Lane in this area; see Lane, 'Economic Consequences of Organized Violence', ibid., 18 (Dec 1958) 401–17, and other articles and essays by the same author in Frederic C. Lane, *Profits from Power* (Albany, New York, 1979).
21. See n. 1, *supra*.
22. This paragraph and the following section draw heavily on my presidential address to the Economic History Association, 'Economic History, Pure and Applied', *Journal of Economic History*, 36 (Mar 1976) 3–27. Given the usual fate of presidential addresses, it is unlikely that many readers will have read it, or remembered its contents if they have. Those for whom it is indelibly engraved in their memories may skip at once to the concluding section.
23. This statement ignores the role of capital; but capital equipment, including structures, is itself embodied technology, and the amount so embodied is a function of total output, individual and social choice, and efficiency of financial intermediation. Much the same can be said for human capital. In other words, in the long run, the amount or value of capital in an economy is a result, not a cause, of development or the lack thereof.
24. North and Thomas, *Rise of the Western World, supra*, n. 20.
25. Carlo M. Cipolla, *The Economic History of World Population* revised edn (Baltimore, 1964) p. 95; John D. Durand, 'A Long-Range View of World Population Growth', *The Annals of the American Academy of Political and Social Science*, 369 (Jan 1967) 1–8. Estimates of experts range from one or two million up to 20 million.
26 Durand, 'Long-Range View . . .' op. cit.

27. Colin Clark, *The Conditions of Economic Progress*, 3rd edn (London, 1957, first published 1940) 'Excursus'.
28. R. Cameron, 'The Logistics of European Economic Growth: A Note on Historical Periodization', *The Journal of European Economic History*, 2 (Spring 1973) 145–8.
29. Fernand Braudel, *Civilisation materielle et capitalisme (XVe–XVIIIe siècle)*, 1 (Paris, 1967) 19; but see R. Cameron, 'Europe's Second Logistic', *Comparative Studies in Society and History*, 12 (Oct 1970) 452–62.
30. North and Thomas, *Rise of the Western World*, pp. 114–5. Immanuel Wallerstein, in *The Modern World-System: Capitalist Agriculture and the Origins of the European World-Economy in the Sixteenth Century* (New York, 1974), also stresses geographical specialisation, economies of scale, and larger markets.
31. Braudel and some other scholars believe that climatic changes in the fourteenth and seventeenth centuries account for the cessation of population growth; but see Cameron, 'Europe's Second Logistic', n. 29 above.
32. William H. Te Brake, 'Air Pollution and Fuel Crises in Preindustrial London, 1250–1650', *Technology and Culture*, 16 (July 1975) 337–59.
33. John U. Nef, *The Rise of the British Coal Industry*, 2 vols (London, 1932) passim.
34. Charles K. Hyde, *Technological Change and the British Iron Industry, 1700–1870* (Princeton, 1977) pp. 29–41, 56–62, 197–209.
35. R. Cameron, 'Profit, croissance et stagnation en France au XIXe siècle', *Économie appliqué*, 10 (Apr–Sep 1957) 427–33; R. Cameron, *France and the Economic Development of Europe* (Princeton, 1961) pp. 387–97; Peter Temin, *Iron and Steel in Nineteenth Century America: An Economic Inquiry* (Cambridge, Mass., 1964) Chap. 3.

4 Stages and the State: How do they Relate?

S. G. CHECKLAND

THE STATE AND THE LONG-TERM THEORY OF GROWTH

If we take the 'long view' at its face value we land of course in the midst of the grand theories of the evolution of human societies. Such theories are difficult to tame, to discipline them into frameworks that make them operational by even the most tolerant of standards. The problems are compounded if we try to see such theories in relation to the political will, seeking clarification of what the role of the state should be in such constructs. But without taking significant account of the state, theories of stages are seriously incomplete. The present essay considers some of the problems that confront grand theory when the claims of the state are made explicit.

To try to formulate links between the state and a long-term theory of growth with a view to providing a unified guide to policy would be, in the vocabulary of Adam Smith, an impertinence. The concepts employed are too diffuse and the linkages between them too loose for such a purpose. But as an exercise in thinking and in teaching such an attempt may be of value, not in terms of generating universal and stable propositions concerning the state and the economy in generalised symbiosis, but as a means of testing our thinking in the long term about both.

The present essay considers the attempts that have been made and are in progress to structure societal systems, doing so over a very long period of time, taking account of a continuously accelerating rate of change, linking in with the present condition of things, with some implications for prognosis and future policy. Such formulations have had to embrace both the spontaneous actions of individuals and groups, and those of the state, together with the interaction between the two. This approach means that although the objective evolution of nation-states and the system they compose, of course, provides the basic reality to be explained, it is not our starting point here. Instead the emphasis is on the explainers – those who have struggled to elaborate theories of greater or lesser scope that will make it possible to penetrate beyond surface experience. Nor is it superficial to make this historiographical approach, for an assessment and reconciliation of conceptualisations, though a tool-box task, is essential. In any case it should drive the student back to reality in the search for it.

Indeed we should always have well forward in our minds the real societies whose experience we are trying to reduce to order. The phenomena that long-term theorists have sought to structure have been European. Only Europe can provide the terrain for the really long view if it is to be taken in terms of dynamic change. For as R. S. Southern has reminded us, 'For a thousand years Europe has been the chief centre of political experiment, economic expansion and intellectual discovery in the world' (Southern, 1953, p. 12). There is undoubtedly a sense in which Europe has been a historical unit against the rest of the world. It was unified in medieval times by the Latin language, the code of chivalry, the Church, the guild system, the merchant corporations, the towns, the fairs, and perhaps especially the legal concepts of Roman and canonic law (Heckscher, I, 1931, pp. 34–5). After the Renaissance it found a new kind of unity in the new rationalism which distinguished it from the rest of the world and out of which came the scientific revolution. But it was also in Europe, partly in consequence of the scientific revolution, that the human system went critical in the sense of generating the Industrial Revolution. This brought divergence of national experience. We must be even more specific. Within Europe the states whose history has chiefly concerned those who have sought for a theory of industrialisation have been Britain and Holland, the German lands and France, together with Russia. In very general terms these were the dominant elements of northern Europe, that small part of the world that from the later sixteenth century had seized the initiative from the societies of the Mediterranean. Historically they arranged themselves conveniently on a west-to-east spectrum across the north European plain, with the west leading in economic achievement and the east lagging. In terms of time the expanse that is relevant to a consideration of the problem of the long-run relationship between stages and the state runs from the rise of the European nation-states in the later middle ages to the present, straddling the period of Europe's cultural unity and its industrial diversity.

Europe was a system of political units, each of which determined the shape of the others, and which was in turn determined. But none succeeded in reducing the others to its will. At the same time the more western of these states were capable of thrusting outward by sea to the rest of the world to produce vast and rival empires, penetrating inward from the edges of the continents. So obvious was all this to those who pondered the longer-term performance of mankind from the Enlightenment onward that they knew, without having to remark upon it, that their thinking was Eurocentric, and did not question this perspective.

The rest of the world existed as exhibiting a contrast. China especially was treated as the antithesis of Europe – an area where an immense and dormant cultural unity under a single state could prevail. The Enlightenment thinkers and their successors, in constructing their long view as it related to the state, thus had two great models, namely the diverse dynamism of Europe and the unitary stagnation of China, one at each end of Eurasia. China could provoke conjectures as to the conditions of stagnation;[1] only Europe posed the challenge of explaining long-term cumulative change, together with the relationship of the state to it. Weber, like other grand-scale speculators, enjoyed using the Europe–China antithesis, writing of the occident's power to generate the rational as well as the national state, a feat of which the orient was incapable (Weber, 1927, Chapter XIX). As to the peripheral world of primary producing countries where the maritime empires were formed, they hardly entered into the formulation at all, for there was relatively little concern with the processes that had been set at work in them until the late nineteenth century.

THE THREE IDIOMS

In conceiving of a theory of stages of societal development at the conceptual, as opposed to the historical level, there are two ways of proceding. One is to leave the state to one side at the outset, and to think in terms of the spontaneous forces generated by individual or group actions, and then, at a later stage, to insert the state into the model. The alternative is to have the state present from the outset, seeing its actions as being in some sense concurrent with those that derive from spontaneity, and interacting with them. In general there has been a tendency to do the former, leaving the state to be assimilated at a later stage. This is broadly what Adam Smith (1723–90), Karl Marx (1818–83) and W. W. Rostow (1916–) have done. This has been partly due to the fact that it is difficult to carry both sets of initiatives simultaneously as the model is being brought into being. But all stigmatisers must procede in terms of some kind of societal unit, otherwise no kind of coherence of experience can be envisaged. Thus all such models must assume at least implicitly, group identities, but most leave the political structuring of them to a later stage in the argument.

It is partly because of the difficulties of merging the spontaneous actions of men in adjusting to their natural environment with the actions of authority that stem from their corporate identity that three general modes of structuring long-term experience have come into being. These three are not mutually exclusive, but represent differences of starting point for different scholars.

The first idiom has four characteristics: it is internalised within each society, it is universal, it is linear, and it treats economic processes as primary over those of the state. In it a sequential or stages experience of an ascending order is envisaged as being domestic to each. It is the fruit of Smith's conjectural history, reappearing as Marx's historical materialism; theoretical formulations that derive from it have their starting point and their principal emphasis within each society, viewed as discrete entities. The essence of this perspective is that the basic determinant of the nature of each society is its mode of subsistence or production. This mode is either static, or pursues an ascending order of productivity as propelled by technological advance. But though the experience of societies is thus viewed in internalised terms, all societies share the same experience to the extent that they are able to make the ascent, in a prescribed sequence, from the more primitive modes of production to the more sophisticated: internalisation is thus accompanied by universality. Nature or natural endowment does have a part to play, not by generating distinct societal experiences, but in the sense of determining the cut-off point on the scale of ascent that may be reached by the less well endowed societies. The interplay between states, politically and in terms of war, is overshadowed by their internal dynamics.

This way of thinking depends of course upon the societal unit of thought employed. The earlier in the sequence of stages, the more ill defined the unit will be. Two watersheds are involved. One concerns the advent of the nation-state – before its consolidation from the later middle ages both the geographical and the political aspects of the state were ill defined. Secondly it is with the commercial revolution, and more especially with the Industrial Revolution, that great differentials are introduced between the economic performances of societies. It is only then that it is really necessary to regard the processes involved as being internalised within nation-states; before the coming of these great changes the differences in economic achievement were sufficiently minor as not to call for a theory that provided a kind of economic and societal ladder of ascent to higher output and more sophisticated state forms.[2]

Moreover the forms assumed by the state are of two kinds, embodying the political will (that of the sovereign) and the executive. The two did not greatly diverge over Europe before the late eighteenth century (with the exceptions of England and Holland); in nearly all cases absolutism, with its divine right of kings, had at its service a bureaucracy which, though often large and far-reaching, was truly the instrument of the political will, with a good deal of philosophising about how the one could best serve the other (Small, 1909). As the industrial and commercial revolutions made their impact the bureaucracy also grew, though not always (as in the case of Russia), in response to these influences but to others, including the extension of empire. With the growth of empire the bureaucracy could assume in some degrees an identity and a set of objectives of its own. The question arises therefore whether and how the theory of bureaucracy should be assimilated to the theory of stages. How far may the evolution of bureaucracy be seen as something common and uniform in states at the same stage?

The universalised, linear, internalised, economic formulation is the oldest of the three, stemming from the Enlightenment. Its most celebrated exponents have, of course, been Adam Smith and Karl Marx. Though there are fundamental differences between the two, the ultimate basis of their reasoning is the same, namely that there is a chain of causality running from the mode of production or forces of production within a given society, via the property relations appropriate to that mode, to the general structure and functioning of that society. This perspective means, of course, that the state both as lawmaker and bureaucracy is seen as secondary; variations in its form and functioning can affect the outcome in a subordinate way only. Marx, moreover, went a stage further in internalisation than did Smith; his law of movement, the dialectic as operating between classes, did so *within* each society.

The second idiom in which historical synthesis has been expressed is also internal, but it stresses the unique elements of particular societies, and may in consequence reject linearity of experience. It is thus antagonistic to generalised, universal sequential paradigms. Moreover it regards the state as having a distinct role to play, being not merely derivative from the mode of production and the property relationships, but being capable of operating quite vitally on society: in short the state can have a degree of independent and determining existence.

This perspective rests on a basis fundamentally geographical or spatial. Not that uniqueness of place and context is absolute, producing an entirely different history for each society: on the contrary, there is a sufficient similarity in various parts of the world to permit comparisons, analogues and even an element of 'theory'. Indeed for any sort of synthesis to emerge there must be a degree of escape from uniqueness. But it is never more than a limited one. By the very nature of things those speculators who start from a form of theory that emphasises differences in experiences rather than similarities, and which stresses nature not in terms of universal laws, but rather nature in the sense of an arbitrary and widely differing distribution of resources and natural contexts for man, must be content with a lower degree of universalism. They are happy to concede much more to contingency and to the irrefragable variations of conditions under which various groups of men have lived their lives. In particular, the state and its role in terms of growth may be a very different thing in the various contexts thus determined, both as framing laws and causing them to be implemented through the bureaucracy.

The idiom of the internal uniqueness has been later in finding exponents than its rival. It is true that the traditional history of nation-states has always depended on the concept of uniqueness, insisting that the experience of each nation has been peculiar to itself and should be viewed in such terms. History could thus easily become a projection of nationalisms, a means indeed of confirming national identity and justification. Such history has little sympathy with explanations that are rooted in determining circumstances, ultimately deriving from the physical environment. Moreover a theory that starts from such differences lacks unifying power, producing explanations that are concerned with fragments of human experience that cannot be readily assimilated to any universal schema of the kind sought by the Enlightenment and its successors. For some protagonists, indeed, this approach is a virtue, blocking attempts at too ambitious a synthesis of human experience. Three leading exponents of historical difference have been the geographer Halford Mackinder (1861–1947), the sociologist Karl Wittfogel (1896–), and the historian Alexander Gerschenkron (1904–78). In a sense all three of these rooted their thoughts in the distinctive and irreducible circumstances that have prevailed in some parts of the world as opposed to others. In spite of their differences they share the characteristic that they emphasise the compelling dissimilarities between societies, ultimately rooted in their physical locations and endowments, which determine divergencies both of private and state action.

The third idiom starts not from universal aspects common to all economies and nation-states, nor from the circumstances that determine major differences between them. Instead it is couched in terms of all of them together, seen as composing a global system of mutual interaction. This is the youngest of the three formulations, with its effective beginning in the modern sense in the later nineteenth and early twentieth centuries with theories of imperialism from the time of J. A. Hobson (1858–1940) who, in 1902, saw Britain's renewed imperial drive as the result of a search for investment opportunities by British capitalists. It has arisen from the recognition that societies and states, though part of their lives is internal and can be approached in such terms, another part, and perhaps a predominant one, arises from international or even world interaction in terms both of economics and politics. In very general terms the more advanced the leading countries are in their economic development, the more pressing is their need to understand the phenomena associated with their interaction, both with peer countries and with those at an earlier stage of development. It is true that the mercantilist thinkers had this aspect as one of their principal preoccupations. But the thinking of a mercantilist was not aimed at understanding the pattern of interdependence in any objective and generalised way, in search for world equity, stability and freedom from war, but rather in terms of matrix upon which his own state could operate to promote its own advantage, or even more specifically, identifying the most formidable commercial enemy and so acting as to obstruct it to the greatest degree, doing so without any great misgiving if war should come.

The global agenda is a formidable one. It has two main components. The first has to do with the relationships between the more advanced and the less advanced economies. How far is it the case that the nations that are approaching or which have reached maturity and high mass consumption have done so through exploitive dependence on the less advanced? Can the world pattern be projected in terms of a core–periphery analysis, with the advanced countries constituting an element of economic dominance, systematically related to the less advanced with their monocultures and feeble states? The emergence of such a pattern may have taken place in a manner which involved no exploitation or coercion, being the effect of 'objective' market forces. Even on such assumptions, however, there are serious questions concerning the long-term stability of such a relationship. Or it may have been the result of unjustified exploitation because the market has not been a neutral mechanism linking equals, or because of direct political manipulation. Moreover the argument that the core is able indefinitely to dominate the periphery is partly obsolescent; already it is apparent that some elements of the former periphery, especially the oil producing countries, are able, under the market conditions generated by the advanced countries as the blind technology they have created redeals the cards, to act as stern monopolists against the core and indeed against other parts of the periphery. Further, as a countervailing force in a sense unifying the core countries and sustaining their position, there are the great multinationals.

But not only is the relationship between core and periphery not fixed in favour of the former, there is also the phenomenon of shifting status at the core itself. Societies and their states have emerged as large and powerful, able to use their political structure to impact outside themselves, both in terms of other core countries and the periphery, but which have then receded to a secondary role: the great exemplar of this is, of course, Britain, the first core country of the industrial age. Part of the explanation of this cycle in terms of international status lies in the profound feedback in the case of a core country upon its own internal structures of this apparently irresistible thrust. States as they have ascended the scale of coherence and wealth have not typically sought an equilibrium relationship with the rest of the world until it was too late, that is, until the dynamic urge itself was fading. Instead they have been subject to the compulsion of self-assertion, both in terms of private business and state action. Moreover, just as one country, Britain, could occupy the core and then recede from it, so too other countries, formerly peripheral, have been able to become core: the leading cases are, of course, Germany, the United States and Japan (Rubison, 1978, pp. 39–74). But in order to explain how these countries found the necessary dynamic it is not possible to refer to a set of general principles operating uniformly in all of them. On the contrary, three highly specific explanations are required, each running largely in terms of internal forces and the relationships they have generated. In the cases of Germany and the United States it can be argued that these forces operated in regional terms, arising from the challenge to reconcile and unify divergent economic interests that had their roots in regional sub-economies; in short the idiom of geographical particularism is employed.

As to the exponents of the global approach, Adam Smith largely falls out of the running, stopping as he did at what he called the commercial stage of development, with industrialisation merely embryonic. Large parts of the world, like China and India, appeared to be dormant in his time, and the primary producing countries, under the operation of the principle of comparative advantage, were regarded as gainers along with the other participants in world trade. On the other hand, Smith was well aware of the struggle between Britain and France for the status of core power, reaching its penultimate climax in the Seven Years' War (1756–63), fought on a global scale at the core of Europe, at sea and in the peripheral countries. Partly because of the general acceptance of the view that the extension of trade was beneficial to all participants, the Smithian system of natural liberty did not inspire in those who stood in his tradition any serious attempt to think of the international system as being composed of dominators and dominated.

Hobson's influence lay not so much among the liberal thinkers, but with Lenin who was seeking an answer to the enigma of why revolutionary conditions had not appeared in the advanced countries as demanded by a theory that rested on discrete national entities (Fieldhouse, 1972). It can perhaps be said that the liberal attempt at globalism is very late, with Rostow making the most sustained effort in this direction, especially in his *Politics and Stages of Growth* of 1971 and *The World Economy. History and Prospect*, of 1978.

Marx, on the other hand, was moving in a global direction, seeing the bourgeoisie both as building a world system dominated by the advanced countries, and as disturbing the ancient stagnation of eastern countries, especially perhaps India. Moreover the idea of capitalism as a total social formation has always implied globality. But Marx's dicta in this direction are not highly developed. Also, some of the elements of the basic part of his system, namely those which stemmed from the internalised account of the behaviour of the capitalist states and their ruling bourgeoisie, set up propositions that could encumber the attempt at globality. Thus if one thinks in terms of a logic deriving from the structuring of a world system perspective, that system may impact upon the constituent societies in such a way as to impair their autonomy of action, thus limiting the ability of the capitalist ruling class to develop a clear sense of internationality and the ability to wield the state in furtherance of it (Block, 1978). Moreover Marxian theory has encountered difficulties in accommodating to the proliferation and structuring of bureaucracy in the modern world. Some Marxists have moved with James Burnham in the direction of recognising a managerial revolution which has led to the development of a new class, namely state managers (politicians and bureaucrats). They stand between the capitalist ruling class and the nation as a whole and might indeed expropriate the capitalist class. (Burnham, 1941; Krygier, 1979). From the 1970s Marxist scholars have renewed the effort to develop a 'political economy of the world system'. The sociologist Immanuel Wallerstein (1930–) has been a principal inspiration of this attempt.

It would thus appear that the historiography of stages thinking itself falls into stages – represented, in sequence, by universalism based upon the nation-state, by an insistence on a degree of national uniqueness, and finally by an attempt to rise above the nation-states to some kind of structure of world interaction. But from whichever emphasis a thinker starts he will find himself involved, by extension of logic and a widened scrutiny of history, in the other two. The problem is to enunciate propositions at each of the three levels such that they are meaningful in themselves but are not exclusive of the other two perspectives. No one with any sense of reality, least of all an historian, could hope for anything remotely approaching conclusiveness in such an enterprise. But the fact that these perspectives cannot be unified for all time and space in the form of a single set of propositions, does not, of course, invalidate them.

Instead they pose the challenge of seeing how valid the triple idiom really is, how close it is possible to bring it to synthesis, and what are the circumstances that impose the shortfall. Some further consideration of the three modes of thought, expressed largely in terms of their leading exponents, may help in this.

THE TWO TITANS OF INTERNALISM: SMITH AND MARX

Smith and Marx may be taken as the two great exponents of universalised, linear internalism. Smith proposed four stages that would provide an organising principle behind the treatment of progress (Skinner, 1979, p. 3): these were the hunting and gathering, the pastoral, the agricultural and the commercial. There he stopped, leaving the future to take care of itself. Marx proposed epochs somewhat differently conceived, namely the Asiatic, the ancient, the feudal and the capitalist, projecting these into the future with the socialist and communist.

Both systems pose severe interpretative difficulties. In the case of Smith it is necessary to gather together his stages formulation in the paradigmatic sense, his account of what happened historically in Europe, his dicta on political institutions, and the implications for his historical perspective of his economics. Similarly with Marx and his collaborator Engels: their exposition relative to stages and the state exists partly as an attempt to present a system that provides a time perspective for a view of the industrialisation they saw proceeding around them, and partly in terms of interpretations of particular situations, both historical and contemporary. Comments on the particular are sometimes difficult to reconcile with the basic propositions of the general. This has led some Marxists to express the relationship of the state to stages theory in relaxed terms, easing the conceptual distinction between the stages, admitting overlaps between them, and softening the political transition from one stage to the next.[3] In both Smith and Marx there was, too, a tendency to make propagandist simplifications of matters both knew to be highly complex, and to indulge in aphorisms, temptations to which Marx was especially prone.

Smith moved sequentially in his reasoning within each stage from the mode of production to the prevailing property relations. But he stopped short of the third step in the argument, the sovereign. For whereas the property pattern is in such close symbiosis with the mode of production as to be deducible from it (and presumably vice versa), the state as a further extension of this deductive pattern cannot really be derived in any but the vaguest of terms. As A. Skinner puts it, Smith finds it 'easy to describe the characteristics of the fourth economic stage, but virtually impossible to predict the social constitution of the state and its political "superstructure"' (Skinner, 1981; Cropsey, 1957, Chapter II). This, of course, is the liberal–pluralist view of historical materialism. It is true that Smith anticipated Marx in saying that a primary function of the state is to defend a pattern of property rights. But with Smith, as with Locke, property was also a defence against the state; it was the fundamental component, along with markets, of the system of natural liberty. Property and the market diffuse power through society and so liberate men from dependence upon the state and subjection to it. In so doing property and the market release energies that turn to economic initiatives. The existence of property is thus an important factor determining the shape and power of the state, but not in a simply deducible form. In consequence these aspects of Smith's thought do not lead to a delineation of the state, nor do they enter into the question as to how far the state can be regarded as an autonomous entity, imposing a pattern that derives from itself.

For Marx, on the other hand, the state is indeed immediately deducible from the pattern of property relations – it is simply the weapon of the ruling class, the chief property-owning group; it derives its origins and its form from property, and would not exist without it. Politics, as Engels insisted, has no primary role, but is super-structure, a basically derived phenomenon. The state is thus used to defend the existing structure of society by those who dominate and exploit it in any given phase of development; it was, under capitalism 'but a committee for managing the common affairs of the whole bourgeoisie'. And yet, for Marx the state is ultimately a feeble weapon: it cannot be used to arrest the fundamental dynamic of history, namely the self-generative movement from one mode of production to its successor, especially from the feudal to the capitalist mode of production and from the capitalist to the socialist. The bourgeoisie was 'like the sorcerer, who is no longer able to control the powers of the nether world whom he has called upon by his spells'. Under capitalism the state thus has two functions, namely to preside over the extraction of surplus by the bourgeoisie from the proletariat while this continues to be possible, and to perform the rearguard role as crisis approaches of trying, quite hopelessly, to prevent the supercession of the obsolete owning class who are its 'master'. It could be argued that the very clarity of the Marxian view of the state sterilises it as a historical tool.

But whereas Smith could dispose of the problem of bureaucracy by relegating it to insignificance along with his minimising of the state, Marx could find no easy solution to the problem of the executive. The young Marx growing to manhood in Germany before 1843 seems to have been developing a kind of sociology of bureaucracy, seeing it as growing out of the necessary functions of the state at a particular phase of societal development, able under certain conditions to assume its own identity, a kind of estate of the realm, maintaining the general interests of society against predatory classes (McGovern, 1970, p. 466). But later on it became necessary to assimilate bureaucracy to his general theory of property and class. That theory demanded that officialdom, like the state itself, be derived from the class divisions in society, arising as these do from the material conditions of life. With bureaucracy thus seen as derivative, Marx, like Smith, could dismiss it as not being a primary or even a significant focus of attention. But the *coup d'état* of Louis Napoleon of 1851 seemed to confound this assimilation. The coup could be interpreted as the eclipse of the bourgeoisie by Napoleon and the apparatus; thus the bureaucratic state had taken power in France, against which the bourgeoisie was impotent. By admitting the possibility of bureaucratic dictatorship Marx impaired, or at least greatly complicated his central theoretical unity, opening the possibility of the state having an autonomous reality above class.

We are thus deprived by both Smith and Marx, in their different ways, of the possibility of a set of political systems that are correlative over time with stages of growth. Smith, in his cautious way, rejects the possibility of extrapolating the form of the state from the production and property pattern; Marx deduces from his general system a proposition concerning the nature of the state that is so drastic as to make a more specific picture otiose. Marx projected a further volume on the state in which this matter might have been resolved, but perhaps it is no accident that this intended element of the canon receded in his mind so as never to appear.

As to the respective treatments by Smith and Marx of the historical as opposed to the conceptual, here again they diverge. Smith in his historical vein proceeded at long term, trying to combine the generality of European experience (the emergence in post-Roman times of coherent states in terms of absolute kingships), with the uniqueness of England's capacity to escape from the constraints of absolutism and to provide leadership into the commercial stage of society. Smith thus writes his history in terms of a continuous and coherent picture. Marx, on the other hand, treats history much more in terms of incidents and critical conjectures, as in his discussion of the French Revolution, the 18th Brumaire or the Paris Commune.

As to the epigoni of Smith and Marx in this matter of the mechanisms internal to society, and in particular the relationship between the economic and the political, both have inherited severe problems. Marxists are in a dilemma: they must strive to maintain a unity, there being in their view but a single history not capable of disaggregation into the economic, the social and the political; in seeking to maintain this perspective as it relates to the state and the political process the propositions laid down by Marx are not very helpful. The successors of Smith also have a dilemma. Rostow is one of the few on the liberal-pluralist side who have sought to assimilate the economic to the political. This has partly derived from his attempt since the early 1950s to solve 'the problem of formulating an alternative to the Marxist system' (Rostow, 1953, p. 9). Having set out his systematisation of stages of economic growth in 1960 he stands by the framework there provided: it is, he said in 1971, 'useful, in politics as in economics, to view the contemporary world as made up of nations at different stages of growth, whose problems bear a family relationship to those of nations at similar stages in the past as well as in the present'. In this connection Rostow refers to 'the remarkable consensus among economists concerning economic growth' (Rostow, 1971, p. 4). By contrast 'the inherent complexities of politics are such that pure theory can take us only a little way forward in our understanding', politics being 'a kind of biological science and art'. On this view the response of the various societies as they absorb new technologies is predictable in the economic sense at a certain level of generality, but the political has a large element of the inscrutable. This is very much in the tradition of Smith.

A line of thought which confirms the approach internalised within the nation-state relates to fiscal need. This emphasis, basic both to cameralists and mercantilists, has recently been revived in characteristically vigorous form by North and Thomas (1973, p. 96 *et seq*.). Because fiscal crisis was endemic in the pre-industrial states of Europe, private property rights were always at risk. Those emergent nation-states that could meet their fiscal challenge in such a way as to do minimal damage to property, thus leaving economic gains in the hands of those who generated them (as in the case of England and the Netherlands), brought about a new and cumulative release of energy and initiative within the nation. Sir John Hicks takes a view of the links between the state and economic growth that could bear a relationship to the North–Thomas thesis. He suggests that the mercantile economy in its first phase (that of the widening of trade by city-states) was an escape from political authority, that in the second phase, when the city-states fell under the political authority of princes, that authority was not strong enough seriously to impede a now thriving commerce, but that in the modern phase in which we find ourselves today, political control over the market has become immensely easier and more powerful (Hicks, 1969, p. 100).

THE PROTAGONISTS OF NATIONAL DIVERSITY

We turn now to those who start from within certain societies in which the arbitrary forces of geography and those developments that are derivable from them have been predominant or at least powerful. This approach gives rise to a set of national experiences each of which is in a sense *sui generis*.

Mackinder started from the notion of the natural region – one that provided a coherent entity in spatial terms, for purposes of effective government. The world for him since the coming of steamship had become one closed political system; this being so the question arose of the manner in which the regions of which it was composed were determined, and how they would relate to one another. He concluded that the central part of Eurasia was the heartland of the world, the pivotal region of the world's politics. Mackinder thus combined the idiom of national diversity with a form of globalism, with the Eurasian heartland constituting the core. Out of his thinking came the discipline of geopolitics, a good deal pursued in Germany, aimed at explaining and indeed predicting patterns of political potential in areal terms.

Wittfogel, like Mackinder, rejects universality of societal experience. He too roots his thinking in the physical framework within which societies and their politics function, and so arrives at differences rather than similarities. In particular Wittfogel derived his concept of oriental despotism from the physical conditions dominant in certain parts of the world. Where it is necessary to conserve and regulate the water supply through large-scale hydraulic works a characteristic form of society will arise. It will do so because of the demands made by the building and maintenance of such works. It will be hierarchical and authoritarian to the point of despotism. Such societies, having raised themselves to a new plateau of output by hydraulic control, become imprisoned by the political structuring which necessarily results. Such societies, their basic nature being determined by particular ecological conditions, will, of course, have a very different pattern of experience from those in which the water supply is delivered more or less uniformly over the year, the characteristic of temperate zone northern Europe. Under the conditions envisaged by Wittfogel property of the kind on which Smith and Marx built their systems cannot exist. Oriental despotism, or the Asiatic mode of production, or what Wittfogel also called the hydraulic or agro-managerial system was not original with him: Marx in his earlier writings delineated some such conditions and their implications. But absolute state power was inconsistent with the general system evolved by Marx, for in it the state could have no primary identity deriving from unalterable ecological conditions. It is, of course, possible to extend this approach by postulating other forms of ecological condition that could produce such a result in whole or in part. A further step would be to envisage despotism as arising from the very size of countries like China and Russia, these being vast empires of propinquity, imposing a powerful and distinctive bureaucracy and militarism, a command society, as a condition of their survival. This line of reasoning of course invites a link between the peculiarities of national experience and the global approach through core and periphery.

Gerschenkron offers one of the most interesting attempts at analysing the differences between national experiences, but at the same time unifying them into a general perspective. The focus of his scholarship was Russia from the time of Peter the Great (1672–1725). It was a society in which the state was both absolute and could act in a demiurgic way. Peter's effort to modernise Russia imposed immense costs, determined the shape of the state power, and so confirmed the position of the serfs as to make their debasement a primary condition limiting further progress, not merely down to their emancipation in 1861, but for long thereafter.

Gerschenkron describes Peter's programme down to 1715 as inspired by 'the daemonic feeling that development was a function of will power translated into pressure and compulsion' (1970, p. 72). The state was the prime mover; it was the state that created the classes and not the other way round. It is the classes that are derivative and not the state. Thus Russia becomes 'the naked power point . . . in the east of the continent' (p. 87).

But Russia is only the strongest exemplification of a general phenomenon. Westward of Russia was Prussia, in which the absolutist state was exemplified to only a degree less than the giant of Eurasia. Size of state is not of course an explanation in this case, but propinquity to a giant may have been a contributing factor. Moreover it may be argued that the political fragmentation of Germany stemmed at least in part from the geography of middle Europe. In any case the German lands before the mid-nineteenth century join Russia as exemplifying the absolutist principle, though in the German case there was often a much stronger paternalistic welfare element. Thus Gerschenkron arrives at his governing concept of economic backwardness, expressed on a geographical scale ranking countries in terms of an east to west scale. Backwardness provides an entire historical paradigm. To the degree that backwardness is present the state must be the vehicle of growth if it is to take place at all, and not the free market; as backwardness yields to 'forwardness' in the west, especially in the British case, the source of dynamic is reversed.

Both Wittfogel and Gerschenkron contain the possibility of cultural momentum, under which societal forms developed under one condition have had the ability to perpetuate themselves long after their originating conditions have disappeared. One of the most interesting examples of this is German and Austrian cameralism. The system of government prevalent in the German lands from the mid-sixteenth to the late eighteenth century was characterised by absolutism: the state was embodied in the prince, who was answerable to no human agency, but to God. The sovereignity and independence of the individual state was confirmed by the Thirty Years' War (1618–48), internally, after so bitter and destructive a period of warfare and confusion most people accepted the position of Jean Bodin (1529–96) that there should be in every state a single recognised law maker, or sovereign, capable of imposing a coherent legal order. Thus it was that the purposes of the state, as embodied in the ruler, were accepted as paramount over the claims of individuals or groups. The state conducted a national management of morals, education, religion, politics, finance, diplomacy and war, developing and confirming the bureaucracy necessary to do this. Consequently the state needed resources. It could and did tax at will, but its ability to sponsor economic development in order to increase the tax base was severely limited by its own role. But the value system that came out of this fragmented pre-industrial Germany, with its inhibitive effects on economic growth, could, after 1871, become an essential component in a mighty burst of state-sponsored economic development. Indeed one of the great determinants of German life from feudal times to the age of high mass consumption, has been its bureaucratic tradition; who could have deduced this mutating momentum? (Kocka, 1981).

THE DEMANDS OF GLOBALISM

At the world level it is perhaps not unreasonable to identify as the heirs of Smith and Marx respectively, Rostow and Wallerstein. Both Smith and Marx, though their starting point was within given societies, were well aware of the problem of the relationship between societies and the consequent effect of these in domestic terms. Indeed no thinker could fail to take account of the phenomena associated with the interactions between economies, least of all such men. But the evolution of their respective thought systems did not carry them to the point of a radical transfer of emphasis. Rostow, too, in his *Stages of Economic Growth* began with the internalised idioms. But from the early 1970s he has moved toward the other perspective, that of interaction, inspired to do so partly by the problem of poverty in the Third World and by the prospect of world war. Wallerstein also has evolved out of internalism to a global perspective, but one very different from that of Rostow.

Neither makes mention of the other; both hold seminars and conferences in which the rival view is not mentioned. Both deploy a formidable battery of scholarship data, but they are of very different kinds. Partly this mutual exclusiveness arises from what appear to be irreducible differences both of disciplines (the sociologist versus the economist), and of convictions. Each protagonist is disposed to test his approach through amplification rather than confrontation. But presumably both would accept Wallerstein's dictum that

'Man's ability to participate intelligently in the evolution of his own system is dependent on his ability to perceive the whole' (Wallerstein, 1974, p.10). This would suggest that attempts should be made to ease the historiographical tension by seeking to define the points of divergence to see whether they are in reality irreducible, and if so why. Or are we to conclude that fruitful dialogue is impossible?

Wallerstein began with political conflict in the United States and its social basis (1974, p.3). This led to the question as to whether indeed 'all history is the history of class struggle'; to deal with this a larger perspective seemed required. So he turned to Africa (1961, 1966) and the 'colonial situation'. What unit of analysis could embrace both? Only the global, using the concept of core and periphery. How were such concepts to be exemplified historically? By turning to Europe in the early modern period, that is from the early sixteenth century. This progression has given rise to a developmental schema or implicit notion of stages of development on a global scale. Four major epochs are proposed, namely 1450–1640 as embracing the origins and formation of the world system, 1640–1815 as covering the consolidation of the system, 1815–1917 as seeing 'the conversion of the world economy into a global enterprise' through technological transformation and advanced industrialism, and, finally, the years since 1917 bringing the consolidation of the capitalist world economy.

The generalised argument used by Wallerstein is that capitalistic interdependence between societies on a significant scale has prevailed since the sixteenth century. But it has been one which has rested not upon the hegemony or empire of a single power; capitalism on the contrary has operated within an arena that no single political entity could control (1974, p.348). The freedom of capitalists was thus 'above' the power of states: their actions under such conditions have caused a continuous expansion of the world system. But within this apparently inchoate picture there was structure, namely that of the core states versus the peripheral ones, with a heavy skewing of rewards in favour of the former. The core economies are such, to a significant degree, by accident, represented by a combination of natural endowment and location and the ability to generate a strongly integrated and motivated society with an effective state machine. Thus 'national homogeneity within international heterogeneity is the formula for the world economy'

(1974, p.353). The peripheral economies, also apparently fortuitously, lack these attributes, both physical and social. Though Wallerstein's approach is, of course, an indictment of capitalism, in the Marxist tradition it regards the system as the product of historical forces to which no blame attaches. But it rests on the basic notion of confrontation and conflict between classes, elevated from the national to the world perspective.

Rostow by the mid-1970s had reached in his personal pilgrimage the challenge of integrating his thought system in terms of the world economy for the world's consideration. He found, however, like Wallerstein, that he had first to recoil far back into the past, back indeed to feudalism. This was in order to provide a world historical exemplification of the traditional society, his first 'stage'. This involved him in a demonstration of the closed circle in which such societies were locked, making it impossible for them to break the Malthusian barrier. He concludes that the locking mechanism was a condition of mind – an inability of those with access to resources to grasp that 'the physical world could be understood in ways that permitted it systematically to be transformed to their advantage' (1975, p.31). Once this cultural and mental obstruction had been removed by the implementation of post-Newtonian science (a concept with which historians of science seem to have some difficulty),[4] it was possible to think, in consequences of the interactions between societies thus provoked, in terms of an articulated system, a world economy. Thinking at this level has convinced Rostow of the inadequacy of 'conventional neo classical and neo Keynesian theory' (1971, p.xxxv), largely because of its failure to move to the world level. But in his *The World Economy. History and Prospect* of 1978, the state, Rostow's principal preoccupation in 1971, reverts to a minor role; he is concerned once more, as in the *Stages*, very largely with private initiatives as they implement new technologies. Here, in a manner in striking contrast to most Marxian writers (so often with a sociological bias), he treats the great economic variables, projecting them on a world scale: these are population, prices, industrial growth and the structural responses to it, the terms of trade between primary and industrial producing countries, together with the elements of trend and stability at work in the world system. He then turns to its national components (twenty of them) as seen in the perspective of his five stages of economic growth. There is a splendid array of data at both world and national levels. Finally Rostow projects into the future, again in economic rather than in political terms. Policy matters are deferred to a later volume.

Proceeding in this way Rostow sees no inherent contradiction or confrontation either within societies or between them. But the conditions of avoidance of conflict will not simply present themselves by the automatic action of the market or any other agency: they must be sought for and carried out, presumably through the political mechanism. In world terms this search may well be eased by market factors: late comers to economic growth can, indeed, 'catch up with the early comers' (1978, p.656). Not all can do so; there is the problem of those that are too poorly endowed: their salvation may be to seek union with a more fortunate country if this can be done. How may the catching-up take place? There are three possibilities: by the slowing down of rates of growth in the more advanced countries, by the fuller implementation of post-Newtonian science in the less advanced, with consequent increases in output per unit of input, and by the market adjusting the ratio of exchange between manufacturing countries and primary producers in favour of the latter.

As between Wallerstein and Rostow the great difference lies in the question of exploitation and confrontation. Are these inherent and universal in a system resting upon private property and the market, or can conflicts, real as they are, be solved or at least reduced to the level of tolerance?

THE CHALLENGE OF SYNTHESIS

Our three levels of thought (the internally universal, the internally unique and the global), pose challenges for the theorist, the historian, the politician and the bureaucrat. The internalised approach suggests that a common paradigmatic ladder of ascent confronts all societies and nation-states, to be climbed as high as resource endowment as mediated by technology, together with national coherence and motivation, permits. Moreover each society can be notionally located on this ladder. The second formulation insists that there is a different, not to say unique ladder of ascent confronting each society. This derives ultimately from basic differences in natural environment and location, but also from cultural elements of outlook inherited from the past, especially those concerned with the nature and role of the state and its bureaucracy. In the case of each nation a conception of societal experience must be formed in its own terms such as to reconcile the generalised with the particularist perspectives. But in terms of globality, each state must locate itself within an evolving world framework. On this basis it must do two things: it must preserve the national interest against other states so far as it is able to do so, and so far as this is legitimate, and it must make its contribution to the obviation of conflicts that could be destructive to all. In these tasks the historical perspective is essential.

NOTES

1. For a modern attempt on the Chinese enigma see Elvin, 1973.
2. Indeed before the mid-eighteenth century long-term theory was not linear, but cyclical: Ibn Khaldun (1332–1406), and Vico (1668–1744) rationalised the processes whereby societies entered upon economic and cultural advance, thrived and sophisticated, until they met the constraints of demography, technology, political and social incoherence and loss of moral fibre. Contraction, collapse or conquest followed. Such thinkers sought to locate societies in terms of their observed places in this postulated cycle of rise and decline (Mahdi, 1958; Capronigri, 1953).
3. Thus we are told by one scholar that for Marx 'feudalism and capitalism' (and presumably their predecessors) were 'like all his categories, abstractions, similar to Weberian ideal types', that 'they were not discrete stages to be found in the past', and that 'the passage from feudalism to capitalism was the history of the last millenium in Europe'. Marx's schema is a 'far more subtle and complex model . . . than most historians and many Marxists have been willing to admit' (Neale, in Kamenka and Neale, 1975, p.11). When any system of thought develops or acquires incoherent appendages beyond a certain point, that system can either be abandoned to be replaced by a new one, or its rigour can be relaxed by lessening its claims, loosening its categories and retreating from their strict articulation.
4. The origins of this fundamental change is a permanent challenge to those who concern themselves with the relationships between science and society (Merton, 1970). Did it originate in the inherent inquisitiveness of man so that, by his very nature, he must have ascended to some such perception of the natural world? If so, why only in Europe? Was it brought about by propitious social conditions deriving from the economic: that is, did the progress of commerce generate a merchant class who in some sense could indicate constraints on exchanges and productivity, and so provided a market incentive for the breaking of these through an advance in physical knowledge? Or is the driving force to be located in a non-materialist motivation stemming from religion: did the puritan ethic see in the inquiry into man's physical setting a form of the worship of the Deity? Or was there some combination of these, together with other factors?

REFERENCES

Bailey, A. M., and Llobera, J. R., 'Karl A. Wittfogel and the Asiatic Mode of Production: a Reappraisal', *The Sociological Review*, 1979.
Block, F., 'Marxist Theories of the State in World Economic Systems Analysis', in Kaplan (ed.), *Social Change in the Capitalist World Economy* (Beverly Hills, 1978).
Burnham, J., *The Managerial Revolution* (London, 1941).
Capronigri, A. R., *Time and Idea: the Theory of History in Giambattista Vico* (London, 1953).
Cropsey, J., *Polity and Economy. An Interpretation of the Principles of Adam Smith* (The Hague, 1957).
Deutch, K. W., 'The Growth of Nations: Some Recurrent Patterns of Political and Social Integration', *World Politics*, 1953.
East, G. W., 'How Strong is the Heartland?', *Foreign Affairs*, 1950.
Elvin, M., *The Pattern of the Chinese Past* (London, 1973).
Fieldhouse, D. K., 'Dissecting the Hobson–Lenin Model', in M. Wolfe (ed.), *The Economic Causes of Imperialism* (New York and London, 1972).
Gerschenkron, A., *Economic Backwardness in Historical Perspective; a Book of Essays* (Cambridge, Mass., 1962).
Gerschenkron, A., *Continuity in History and Other Essays* (Cambridge, Mass., 1968).
Gerschenkron, A., *Europe in the Russian Mirror, Four Lectures in Economic History* (Cambridge, Mass., 1970).
Heckscher, E. L., *Mercantilism*, 1931, rev. ed., E. F. Soderlund (ed.), (London, 1955).
Hicks, J., *A Theory of History* (Oxford, 1969).
Hobson, J. A., *Imperialism, a Study* (London, 1902), quoted in Wolfe, *The Economic Causes of Imperialism*, 1972.
Johnson, H. C., 'The Concept of Bureaucracy in Cameralism', *Political Science Quarterly*, 1964.
Kamenka, E., and Neale, R. S., (eds), *Feudalism, Capitalism and Beyond* (London, 1975).
Kamenka, E., and Krygier, M., (eds), *Bureaucracy. The Career of a Concept* (London, 1979).
Kaplan, B. Hockey (ed.), *Social Change in the Capitalist World Economy* (Beverly Hills, 1978).
Kocka, J., 'Capitalism and Bureaucracy in German Industrialisation' Tawney Memorial Lecture, Economic History Society, April 1980 forthcoming, *Economic History Review*, 1981.
Krygier, M., in Kamenka and Krygier, 1979, op. cit.
Mackinder, H., 'The Geographical Pivot of History', *Geographical Journal*, 1904.
Mahdi, M., *Ibn Khaldun's Philosophy of History* (London, 1958).
McGovern, A. F., 'The Young Marx and the State', *Science and Society* (1970–1).
Meek, R. L., *Smith, Marx and After: Ten Essays in the Development of Economic Thought* (London, 1977).
Merton, R. K., *Science and Technology in 17th Century England* (New York, 1970).
North, D. C., and Thomas, R. P., *The Rise of the Western World. A New Economic History* (Cambridge, 1973).
Rostow, W. W., *The Process of Economic Growth* (Oxford, 1953).

Rostow, W. W., *The Stages of Economic Growth. A Non-Communist Manifesto* (Cambridge, 1960).
Rostow, W. W., (ed.) *The Economics of Take-Off into Sustained Growth* (London, 1963).
Rostow, W. W., *Politics and the Stages of Growth* (Cambridge, 1971).
Rostow, W. W., *How It All Began. Origins of the Modern Economy* (London, 1975).
Rostow, W. W., *The World Economy. History and Prospect* (London, 1978).
Rubison, R., 'Political Transformation in Germany and the United States', in B. H. Kaplan (ed.), op. cit.
Sawer, M., *Marxism and the Question of the Asiatic Made of Production* (The Hague, 1977).
Skinner, A. S., *A System of Social Science: Papers Relating to Adam Smith* (Oxford, 1979).
Skinner, A. S., 'A Scottish Contribution to Marxist Sociology', in I. Bradley and M. Howard (eds), *Classical and Marxian Political Economy. Essays in Honour of R. L. Meek* forthcoming, 1981).
Small, A. W., *The Cameralists. The Pioneers of German Social Policy* (Chicago, 1909), new edn (New York, 1962).
Southern, R. S., *The Making of the Middle Ages* (London, 1953).
Ulmen, G. L., *The Science of Society. Toward an Understanding of the Life and Work of Karl August Wittfogel* (The Hague, 1978).
Wallerstein, I., *Africa, the Politics of Independence* (New York, 1961).
Wallerstein, I., *Social Change: the Colonial Situation* (New York, 1966).
Wallerstein, I., *The Modern World-System. Capitalist Agriculture and the Origins of the European World-System in the Sixteenth Century* (New York and London, 1974).
Weber, M., *General Economic History* (1927, new edn London, 1953).
Wittfogel, K. A., *Oriental Despotism: A Comparative Study of Total Power* (New Haven, 1959).
Wolfe, M., (ed.), *The Economic Causes of Imperialism* (New York and London, 1972).

5 The Impact of the Depression on Economic Thought*

P. TEMIN

The aim of this paper is to integrate the well-known changes in economics during the Depression into a longer history of economic thought. This will require looking at Keynesian theory from a somewhat unusual viewpoint. It will require looking at Keynes's psychology rather than his economics. This implicit psychology, which might as well be called an implicit sociology, has its parallels and connections with both earlier and more recent thought.

Being a historian, I start at the beginning. The American Economic Association was formed in 1885. Coming more than a century after *The Wealth of Nations*, this event cannot be counted as the beginning of economic thought, but it may be accorded status as a pivotal event in the origin of the profession of economics. The Association was formed at roughly the same time as other social-science associations, and it was a reflection of the growth of professionalism in the late nineteenth century.

People living through the last decades of the nineteenth century in America felt themselves to be in a period of massive change. The established boundaries of economic and social discourse were being breached by new forms of communication and interaction, and new, larger business organisations were growing to take advantage of the wider stage for their actions. People, particularly upper middle-class articulate people, felt themselves under pressure by

* The research for this paper was supported by a grant from the Sloan Foundation to the Department of Economics, MIT, on the Public Control of Economic Activity.

this process. They were oppressed by – or maybe just obsessed with – the growth of large business organisations and the decline of local social and economic units.[1]

T. Haskell has conceptualised recently the changes of the late nineteenth century as a growth of interdependence. He refers to the geographic growth of markets, the rising speed of communication and transportation, and the increased specialisation of labour as aspects of the growing interdependence. In his metaphor:

> Like a sheet of chain mail stretched taut, the individual links of what had been a remarkably slack society lost a degree of freedom and found themselves constrained by forces transmitted through adjacent links (Haskell, 1977, p. 36).

Haskell then reformulates White's 'anti-formalist revolt' of these years into a growing consciousness and articulation of interdependence. This change in thought patterns had two consequences. First, people found it necessary to analyse events in the context of other events, linked both by time (history) and space (contemporaneous events). Second, people found it hard to attribute causation in any simple fashion in their interdependent conceptualisation.[2]

It was in this context that the AEA appeared on the American scene. Started by Richard T. Ely, it was to be a forum from which to attack laissez-faire ideology and policies. As such, it was to be a recognition that the formal economic analysis deriving from the English Utilitarians was inadequate to modern conditions, precisely because it did not take into account the influence of history and the interconnections between economic and other events. But the membership to whom Ely appealed did not share his conception of economics, and leadership of the AEA quickly passed to the supporters of classical economics. Ely's statement of principles was dropped in 1888; he was forced from his post as Secretary of the Association in 1892 (Haskell, 1977, pp. 181–7).

Economics therefore repudiated the emphasis on interdependence and the need to appeal to history and other social sciences in the analysis of economic events. Economists who did not share this vision, who emphasised the importance of history or of sociology, were relegated to the fringes of the profession. The discipline of economics dedicated itself to understanding the implications of a simple Utilitarian psychology in which people acted consistently and independently in pursuit of stable goals. As H. L. A. Hart expressed it while discussing John Stuart Mill:

> Underlying Mill's fear of paternalism there perhaps is a conception of what a normal human being is like which now seems not to correspond to the facts. Mill, in fact, endows him too much of the psychology of a middle-aged man whose desires are relatively fixed, not liable to be artificially stimulated by external influences; who knows what he wants and gives him satisfaction or happiness; and who pursues these things when he can (Hart, 1933, p. 33).

Even though the profession of economics followed along the lines laid down by Mill and explored the implications of the psychology he assumed, economic policy remained far more eclectic. In fact, one could reasonably assert that people excluded from the AEA had more influence on policy than those included within it. The growth of Progressivism, with its attempts to control the growing interdependence and the large business organisations that it fostered, is evidence of the dominance in policy circles of a more eclectic ideology (Fine, 1956).

Teddy Roosevelt popularised and implemented the policies of Progressivism, and Franklin Delano Roosevelt was educated in the Progressive tradition (Fusfeld, 1954). The Democratic Roosevelt consequently saw the Depression as the result of a lack of coordination or of integration of the different parts of the economy. Unfortunately, his Progressive training led him to deal with each of the parts – agriculture, industry, banking – rather than with variables that affected them all.

While we do not think those policies were the best that could have done, it is well to remember that no one at the time had an integrated view of the Depression to oppose to the Progressive vision of a complex machine in need of oiling. The academic literature of business cycles concentrated on price fluctuations and had little to say about employment. The popular press, lacking even a view of price fluctuations, sought the causes of the Depression in moral failings.

Businessmen were to blame, said one camp, because they had been responsible – or at least had claimed they were responsible – for the preceding prosperity. The argument was by a kind of symmetry; businessmen were responsible for the economy for better or for worse. To the question of how businessmen had caused the Depression, no clear answer was given, but the tone of the discussion implied strongly that it was the businessmen's personal lack of concern for society at large that had produced the economic decline.

The reply from the business community was that the workers were responsible for their own suffering. The president of the NAM asked in late 1930, if workers 'do not . . . practice the habits of thrift and conservation, or if they gamble away their savings in the stock market or elsewhere, is our economic system, or government, or industry to blame?'[3]

In keeping with the tone of these comments, the Depression appeared as the failure of the economic system or the end of economic growth or the disintegration of society. In no case was there an explanation of the Depression that led to policy prescriptions liable to increase employment (Leuchtenburg, 1963, pp. 18–30.) Economic policy, consequently, worked against recovery as much as for it.

For example, Herbert Hoover decided to raise taxes after Britain left gold in 1931. As he saw it, taxes needed to go up to keep the government from trying to borrow, increasing the supply of bonds, lowering bond prices and increasing bond yields. He was trying to stimulate investment by keeping down interest rates, by avoiding 'crowding out' in modern terminology (Stein, 1966, p. 32). The argument is sound as far as it goes, but it misses the point. Economists today disagree on the extent to which crowding out offsets the primary effect of changing government taxes or expenditures, but everyone agrees that the effect on demand – which works in the opposite direction to the crowding out – is at least as large as the crowding out itself. Hoover, by contrast, was thinking of the business sector alone, without reference to the economy as a whole.

Similarly, Roosevelt reduced federal expenditures to veterans and federal employees by half a billion dollars within a few days of taking office; the management of aggregate demand clearly was not the issue. The special session of Congress in 1933 passed a whole raft of bills aimed at helping one or another part of the economy. The Agricultural Adjustment Act was to help agriculture; the National Industrial Recovery Act, to help industry; the Securities Act, the stock market; and the Glass–Steagall Act, banks (Leuchtenburg, 1963, pp. 41–62). The economy was seen as the sum of its parts, and aid to all of its parts was the same as aid to the whole. In modern terminology, Roosevelt tried to solve a macroeconomic problem with microeconomic tools, because neither he nor anyone else had a way of utilising the awareness of the economy's interdependence to ease the pain of the Depression.

The integration of the concept of interdependence and plans for economic policy was the work of John Maynard Keynes. *The General Theory of Employment, Interest, and Money*, published in 1936, brought Keynes's insights as an intellectual to bear on the economic problem of unemployment. It is not for me to explain why Keynes, rather than someone else wrote *The General Theory*. But a recent article by Dorothy Ross suggests that he was more likely to have been English than American. Ross argues that the greater rigidity of English society paradoxically allowed social thinkers more latitude in their approach to public policy. This argument is used to explain why English Fabianism flourished while American socialism was banished from respectable forums in the late nineteenth century. (Ross, 1978). It may not be too much to suggest that the same forces allowed Keynes more freedom to utilise ideas from outside economics proper – as represented by the ideological thrust of the AEA – than a similarly-placed American.

It is obvious to any reader of *The General Theory* that Keynes painted on a wide canvas. The recurrent references to psychology are both unusual in economics treatises and an indication of the interdependence of the social sciences in Keynes's mind. Two examples may be noted to prepare the ground for later discussion. The shape of the consumption function, a basic building block in *The General Theory*, was justified on the basis of a 'fundamental psychological law, upon which we are entitled to depend with great confidence both *a priori* from our knowledge of human nature and from the detailed facts of experience' (Keynes, 1936, p. 96). Similarly, the decision to invest in the face of uncertainty about the future was seen as the result of 'animal spirits' rather than careful calculation. In Keynes's rather famous words:

> Most, probably, of our decisions to do something positive, the full consequences of which will be drawn out over many days to come, can only be taken as a result of animal spirits – of a spontaneous urge to action rather than inaction, and not as the outcome of a weighted average of quantitative benefits multiplied by quantitative probabilities (Keynes, 1936, p. 161).

As everyone knows, Keynesian economics did not replace the existing economics. It was placed over the existing theories as a kind of umbrella, keeping its identity separate. The split within economics that resulted – between macroeconomics and microeconomics – corresponds to the split in the nascent social sciences of the late nineteenth century between the thinkers who emphasised the interdependence of human affairs and the people who denied the importance of history or other social sciences for the study of economic phenomena.

The split between heterodox Keynesianism and orthodox microeconomics was built into the structure of textbooks and course offerings. One of the more influential documents to solidify the dual nature of economics was Paul Samuelson's elementary textbook, *Economics*. First published in 1948, this book was divided into three parts. The first part provided a wide range of information about the American economy together with an introduction to the economist's jargon. The second part expounded Keynesian theory, 'to help fill the long-felt gap in introductory textual material on the theory of employment' (Samuelson, 1948, p. vii). And the third part presented the traditional theory of value. The structure of the book therefore embodied the division within economics: after an initial introduction, the book split into two admittedly self-contained parts. It is apparent that the two parts were independent of each other, because the order of presentation was not important. As Samuelson explained in his introduction, the Keynesian theory was placed first because, 'introductory analysis of income determination is easier and more interesting than introductory "value and distribution theory"' (Samuelson, 1948, p. vi).

This phenomenally successful textbook molded the conception of economics of a generation of economists.[4] One has only to notice the similarity of organisation of almost all current best-selling introductory economics texts to Samuelson's first edition to realise how pervasive this influence has been. The split within economics has been embodied in countless course offerings and texts, and most economists today define themselves in terms of it – as macroeconomists or microeconomists. It is perhaps not surprising that Samuelson's tenth edition, almost thirty years later, retains the same organisation as the first with the addition of parts on international trade and current problems (Samuelson, 1976). But it is also true that even new and putatively innovative textbooks also follow this organisation. The recent elementary text by Baumol and

Blinder, for example, has an introductory part (one), followed by macroeconomic parts (two and three), followed in turn by microeconomic parts (four to eight), an international part (nine), and concluding comments on items that don't fit the preceding organisation (Baumol and Blinder, 1979).

While the two aspects of economics coexist neatly in most textbooks, they often come into conflict in professional discussions. In fact, there have been continual border skirmishes, similar in spirit to those between the Chinese and the Russians in Mongolia. The microeconomic camp has tended to win these skirmishes, and Keynesian economics has been slowly yielding intellectual ground. We can examine some of these conflicts and document their outcomes and then try to anticipate the future of this territorial struggle.

The conventional distinction between macroeconomics and microeconomics hinges on their subject matter. But that is not the important distinction here. Since we are examining competing approaches to the same questions, a division based on subject matter will not help us. Instead, the two lines can be disentangled by examining the implicit psychology in any economic model. A writer in the microeconomic tradition will assume that people fit the description given above of Mill's psychology. Authors writing in the macroeconomic tradition, by contrast, will assume that individuals respond to changes in the 'animal spirits' noted by Keynes, that they act in concert with other people, and that the history of their behaviour is an important variable. While these divergent assumptions often are hard to spot, there are a few cases where they are highly visible.

The first example concerns the theory of consumption. Stimulated by Keynes's ideas on the determinants of consumption, economists collected data on the relation between consumption and income at different times. The data exposed an apparent contradiction. If one compared different people at any one time, the proportion of income consumed fell as income rose. But if one compared the national ratio of consumption to income over time, it had not fallen as national income, and therefore the incomes of individuals within the national aggregate, had risen. The first result indicated that consumption rose less rapidly than income – Keynes's fundamental psychological law; the second, that they rose at the same rate.

The contradiction arose out of Keynes's theory, which predicted that consumption was a simple function of income, and which did not recognise any differences between comparisons between people at a given time and between national aggregates at different times. The way out of the contradiction therefore was to revise the theory. James Duesenberry suggested in the late 1940s that the theory be revised by abandoning the assumption of independent preferences. In his words:

> There are strong psychological and sociological reasons for supposing that preferences are in fact interdependent (. . .) For any given relative income distribution, the percentage of income saved by a family will tend to be a unique, invariant, and increasing function of its percentile position in the income distribution. The percentage saved will be independent of the absolute level of income. It follows that the aggregate savings ratio will be independent of the absolute level of income (Duesenberry, 1949, p. 3).

Appealing across disciplinary lines, Duesenberry asserted that the two bodies of data were the products of two entirely different processes. The comparison of two people at a single point in time showed what happened to the ratio of consumption to income as position within the income distribution, and therefore the social structure as well, varied. The comparison of national aggregates at different times showed the effects of shifting the whole distribution without changing the distribution itself. Variations in the ratio of consumption to income are the result of moving within the social structure, of changing relative position. They are to be expected when looking within the national aggregate, but not when looking at the aggregate itself.

Economists did not flock to the intellectually eclectic standard raised by Duesenberry. Instead, they continued to seek an explanation for the apparent contradiction consistent with the micro-economic assumption of completely rational, individualistic behaviour. Such an explanation was found in the 1950s. It has two variants, referred to as the 'life-cycle' or 'permanent-income' hypothesis (Modigliani and Brumberg, 1954; M. Friedman, 1957). Differing in details, the two variants make the same assumption that people make consumption plans for a long period – for their whole lifes according to the life-cycle variant. Their consumption at any moment is determined by the plan, not by their current income.

Current incomes vary, and people experiencing high income for the moment will show low ratios of consumption to income, while people with temporarily low income will show a high ratio. At any moment of time, a disproportionate number of people with high incomes will be above their average or planned income, while a disproportionately large proportion of people with low incomes will be below this level (which is different for each person). Comparing different groups within the population, therefore, shows that people with higher incomes consume less of their income than people with lower incomes, as expected. But comparing national aggregates at different times does not show a similar result because the proportion of people experiencing temporarily high income is balanced by the proportion receiving temporarily low income. As in Duesenberry's theory, the apparent contradiction vanishes.

Once the contradiction was eliminated, it ceased to be more than a historiographic curiosity. The new theories found their place in the explanation of the short-period stability of consumption when income fell during recessions. And here both types of theories gave pretty much the same explanation. They both appealed to the durability of consumption plans and the time needed to change them. Duesenberry emphasised the difficulty of reducing consumption expenditures, in part due to the implied loss in social standing, which he compared with the ease of raising them and advancing in the social structure. The later theorists simply noted that the proportion of people with income below their long-run expectations is larger in recessions than the proportion of people earning more than this level. It follows that the proportion of people with relatively high consumption-income ratios is higher than the proportion with relatively low ratios, and the aggregate ratio is high. The ratio of consumption falls less than the level of income.

This brief discussion shows that – at least to a first approximation – the two types of theories explain the same previously puzzling phenomena. Yet the life-cycle and permanent-income theories have been incorporated into the mainstream of economic analysis, while the relative-income hypothesis of Duesenberry has been left to languish as a historiographical curiosity, similar to the one it was formulated to explain.[5]

Despite the relative income hypothesis' lack of development, however, it did not vanish entirely from the economic literature, and recently it has received renewed attention. Several authors have expressed a growing disenchantment with the goal of continuous economic growth in terms of the relative-income hypothesis. The argument, with variations, goes like this: Any individual wants to increase his income in order to make progress within the social structure. But when everyone increases his income, no-one has risen relative to others, and everyone's aspirations to rise in a stable social hierarchy are frustrated. Even though everyone desires economic growth, everyone is disappointed by the result. The parallel with Duesenberry's explanation of the anomalous consumption behaviour is obvious, as is the reliance of this view on Duesenberry's resolution of the consumption puzzle, not the more orthodox theories.[6]

A second example of work at the boundary between the two branches of economics concerns uncertainty. The theory of pure competition assumes that information is costless and that all consumers and producers know all information relevant to the decisions they make. This clearly is false, and two models to deal with the costs of information were put forward around 1960. One stayed within the boundaries of conventional microeconomics and has been incorporated into the mainstream of the discipline. The other breached the intellectual walls and has been neglected by economists as a result.

As with consumption, the earlier theory was the heterodox one. Herbert Simon proposed that the assumption of continuous maximising behaviour be replaced by the assumption of 'satisfying' behaviour. This new term described behaviour that did not ceaselessly strive for efficiency, but rather followed tradition or habit if the results – measured in some crude way – were not too bad. When the result of this customary behaviour diverged too far from the goals of the person or organisation acting, search behaviour was instituted to find a better way of operating. As described by Simon, searching is an example of maximising behaviour, and the transition from satisfying to searching in his model is a change in the way people act. Going further, Simon noted that if the divergence between experience and goals was too great, 'emotional' behaviour might result. Simon clearly had in mind a third mode of action, although the precise nature of 'emotional' behaviour was not spelled out. Nevertheless, Simon clearly articulated a theory based on discrete modes of behaviour in which people did not maintain the type of behaviour assumed in microeconomic models continuously over their careers (Simon, 1957, 1959).

The motivation for this theory was Simon's contention that it was too costly for people or for organisations to process continuously the information needed for even moderately complex decisions. To avoid these costs, people switched from instrumental to customary, satisfying, behaviour. In contrast to Duesenberry's argument, the social aspects of personality play no role. Instead, the noise in the environment and the lack of simple connections between actions and results promote the use of customary behaviour.

George Stigler, writing shortly after Simon, looked at the other side of the information problem. Retaining the assumption of continuous maximising behaviour, Stigler asked how much costly information would a firm supply or a person acquire. The answer was that the firm would provide information up to the point where the expected gain of issuing the last scrap of information equalled the cost of issuing it, and that the person would accumulate information up to the point where the value of the last unit of information gathered, equalled the cost of obtaining it. In economic language, they would issue and gather information until the marginal value of the information equalled its marginal cost (Stigler, 1961). On this foundation, Stigler and later writers constructed a theory of economic search, investigating the costs and gains from different stopping rules, the responses to different costs of information, the price structure compatible with costly information, and the role of costly information in explaining unemployment.[7]

As with the consumption function, the orthodox theory of Stigler has been extended and elaborated by economists until it has become an integral part of economic theory, while the heterodox theory of Simon has not. And as with the heterodox theory of consumption, neglect by economists does not mean total neglect. Simon's ideas have been widely used outside of economics, and they have recently received some attention from economists as well. Attempts have been made to formalise the concept of satisfying behaviour and to draw implications from these formulations about economic behaviour.[8]

Border skirmishes have a way of escalating into full-scale war, and the disagreements I have mentioned have been broadened into a disagreement about the nature of the Depression itself. Since the interdependent school of economics got its greatest boost from its ability to explain the Depression, a challenge to that analysis was a serious challenge indeed.

Keynes himself gave the first expression of what was to become the Keynesian view of the Depression. In the *Treatise on Money* he said, 'The boom of 1928–9 and the slump of 1929–30 in the United States correspond respectively to an excess and deficiency of investment'. Looking for the cause of this change from excess to deficiency, he continued,

> I attribute the slump of 1930 primarily to the deterrent effects on investment of the long period of dear money which preceded the stock-market collapse and only secondarily to the collapse itself. But the collapse having occurred, it greatly aggravated matters, especially in the United States, by causing a disinvestment in working capital (Keynes, 1930, vol. 2, pp. 194, 196).

Subsequent writers adopted Keynes's framework of thought without attributing the same importance to the level of interest rates. Keynes himself presented a modified position in *The General Theory* when he said that the marginal efficiency of capital, as he then termed it, fell because of the large previous investment (Keynes, 1936, p. 323). This is the form in which the spending hypothesis has received support from later investigators, although the stock-market crash reappears in some studies as an explanatory factor in the Depression. The first serious studies of the Depression to embody the Keynesian point of view were done by Hansen and Wilson at the start of the 1940s. Their conclusion, in Wilson's words, was that 'The collapse (of income) occurred only because the development of underconsumption was accompanied by a declining demand for houses and a serious exhaustion of investment opportunities' (Wilson, 1942, p. 156).

With the exception of the archaic term, underconsumption, this sentence ably summarises most of the succeeding empirical literature on the Keynesian view of the Depression. It has been stated in several different ways, but an emphasis on the decline in housing expenditures, in investment opportunities in general, or in both, identifies a proponent of this point of view.

The informal approach used by Hansen and Wilson was extended by Gordon in a series of studies published approximately a decade later. His work contains what is probably the most comprehensive statement of the Keynesian analysis of the Depression, giving due allowance for a variety of factors, but concentrating on housing and the exhaustion of investment opportunities. A paragraph from a recent restatement of his position will show the direction his elaborations took:

> It is possible to find in the situation prevailing in 1929 important elements of weakness that were sufficient to create a depression more severe than that of 1924 or 1927. It is clear that the rise in output of durable goods in 1928–1929 was too rapid to be long maintained. Excess capacity was developing in a number of lines, and this meant a decline in demand for capital goods. As a matter of fact new orders for some types of durable goods declined fairly early in 1929. The automobile market was clearly oversold; in addition, the industry's capacity exceeded even the peak production of 1929. The tire industry had been overbuilt, and the tire production had fallen sharply in the latter part of 1928. The textile industries had been suffering from overcapacity for some time. Residential construction had been declining sharply since the beginning of 1928, and an overbuilt situation obviously existed in that area. Some of these developments may be described as a result of the belated and rough working of the acceleration principle, although it should be emphasized that we can trace no simple correlation between the short-term changes in the rate of increase in output and the demand for capital goods (Gordon, 1974, pp. 43–4).

This account of the Depression dominated academic and popular discussion for 30 years. The reaction came in 1963 with the publication of Friedman and Schwartz's classic study, *A Monetary History of the United States* (M. Friedman and Schwartz, 1965). The *Monetary History* appeared at the same time as two articles co-authored by Friedman that provide a context for the historical analysis in the book. In one article, Friedman and Meiselman showed that the level of income was more closely correlated with the stock of money than with a measure of 'autonomous spending' over almost a century. While a correlation is not evidence for causation, the results were striking and suggestive.[9]

The argument was carried further in a contemporaneous article by Friedman and Schwartz. They rejected the idea that the correlation found between income and money could be coincidence and asked how the two could be related. The choice they presented was simple: either changes in the stock of money caused income to change, or vice versa. The resolution was equally simple. The stock of money was determined by a variety of forces independent of the level of income, according to Friedman and Schwartz, and the direction of causation therefore must be from money to income, not the other way.

The *Monetary History* completed the argument. The historical determinants of the stock of money were only briefly sketched in the article, and the encyclopedic discussion of the book provided the details. The book thus contains the evidence on which the conclusions of the article are based.

The *Monetary History's* story of the Depression has been summarised elsewhere by Friedman and Schwartz.

> An initial mild decline in the money stock from 1929 to 1930, accompanying a decline in Federal Reserve credit outstanding, was converted into a sharp decline by a wave of bank failures beginning in late 1930.
>
> The quantity of money (. . .) fell not because there were no willing borrowers – not because the horse would not drink. It fell because the Federal Reserve System forced or permitted a sharp reduction in the monetary base, because it failed to exercise the responsibilities assigned to it in the Federal Reserve Act to provide liquidity to the banking system (M. Friedman, 1969, pp. 97, 218).

This reconstruction of the events of the early 1930s was a direct attack on the Keynesian view of the Depression and an indirect attack on the heterodox, interdependent mode of thought characteristic of macroeconomic analysis. It is no surprise, therefore, that Friedman and Schwartz's general empirical results as well as their specific story of the Depression have been questioned by many authors, including myself. Restricting the discussion to the Depression, the conclusion for the moment seems to be that neither view – the Keynesian nor the monetarist – has a clear advantage in explaining the Depression. I think that the Keynesian view fits the observed data better, but not everyone agrees (Temin, 1976; Brunner, 1981). In fact, recent attempts to compare the explanatory power of different macroeconomic models have yielded more heat than light. This seems to be true of conferences on macroeconomic models in general as well as on the causes of the Great Depression (ibid.; Stein, 1976). It is certainly true of recent newspaper and magazine articles.

Comparisons of alternative models increasingly have been made in terms of the underlying psychology of the models rather than their empirical macroeconomic implications. The discussion has centred on 'rational expectations', the theory that asserts that people form expectations by using all available information. Whatever the merits of this debate, it reveals more clearly than the comparison of macroeconomic predictions, that the difference between economic models is a difference of psychology, that is, of the assumed behaviour of individuals.[10]

Stimulated in part by Friedman and Schwartz's exposition, economists have tried to provide explanations for macroeconomic events using traditional behaviourist assumptions. The title of an important book in this area, *Microeconomic Foundations of Employment and Inflation Theory*, explains succinctly what is being sought (Phelps, 1970). This book emphasises the effects of uncertainty, following Stigler's conceptualisation of people's reaction to it. Alternative approaches emphasise liquidity constraints facing individuals, explaining their behaviour by a combination of traditional economic psychology and external constraints on behaviour (Barro and Grossman, 1976). Economists generally have begun to talk of the 'neoclassical synthesis', a term that tends to mean the exclusion of theories emphasising interdependence and complex psychologies.

Economic policy often follows economic thought, albeit with a lag, and current economic policy proposals seem closer to those popular before the publication of *The General Theory* than the ones preferred after the Second World War. President Carter argued in April 1978, that, 'The two most important measures the Congress can pass to prevent inflation . . . (are) the airline deregulation bill . . . (and) hospital cost containment legislation' (*The New York Times*, 12 April 1978). The attempt to deal with a macroeconomic problem – inflation – with microeconomic tools is highly reminiscent of the New Deal.

President Carter went further at about the same time, asserting that his recommended $25 billion tax cut was not inflationary (*The New York Times*, 24 April 1978). Not only are microeconomic tools effective against inflation, he seemed to be saying, but Keynesian macroeconomic tools will not work. And he gave expression to this view in the Fall of 1978 by appointing Alfred E. Kahn, chairman of the CAB, to head the administration's anti-inflation programme. Kahn is a specialist in regulation; he is a microeconomist. And Kahn's plans as he explained them shortly after his appointment were, not surprisingly, microeconomic in nature. Kahn's stated priorities were to deregulate trucking, encourage the development of vacant land (to reduce housing prices), curtail federal agricultural programmes that reduced the supply of produce, control health care costs, and reduce market power in insurance and ocean shipping (*The New York Times*, 12 November 1978). While only the most foolhardy analyst would make a parallel between Carter and Roosevelt, there is not much trace of the intervening developments in macroeconomic thought in these proposals.

What of the future? The trend within economics seems clear; the heterodox economists are losing ground now just as they did in the formative years of the AEA. Without some dramatic turnabout, the next generation of economists may see the economic thought stimulated by the Depression as a temporary aberration in the line of professional development, as a kind of economic Manicheism. (We certainly hope they will be able to see the events of the Depression as a temporary aberration of economic affairs!)

Having said this, I want to note some straws in the wind that suggest a possible alternative outcome to this intellectual odyssey. There are two kinds of straws, one dealing with thought and one with events. Turning first to thought, it is possible to see a group of economists who take as their starting point the work of Keynes, Duesenberry and Simon and who are developing ideas with the same emphasis on interdependence showed by these men. While the more recent thinkers have shown little cohesion to date, there is no reason to think that they won't come together as they progress. Herbert Simon, in his 1978 Nobel Lecture, argues strongly for an underlying unity of thought (Simon, 1979).

I have already referred to Oliver Williamson's work in connection with Herbert Simon's approach to uncertainty. Williamson has tried to build a theory of organisational behaviour on the assumption that people can only handle limited quantities of information (Williamson, 1975). Richard Nelson and Sidney Winter have utilised similar assumptions to construct a model of the interaction between business organisations (Nelson and Winter, 1973). And other authors have used similar frameworks to examine contracts or regulatory agencies (Goldberg, 1976; Joskow, 1974).

Other economists have turned to macroeconomic questions, using the presence of interdependence as a critical part of their analysis, without relying on Keynes's formulation of its effects. Michael Piore and his students have pulled together a variety of threads coming out of the analysis of technical change and relative wages into an explanatory cloth to be used to explain our current inflationary condition (Piore, 1979). And Richard Easterlin has combined varied behavioural assumptions with demographic analysis to produce a macroeconomic view close to Piore's and similarly far from the current mainstream view (Easterlin, 1978).

Occasionally the two strands of economics appear to coexist in a single line of thought. Kenneth Arrow opens his discussion of organisations by claiming the role of the economist: 'the guardian of rationality, the ascriber of rationality to others, and the prescriber of rationality to the social world' (Arrow, 1974, p. 16). But when Arrow begins to discuss the behaviour of organisations, he turns to Simon's approach to uncertainty. Noting first that individuals will put areas requiring decisions into different classes, Arrow asks how decision areas get moved from one class to another, particularly from his 'passive' or inactive class to one in which information is gathered and/or new actions are contemplated:

> One possibility, is a sharp change in payoffs to terminal acts. In particular, the opportunity benefit, that is the change in benefits due to a change in action, may rise because of a decrease in the return to the present, unexamined, action. In plain language, we have a 'crisis' . . . The sinking of the *Titanic* led to iceberg patrols (Arrow, 1974, p. 52).

The reliance on Simon's Keynesian treatment of uncertainty – as opposed to Stigler's – is clear; Arrow sees no conflict between his standard of rationality and the crisis mentality that introduced iceberg patrols in response to the sinking of the Titanic. Yet icebergs were no more dangerous just after that event than before it.

These essays are all interesting and all provocative. They are still straws in the wind, and only time will tell whether they will be joined by others. Other straws – coming from events – suggest that they will be. Economists are being drawn increasingly into the discussion of public policy problems where a more complex psychology than Mill's is needed. Two examples may suggest the problem. Medical care has become a major national expense, as everyone knows. The debate is only beginning on alternative ways to organise and deliver health care in this country. Since the cost of medical care is a critical element in any reorganisation, economists can expect to play a part in the discussions. But unless they can acknowledge that people – particularly sick people – cannot and will not always act like *homo economicus*, they will be of little use. Similarly, despite the pleas of economists to leave producers alone, there has been a rapid growth in the regulation of consumer products. These regulations are hotly debated, but the economist who simply says that they can be abolished because people make their own choices will have little impact. To combine both examples, the economist who advocates the abolition of the United States Food and Drug Administration (FDA) is liable to be dismissed out of hand.

This is not to say that traditional microeconomics is outmoded or that it should be abandoned in favour of some alternative construction of the world. It is instead an appeal to economists not to isolate themselves from either history or the other social sciences in dealing with certain problems. Economists need to embrace both strands of economics and be able to use either where appropriate. Who can doubt that current energy policy would be improved by attention to some simple economic realities? But who also can doubt that a 'free market' in medical care would be neither popular nor efficient?

NOTES

1. This story has been chronicled in various ways by many people, including Hofstadter (1955), Wiebe (1967), Chandler (1977).
2. Haskell includes White's components of anti-formalism – historicism (the appeal to history) and cultural organicism (the appeal to other social sciences) – as consequences of interdependence. See White (1976, p. 12), Haskell (1977, pp. 11–13).
3. The theme that workers suffered more than businessmen was prevalent at the time. More recently, Chandler reported with apparent approval that 'One unemployed man commented: "I'd rather be me than the boss. I may not have any income, but at least I'm not making losses"' (Chandler, 1970, p. 29).
4. Walt Rostow (1948), it should be noted, was one of the first to apply Keynes's ideas to the study of economic history.
5. An influential review of new theories of the consumption function in the late 1950s did not even mention Duesenberry. Similarly, closely-reasoned attack on the progressive income tax in the same decade did not take note of Duesenberry's demonstration that his behavioural assumptions implied a strong argument in favour of the progressive income tax (Farrell, 1959; Blum and Kalven, 1953).
6. The most complete statement of this view is in Hirsch (1976). See also Easterlin (1973).
7. A good selection of this literature can be found in Diamond and Rothschild (1978).
8. Nelson and Winter (1973, 1975), Radner (1975), Radner and Rothschild (1975), Williamson (1975).
9. Significantly, however, they held true in every decade but one. In the 1930s, the level of income was not more closely correlated with the stock of money than with 'autonomous spending' (Friedman and Meiselman, 1963).

10. As Lucas and Sargent said at a recent comparative conference, 'Since its inception, macroeconomics has been criticised for its lack of "foundations in microeconomic and general equilibrium theory" (. . .) The creation of a distinct branch of theory with its own distinct postulates was Keynes's conscious aim' (Lucas and Sargent, 1978). They were roundly ciriticised, I might note, for failing to take adequate note of the changes in macroeconomics since Keynes – of the continuing tendency to reinterpret Keynesian postulates as examples of admittedly complex maximising behaviour.

REFERENCES

Arrow, Kenneth J., *The Limits of Organization*, (New York: W. W. Norton, 1974).

Barro, Robert J. and Herschel Grossman, *Money Employment and Inflation* (Cambridge University Press, 1976).

Baumol, William J. and Alan S. Blinder, *Economics, Principles and Policy* (New York: Harcourt Brace Jovanovich, 1979).

Blum, Walter J. and Harry Kalven, Jr., *The Uneasy Case for Progressive Taxation* (University of Chicago Press, 1953).

Brunner, Karl (ed.), *The Great Depression Revisited* (Boston: Martinus Nijhoff, 1981).

Chandler, Alfred, *The Visible Hand: The Managerial Revolution in American Business* (Cambridge: Harvard University Press, 1977).

Chandler, Lester V., *America's Greatest Depression 1929–1941*, (New York: Harper and Row, 1970).

Diamond, P. A. and Michael Rothschild (eds), *Uncertainty in Economics: Readings and Exercises* (New York: Academic Press, 1978).

Duesenberry, James S., *Income, Saving and the Theory of Consumer Behavior*, (Cambridge: Harvard University Press, 1949).

Easterlin, Richard A., 'Does Money Buy Happiness?' *Public Interest*, No. 30 (Winter 1973), 3–10.

Easterlin, Richard A., 'What Will 1984 be Like? Socioeconomic Implications of Recent Twists in Age Structure', *Demography*, 15 (Nov 1978), 397–432.

Farrell, M. J., 'The New Theories of the Consumption Function', *The Economic Journal*, 69 (December 1959), 678–96.

Fine, Sidney, *Laissez-Faire and General Welfare State* (Ann Arbor: University of Michigan Press, 1956).

Friedman, Milton, *A Theory of the Consumption Function* (Princeton University Press, 1957).

Friedman, Milton, and David Meiselman, 'The Relative Stability of Monetary Velocity and the Investment Multiplier in the United States', in *Stabilization Policies. Studies for the Commission on Money and Credit*, (Englewood Cliffs, New Jersey: Prentice-Hall, 1963). p. 168–268.

Friedman, Milton, and Anna J. Schwartz, *A Monetary History of the United States, 1867–1960*, (Princeton University Press, 1965).

Friedman, Milton, *The Optimum Quantity of Money, and Other Essays*, (Chicago: Aldine, 1969).

Fusfeld, Daniel R., *The Economic Thought of Franklin D. Roosevelt and the Origins of the New Deal*, (New York: Columbia University Press, 1954).

Goldberg, V. P., 'Regulation and Administered Contracts', *Bell Journal of Economics*, 7 (Autumn 1976) 429–48.

Gordon, Robert A., *Economic Instability and Growth: The American Record*, (New York: Harper and Row, 1974).

Hart, H. L. A., *Law, Liberty and Morality*, (Stanford University Press, 1933).

Haskell, Thomas L., *The Emergence of Professional Social Science*, (Chicago, Illinois: University of Illinois Press, 1977).

Hirsch, Fred, *Social Limits to Growth*, (Cambridge: Harvard University Press, 1976).

Hofstadter, Richard, *The Age of Reform*, (New York: Random House, 1955).

Joskow, Paul, 'Inflation and Environmental Concern: Structural Change in the Process of Public Utility Price Regulation', *Journal of Law and Economics*, 17 (Oct 1974) 291–327.

Keynes, John Maynard, *Treatise on Money*, 2 vols (New York: Harcourt Brace, 1930).

Keynes, John Maynard, *The General Theory of Employment, Interest, and Money* (New York: Harcourt Brace, 1936).

Leuchtenburg, William E., *Franklin D. Roosevelt and the New Deal: 1932–1940* (New York: Harper and Row, 1963).

Lucas, Robert E. and Thomas J. Sargent, 'After Keynesian Macroeconomics', in *After the Phillips Curve: Persistence of High Inflation and High Unemployment*, (Boston: Federal Reserve Bank, 1978).

Modigliani, Franco and R. E. Brumberg, 'Utility Analysis and the Consumption Function: An Interpretation of Cross-Section Data', *The Post Keynesian Economics* (K. Kurihara: Rutgers University Press, 1954).

Nelson, Richard R. and Sidney G. Winter, 'Toward an Evolutionary Theory of Economic Capabilities', *American Economic Review, Papers and Proceedings*, 63 (May 1973) 440–9.

Nelson, Richard R. and Sidney G. Winter, 'Factor Price Changes and Factor Substitution in an Evolutionary Model', *Bell Journal of Economics*, 6 (Autumn 1975) 466–86.

Phelps, E., *The Microeconomic Foundations of Employment and Inflation Theory* (New York: Norton Publishing House, 1970).

Piore, Michael Joseph, (ed.), *Unemployment and Inflation* (White Plains, NY: M. E. Sharpe, 1979).

Radner, Roy, 'A Behavioral Model of Cost Reduction', *Bell Journal of Economics*, 6 (Spring 1975) 196–215.

Radner, Roy and Michael Rothschild, 'Notes on the Allocation of Effort', *Journal of Economic Theory*, 10 (June 1975) 358–76.

Ross, Dorothy, 'Socialism and American Liberalism: Academic Social Thought in the 1980s', *Perspectives in American History*, 11 (1978), 7–79.

Rostow, W. W., *The British Economy in the Nineteenth Century* (Oxford University Press, 1948).

Samuelson, Paul A., *Economics, An Introductory Analysis*, 1st edn (New York: McGraw-Hill, 1948).

Samuelson, Paul A., *Economics*, 10th edn (New York: McGraw-Hill, 1976).

Simon, Herbert A., *Models of Man* (New York: Wiley, 1957).

Simon, Herbert A., 'Theories of Decision-Making in Economics and Behavioral Science', *American Economic Review*, 49 (June 1959) 253–83.

Simon, Herbert A., 'Rational Decision Making in Business Organizations', *The American Economic Review*, 69 (September 1979) 493–513.
Stein, H., *The Fiscal Revolution in America* (University of Chicago Press, 1966).
Stein, J. (ed.), *Monetarism* (Amsterdam: North Holland, 1976).
Stigler, G., 'The Economics of Information', *Journal of Political Economy*, 69 (June 1961) 213–25.
Stigler, G., *The Intellectual and the Market Place and Other Essays* (New York: Free Press, 1963).
Temin, Peter, *Did Monetary Forces Cause the Great Depression?* 1st edn (New York: W. W. Norton, 1976).
White, Morton, *Social Thought in America* (New York: Oxford University Press, 1976).
Wiebe, Robert H., *The Search for Order, 1877–1920* (New York: Hill and Wang, 1967).
Williamson, Oliver E., *Markets and Hierarchies: Analysis and Antitrust Implications* (New York: Free Press, 1975).
Wilson, Thomas, *Fluctuations in Income and Employment* (London: Pitman, 1942).

6 Progress and Dissimilarity in Historical Perspective

R. M. HARTWELL

I

When Edward Gibbon, with magisterial authority, summed up his great work with some 'General Observations on the Fall of the Roman Empire in the West', he wrote:

> The discoveries of ancient and modern navigators, and the domestic history, or tradition, of the most enlightened nations, represent the *human savage*, naked both in mind and body, destitute of laws, of arts, of ideas, and almost of language. From this abject condition, perhaps the primitive and universal state of man, he has gradually arisen to command the animals, to fertilize the earth, to traverse the ocean, and to measure the heavens. His progress in the improvement and exercise of his mental and corporeal faculties has been irregular and various, infinitely slow in the beginning, and increasing by degrees with redoubled velocity; ages of laborious ascent have been followed by a moment of rapid downfall; and the several climates of the globe have felt the vicissitudes of light and darkness. Yet this experience of four thousand years should enlarge our hopes, and diminish our apprehensions; we cannot determine to what height the human species may aspire in their advances towards perfection; but it may safely be presumed that no people, unless the face of nature is changed, will relapse into their original barbarism.

Gibbon concluded: 'We may therefore acquiesce in the pleasing conclusion that every age of the world has increased, and still increases, the real wealth, the happiness, the knowledge, and perhaps the virtue, of the human race.'[1] To Gibbon the contrast between ancient barbarism and modern civilisation was remarkable, and he tried to explain both those forces which had lifted man out of barbarism and also those which on occasions had halted or reduced his progress. Gibbon's problem is still with us, and is indeed perhaps the most difficult and most neglected of all historical problems. This problem is what in the nineteenth century was called 'progress'[2] and today is called 'growth', not short-term growth but long-term growth or, more accurately, very long-term growth. Those modern historians who have been tempted by curiosity or ambition to attempt to explain man's long pilgrimage, and his halts and set-backs, have been severely criticised for simplicity, or, even worse, historicism.[3] This is perhaps not surprising. Historians are more skilled in describing and explaining small events, events that are simple in content and limited in time, than in understanding and analysing larger and longer events; and their training almost invariably predisposes them to avoid the long-term and complex.[4] Short-term history is more comprehensible and more appealing to most minds, since it deals with individuals rather than trends; it has, also, the advantage of concrete reality, since it depends mainly on direct evidence; and it is narrative rather than analytical. The French call it '*l'histoire événementielle*', the history of events, and it has preoccupied most modern historians. This is not to say that the big problems of history – the great trends and the great discontinuities – are not the more important and the more exciting; only that they are more difficult and are tackled with less confidence by historians whose time preferences run to years rather than to millennia. Gibbon was referring in his analysis to a very long process of historical change, at least 4000 years for the period of 'civilization' and a much longer period for 'barbarism'. And how many modern historians are willing to account for a thousand years?[5]

The shortness of the time-horizon of historians can be illustrated by the carelessness with which they use the terms 'in the short run' and 'in the long run'. The partial exceptions are, on the one hand, French historians of the *Annales* school, and on the other, the economic historians. The French have developed a theory of the *longue durée*, involving structures and conjunctures; the economic historian, because of the nature of much of his material, has developed a literature on cycles and trends. Generally, however, there is a neglect of time. Surely this is curious? Whatever else historians are concerned with, they are always concerned with time; they are always ordering events chronologically and measuring their duration. Two recurring questions of history are always: 'When did it occur?' 'How long did it last?'[6] History is a subject quintessentially concerned with time, with dates, years, centuries, millennia, as well as with periods, ages, epochs and eras, the latter concepts all with explicit but not always exact time dimensions. And when historians use phrases like 'in the long run', they rarely make clear what time period is involved, although usually the phrase is used as a prelude to some judgment about the durability of an event. The phrase has no precision, although the context will usually, but not always, give an idea of what time period is involved. And that time period has no uniformity from event to event; there is no chronological precision to this phrase 'in the long run' except in the context in which it is written. So, for the history of an individual, 'in the long run' can mean years; for a country, it is likely to mean centuries, and for a civilisation, millennia. It could even be concluded that the historian's view of time shrinks according to the size of the unit he is studying. But that would be to give more consistency to the historians than they deserve.

Are the modern economists more interested in big problems and long periods than the historians, and are they more successful in explaining them? The answer is an emphatic 'no'. Since the grand dynamics of the classical economists, economists also have been preoccupied with small problems of, in historical terms, short duration. The economist does use phrases like 'in the short run', to clarify decision-making problems in production planning, especially in the theory of the firm. 'The short run', to the economists, is a period in which at least one factor of production is held constant while in others, the variable factors, change. 'The long run' is a period in which all factors vary while the basic structure of industry and of technology remains constant. 'The very long run' is a period in which not only all factors vary but also structure and technology. The adjustment process to equilibrium is assumed to lengthen between the 'short' and the 'long' run, but neither has a fixed time period, and the economist's interest centres on adjustment and equilibrium rather than on time.[7] The economist, however, has found it quite impossible to deal with the problems of real historic growth of any length of time. The problem of explaining man's progress from barbarism to civilisation would dismay him, but he would find it more baffling, only to a degree, than the problem of explaining the industrial revolution or the great depression. From the economist's silence on such matters, and from his profound incompetence in dealing with contemporary, real-world problems of growth, it would seem that the historian has little to learn from him?

History is never about 'equilibrium', in the economist's sense, and almost always about 'the long run', in the economist's sense. There are indeed in history long periods which resemble the economist's 'long run'. in which the underlying structure of the economy remains relatively stable, while some important factor or factors change, for example, population. There are other usually longer periods, resembling the economist's 'very long run', in which the basic structure also changes.[8] In the long run periods, the basic economic problems are solved in a similar way, the economic institutions are stable and enduring, and variable factors operate and work themselves out 'in the long run'. It is this concept of a long-run period which has given authenticity to terms like 'feudalism' or 'medieval economy'. But what of even longer periods? History in 'the very long run' consists obviously of a series of 'long run' periods in which basic structures change, but in which, nevertheless, unless society disappears completely, there are still enduring forces that ensure at least a minimum of historical continuity. Those forces outlive changing structures and other discontinuities and explain not only why man has survived in the very long run but also why he has progressed. Those forces – elementary structures – centre on the material wants of the individual and his family, and on the cumulative nature of technology, and are discussed below. Those forces, moreover, operate differentially, in time and in place, to produce different end-results in civilisation, or lack of it. If man's very long-term remarkable progress is surely a proper subject of investigation for the historian, so is his dissimilarity, for the outstandingly obvious characteristic of the world human situation today is dissimilarity.

II

No historian can look at the world economy today and not be struck by the spectacle of dissimilarity, dissimilarity that is depicted with statistical accuracy. Indeed it is this dissimilarity that leads the historian naturally to the problem of growth, for obviously the differential growths of the past have produced today's remarkable differences between the nations and areas of the world. The historian, also, might reflect on how much social effort goes into proving those differences statistically.[9] The modern age is a statistical age in which governments, firms, professional associations, international organisations, research institutions, universities and individuals are all in the business of manufacturing statistics. All economic 'facts' are quantified, tabled, ranked and compared, and such facts are used to detect differences and to identify dissimilarities. This statistical scrutiny of nations, for example, reveals universal dissimilarity, in levels of income and wealth, in rates of growth, in the structure of economies, in consumption and investment patterns, in distribution, and, among other things, in dependence on international trade. Given these statistics, the aggregate performance of nations, and their success, are judged, usually on the basis of two criteria: on levels of real incomes per capita, and on the rates of growth of those incomes. Given the existing condition of nations, prescriptions for future change are then formulated, almost invariably aimed at inducing higher rates of growth and higher levels of income.[10] Such prescriptions are the preserve of the economist, not of the historian, for economists look forward while historians look backwards. It could seem useful, nevertheless, for the economist also to look backwards, if only to discover why the dissimilarities they are planning to correct already exist.[11] Since present dissimilarity is the end-result of an historical process, perhaps the key to future growth lies in past growth? Certainly when examined historically it becomes quickly apparent that present dissimilarity is the consequence of a process of differentiating growth that goes back a long way. Prescriptions for growth, if they are to be historically based, must be based on long-term or very long-term historical research, not just on a consideration of the successful growths of the last two centuries.

If the economist were to compare present European dissimilarity with past dissimilarity, and also the present and past differences between Europe and the rest of the world, he would conclude indeed that dissimilarity has been long in the making. Not that he could base this conclusion entirely on statistics; he would have to abandon the quest for accurate measurement and would base his generalisation on qualitative as well as quantitative data, and on a wider variety of less comprehensive information than a twentieth century economist would depend on. But the seeking of a wider basis for generalisation should also make the economist wiser and more realistic about social processes in general and about growth in particular. He would find, perhaps to his surprise, that the rich countries of eighteenth century Europe, before industrialisation, are the rich countries of today, and although interesting variations in ranking have occurred, a central core of west European countries were the most advanced economies before industrialisation and are still today.[12] The industrial revolution did not create the dissimilarities the economists now observe, neither within Europe nor between Europe and the rest of the world. The underdeveloped countries of the twentieth century were the underdeveloped countries of the eighteenth century. Africa was poor and backward long before the first adventurous European explorers moved cautiously along its coasts; and it remained poor after the industrialisation of Europe. Industrialisation may have widened the economic gap between Europe and the rest of the world; it certainly did not create it.[13] Indeed, the difficulty which most non-European societies have experienced in achieving even modest growth points unambiguously to the conclusion that growth, at least in its modern form, is a European phenomenon whose explanation must be sought in the long history of Europe,[14] at least back to the Middle Ages, when the gap between Europe and the rest of the world began to widen, and perhaps back to Greece and Rome which contributed so much that is essential to the character and institutions of European civilisation.

If the economist were then to look further back in history, before the expansion of Europe, he would find a different world-pattern of dissimilarity. Far enough back he would discover that Europe was an uncivilised backwater of barbarism when elsewhere in the world there were advanced civilisations that had experienced considerable long-term growth.[15] Some of these earlier civilisations survived a long time, but all finally declined or disappeared, leaving the modern world to be made by Europe. And even before the rise of civilisation, the economist would find change and variety, with wide regional variations in barbaric achievement.[16] The long history of dissimilarity, therefore, raises fundamental questions about the history of growth, not just about the achievements and prospects of today's economies, but of growth in long-term historical perspective. The problems are not only to explain the process whereby man has progressed, in spite of set-backs, from something less than man to the sophisticated urban–industrial creature that he now is over much of the world; but also to explain how, in certain areas and at certain times, some nations and civilisations progressed so remarkably and then declined. These are the problems of *very long-term growth* and *long-term growth*, and *long-term decline*, because the proper understanding of growth must also include explanations of the melancholy phenomenon of the decay of civilisations, of those long-lived civilisations which, like modern Europe, once dominated, but ultimately declined.[17] It is the longer pilgrimage, from cave to skyscraper, with the retreats *en route*, however, which is the phenomenon of 'history' rather than any of its smaller parts. And it is history in this very long-term sense that needs explaining, as much as the shorter episodes, long-term though they may be, which together go to make up the total historical experience of man. And to give the longer problem realistic chronological perspective, it needs only to be pointed out that mankind has been paleologically primitive for most of his history, and that the period of civilisation, and that of European expansion, have occupied only tiny fractions of that total history.[18]

III

The problems of explaining man's long preparation for civilisation, and the first great 'leap' forward, the neolithic revolution, are the most difficult, if only because of the scarcity of evidence. Nevertheless, the first question about growth must be: Why did primitive man not remain locked forever, like the animals he lived with and hunted, in a trap of socio-economic subsistence immobility? Why, indeed, was there ever any growth at all? Historians have identified three broad long-term phases of growth:[19] the food-gathering and hunting phase, the food-growing and agriculture phase, and the industrial phase, each characterised by the dominant activity during that phase of the majority of people. There were no sharp turning-points between these phases and each was long in the making, although the preparation for agriculture was obviously much longer than that for industry. The first phase lasted perhaps half-a-million years and the second only ten to twelve millennia; the third, perhaps eight centuries in the making, has affected more people more quickly than the previous agricultural transformation, although its decisive growth period over the last two centuries can hardly be measured on the time-scale of history. It would appear, therefore, that whatever 'factors' and 'forces' produce growth, they were painfully slow in coming into operation *in the first place*, but thereafter operated cumulatively,[20] speeding up the process, and, in the case of industrialisation, with remarkable results over a short period of time. But the questions still remain: Why did progress begin at all, and when it did begin, why did it not begin everywhere, and why did it stop short with certain peoples in certain places?

The transition from food-gathering to food-growing first occurred in some places about 10 000 years ago, but in other places it occurred later, and in some places it has never occurred. At the same time as cultivation appeared, a more elaborate and settled social organisation in the form of the village community appeared. Some of these village communities later developed into cities, but not everywhere; indeed, in the first place, in only a few centres, and, as with cultivation, in many places villages never became cities.[21] The transition from agriculture to industry began to speed up in the eighteenth century, but again not everywhere, so that agriculturally based societies have persisted into the last quarter of the twentieth century. Many societies which in the past had produced advanced civilisations, with urbanisation and industry, however, stopped short of an industrial revolution.[22] And so the world picture today is one of dissimilarity, with societies of differing degrees of progress, from paleolithic to industrialised, with societies that have stagnated and declined, to which should be added those which have disappeared.

These are, then, four problems about very long-term growth for the historian to solve. Why was growth possible in the first place? Why was it not possible everywhere? Why was it not continuous once it began? Why, at every point of time, was the character of growth different, different in different places and with different people? Or, to phrase the problems differently: What caused growth? What were the obstacles to growth? What halted growth? What caused dissimilarities in growth? Or differently again: What 'forces' or 'factors' over history have been continuously at work to produce growth? Similarly, what forces have frustrated growth? What forces have halted growth and what has reversed it? Why have these forces operated differently in different places at different times? These questions are concerned with *the long run* and *the very long run*, with those enduring forces, those structures, either environmental or human, which have determined the outcomes of history as we observe them. No attempt will be made to answer all these questions, but the problems can be specified, some variables identified, and some solutions suggested.

IV

Edward Gibbon argued,

> The improvements of society may be viewed under a threefold aspect. 1. The poet or philosopher illustrates his age and country by the efforts of a *single* mind; but these superior powers of reason or fancy are rare and spontaneous productions, and the genius of Homer, or Cicero, or Newton, would excite less admiration, if they could be created by the will of a prince or the lessons of a preceptor. 2. The benefits of law and policy, of trade and manufacturers, of arts and sciences, are more solid and permanent; and *many* individuals may be qualified, by education and discipline, to promote in their respective stations, the interests of the community. But this general order is the effect of skill and labour; and the complex machinery may be decayed by time or injured by violence. 3. Fortunately for mankind, the more useful, or, at least, more necessary arts can be performed without superior talents or national subordination; without the power of *one* or the union of *many*. Each village, each family, each individual, must always possess both ability and inclination to perpetuate the use of fire and of metals; the propagation and service of domestic animals; the methods of hunting and fishing; the rudiments of navigation; the imperfect cultivation of corn or other nutritive grain; and the simple practice of the mechanic trades. Private genius and public industry may be extirpated; but then hardy plants survive the tempest, and strike an everlasting root into the most unfavorable soil.[23]

Gibbon went on to point out that during the Barbarian invasions 'the scythe . . . still continued annually to mow the harvests of Italy'.

The continuity of civilisation, then, is assured by the basic needs of survival, needs that are satisfied, as F. Braudel has pointed out, by habit and routine rather than by conscious effort:

> Countless inherited acts, accumulated pell-mell and repeated time after time to this very day, become habits that help us live, imprison us, and make decisions for us throughout our lives. Those acts are incentives, pulsions, patterns, ways of acting and reacting that sometimes – more frequently than we might suspect – go back to the beginnings of mankind's history.[24]

Braudel called this 'material life'; 'activities for survival' might be a more accurate description. Man early differentiated from other animals because of his intelligence and manipulative skill which gave him an adaptability which varied, from problem to problem and from environment to environment. They also enabled him to make tools which from the earliest times enlarged his powers and made it possible for him to manipulate the environment. This made all the difference. As Thomas Carlyle pointed out: 'Man stands on a basis, at most of the flattest soled, of some half square foot insecurely enough. Three quintals are a crushing load for him; the steer of the field tosses him aloft like a waste rag. Nevertheless he can use tools. Without tools he is nothing. With tools he is all.'[25] Intelligence, adaptability and tools gave man choice, and choice made for variation. Differing environments made for different choices and different solutions to the problems of material life; the arts of survival varied, and some have been more successful than others.[26] And, as Gibbon pointed out, unusual talents occur randomly, even though their influence may be decisive in the success of a group or enterprise, and hence on their survival and growth. One pervasive characteristic of man made for progress, his tool-making, which, as C.E. Ayres pointed out, was 'inherently progressive'.[27] As technology improved, so did material life. Certainly progress at first was painfully slow, because the cumulative character of environmental experience and of technological knowledge meant a slow build-up of man's increasing mastery of his environment; and there were halts and reversals, often because of natural disasters.[28] But always progress resumed, and in time went beyond the levels of material life previously attained. Tools, once invented, had greater survival power than the civilisations which produced them, as did the habits and customs on which material life so much depended. Human adaptability and the nature of technology, then, can explain two very long-run characteristics of man's history: dissimilarity and progress. But what explains the shorter-run phenomena of the growth and decline of civilisations?

The growth of civilisation depends firstly on economies to scale in human organisations.[29] Man's survival for so long depended on small-scale social units; civilisation depends on large-scale units. At the level of material life discussed above, the relevant and appropriate social unit for survival, and for the transmission of custom and skills, is the individual and his family, by themselves or in a small community (the village or the tribe). For most of history, and still today in primitive communities, survival has depended on the production of food and a limited range of artifacts by individuals and small groups. More complex societies have been possible only where and when agricultural productivity has been increased substantially.[30] Civilisation grew out of a food surplus, and generally over history agricultural output has increased only very slowly by improved husbandry and more usually by having more men till more land with the same old tools. Even with increasing agricultural productivity, civilisation was rare, touching the minority of mankind, most of whom until very recently lived close to subsistence. And when a progressive agriculture did allow more complex and larger-scale social organisations of civilisation, the chances of failure were also increased. Civilisation, indeed, turned out to be a risky innovation! At the level of material life, the individual depended on the land, his skills, his primitive tools, and the climate; with the invention of civilisation a large new variable complicated this simple picture. As man had invented tools, and a great variety of tools, so also he invented institutions, and again in great variety. These institutional artifacts, however, were not only more varied but also less durable than the tools and habits of material life. Some institutions thrived, others stagnated, others died; and civilisation followed suit. When civilisation stagnated or decayed, however, men could always fall back onto material life, abandoning the refinements of civilisation for the activities of survival. Many writers have recognised that within the national state, for example, institutions decisively affect the capacity for progress. To Adam Smith the limiting factor in growth was always the constitution: 'Nations tolerably well advanced as to skill, dexterity, and judgment in the application of labour, have followed very different plans in the general conduct or direction of it; and those plans have not all been equally favorable to the greatness of the product.' The economy in the modern period which prospered, according to Smith, was the one in which there existed 'the obvious and simple system of liberty'. Inappropriate constitutions meant stagnation. As regards China, Smith wrote: 'It had perhaps . . . acquired that full complement of riches which the nature of its laws and institutions permits it to acquire.'[31] Smith and other writers, also, have recognised characteristics in institutions which led to the decline of civilisation, characteristics that centre in the behaviour of state bureaucracies as they grow powerful, wealthy, conservative, and corrupt.[32]

The survival and success of civilisations depend, secondly, on exogenous forces, of which the most important have been the weather and 'the barbarian invaders'. The weather varies in different ways over different time periods, and its long-run variations have certainly affected history in obvious and influential ways.[33] The end of the ice-age heralded the agricultural revolution and the beginnings of communal living; warm weather in the first millennium B.C. witnessed the rise of Greece, and in the eighteenth century A.D. saw the onset of the industrial revolution in England. The colonisation of Europe after 1000 A.D. coincided with three centuries of relatively good weather. The weather has been a continuous and changing variable in man's history, and seems also to have given some chronological structure at least to the rise of civilisations; the great civilisations of history seem to have developed, in the long-term perspective of the history of climate, in periods of good weather. But civilisations did not develop everywhere, even in good weather, and bad weather did not necessarily destroy existing civilisations. Men and their institutions could always ensure the survival of a civilisation, even in bad weather, or the decline of a civilisation, even in good weather. The relationship, then, between climate and civilisation is important but not decisive. It is also the case with 'barbarian invaders', who have been viewed by some writers, not just as the destroyers, but also as the dynamic of civilisation. Giovanni Vico viewed history as a process in which vigorous barbarians gradually declined because of the triumph of rationalism over energy.[34] W. M. Flinders-Petrie argued that 'there is no advance without strife', and that civilisation is 'an intermittent phenomenon' because the struggle initially with barbarian invaders produces vigour and progress in civilisation, but that in the long run that vigour is weakened by the debilitating consequences of success.[35] If to the ancients time was the enemy of humanity, to modern writers it has often been wealth which allegedly corrupts and weakens, and then destroys. It is interesting to note, however, that the most successful of civilisations, that of Europe, developed on the frontiers of the ancient civilisations of the Middle East by acquiring their technology – their 'material life' – but not their institutions.[36] Perhaps the failure of Asian civilisation to develop beyond a certain point was the absence of a large and populated land mass, of high agricultural potential, at its frontiers? But whatever the judgment of history there is no doubt that barbarian invaders have played an important role both in creating and destroying civilisations.

Dissimilarity and progress *in the very long run*, and the rise and decline of civilisations *in the long run*, can now be separated as distinctive problems with different solutions. Some causes of change in both cases can be suggested, but many mysteries remain. It is a healthy sign of realism in modern historical studies that, along with the preoccupation of so many with social forces, there are an increasing number of historians who once again are interested in the history of progress.

NOTES AND REFERENCES

1. Edward Gibbon, *The History of the Decline and Fall of the Roman Empire*, Chap. XXXVIII (London: Straham and Cadell, 1782).
2. See: J. B. Bury, *The Idea of Progress* (London: Macmillan, 1921) and R. Nisbet, *History of the Idea of Progress* (New York: Basic Books, 1980).
3. The trend may be changing, but see, for example, the hostile reception by professional historians of A. J. Toynbee's *A Study of History* (10 volumes, Oxford University Press, 1934–1961). Part of the reaction to the great systematisers was a reasonable reaction against historicism; see, for example, K. R. Popper, *The Poverty of Historicism* (London: Routledge and Kegan Paul, 1957).

   If great trends are out of favour, great discontinuities are not. No event in modern history has commanded a larger literature, for example, than the industrial revolution of England.
4. University trained historians are 'specialists', concentrating in function and in period, and seldom accounting for more than a century. Teaching and research clearly demarcate the historian as 'economic', 'political', 'social', etc.; as 'modern', 'early modern', 'medieval', etc.; as 'British', 'French', 'American', etc.; and even within functional categories, as 'industrial', 'labour', 'demographic', etc. within economic history. The idea of training an historian to look at the whole of history would be looked on by most historians as both absurd and dangerous, and, in any case, impossible. Occasionally some adventurous historian does attempt to portray the economic history of man from its beginnings; e.g., Carlo Cipolla's *The Economic History of World Population* (London: Penguin, 1965).
5. Except the writers of text-books for those 'survey' courses which introduce students to history but which are not taken seriously as 'contributions' to

scholarship. Yet see the importance of the survey course of an earlier generation of historians, M. Weber's *General Economic History* (translation by F. H. Knight, London: Allen and Unwin, 1928).

6. Obviously an exact chronology is also useful, and often essential, in establishing cause in historical sequences. See J. L. Mackie, *The Cement of the Universe: A Study of Causation* (Oxford University Press, 1974).
7. See, for example, F. H. Knight, 'Costs of Production Price over Long and Short Periods', in *The Ethics of Competition* (London: Allen and Unwin, 1935). For a conventional text-book approach see: R. G. Lipsey and P. O. Steiner, *Economics* (New York: Harper and Row, 1969).
8. I use the word structure in the way in which the French use it, to describe 'the parts of an economic whole which, over a period of time appear relatively stable alongside the others'. See A. Marchal, 'De la dynamique des structures à la dynamique des systèmes' (*Revue économique*, Paris, 1955); quoted in, R. Doehaerd, *The Early Middle Ages in the West* (Amsterdam: North-Holland, 1978). p. v.
9. The outstanding chronicler of dissimilarity, in statistical terms, is S. Kuznets who has spent his life in compiling statistics which reveal the differences between nations. See, for example, *Modern Economic Growth* (Yale University Press, 1966).
10. Growth as a subject of study by economists has become inextricably confused with policy for growth as a desirable objective of politics. Most writing on growth hovers uncertainly between theory and policy, the degree of policy involvement usually being directly related to the degree of political commitment of the growth theorist.
11. Governments always have economic advisers but never historical advisers. The logic of the choice of economists over historians to advise on growth is, at least on grounds of realism, difficult to follow.
12. On quantitative measures to prove this see: P. Studenski, *The Income of Nations* (New York University Press, 1958).
    On qualitative measures, for example, see the volumes for the centuries before 1800 of *The Cambridge Economic History of Europe*. See also: C. M. Cippola, *Before the Industrial Revolution. European Society and Economy, 1000–1700* (New York: Norton, 1976).
13. There is another theory which argues that the rest of the world is poor because Europe is rich, that national wealth and national poverty are fundamentally related. The thesis is unproven.
14. The exception is Japan, but Japan excepted, no non-European society has yet achieved growth comparable to that achieved by Europeans, either in Europe or abroad. The fact that Europeans abroad (in Australia, for example) have achieved growth underlines the specificity of European culture for growth.
15. Europe was the last great civilisation to develop, at the frontier of the ancient civilisations of the Middle East.
16. G. Clark, *Aspects of Prehistory* (University of California Press, 1970).
17. The decline of Europe has also been confidently predicted by many writers. See, for example perhaps the most famous prophecy of western decline: O. Spengler, *The Decline of the West* (translated by C. F. Atkinson, New York: Knopf, 1926).

18. The period of history since the birth of Christ consists of about one five-hundredth (i.e., 0.2 per cent) of history; the period since the beginning of the industrial revolution comprises only one over two thousand five hundredths of history.
19. See Cipolla, *The Economic History of World Population* op. cit., for an explicit long-term history of man in terms of those revolutions. See, also: R. M. Hartwell, *The Industrial Revolution and Economic Growth* (London: Methuen, 1971).
20. The theory that progress is cumulative has been used effectively by C. E. Ayres to explain technological progress; see, C. E. Ayres, *The Theory of Economic Progress* (University of North Carolina Press, 1944). More generally the growth of knowledge has been explained as a cumulative process by K. R. Popper; see, *Conjectures and Refutations: The Growth of Scientific Knowledge* (New York: Basic Books, 1962), p. 129.
21. See Sir Henry Maine, *Village Communities in the East and West* (London: Murray, 1876).
22. As E. L. Jones and S. J. Woolf have written: 'One of the less palatable lessons of history is that technically advanced and physically productive agriculture does not inevitably bring about a sustained growth of *per capita* income, much less promotes industrialization'. E. L. Jones and S. J. Woolf, (eds), *Agrarian Change and Economic Development* (London: Methuen, 1969) p. 1.
23. Gibbon, *op. cit.*, Chap. XXXVIII.
24. F. Braudel, *Afterthoughts on Material Civilization and Capitalism* (Johns Hopkins University Press, 1977) p. 7.
25. Quoted by D. Birdsall and C. M. Cipolla, *The Technology of Man: A Visual History* (England: Penshurst Press, 1979), p. 17.
26. See G. Clark, *Aspects of Prehistory* (University of California Press, 1970) for an excellent account of man's varying response to environmental difficulties, and for a nondeterminist account of cultural differentiation.
27. C. E. Ayres argued that technology was progressive because of 'the tool-combination principle'. 'Granted that tools are always tools of men who have the capacity to use tools and therefore the capacity to use them together, combinations are bound to occur. Furthermore it follows that the more tools there are, the greater is the number of potential combinations.' *The Theory of Economic Progress* (University of North Carolina Press, 1944) p. 119.
28. See E. L. Jones' forthcoming *The European Miracle*. The manuscript of this book was seen only as this article was being concluded; it is concerned with very long-term growth in terms of varying civilisations' divergent responses to natural disasters. It is a brilliant addition to the now growing literature on very long-term development.
29. Only a reasonably large-scale society can provide most of the goods and services generally associated with 'civilization'. The 'golden age' myth of rural life plays no role in serious consideration of civilised living.
30. See G. Childe for a persuasive account of 'the urban revolution' as a consequence of 'the neolithic revolution', especially *What Happened in History* (London: Penguin, 1942).
31. Adam Smith, *The Wealth of Nations* (Modern Library Edition, edited by E. Cannan, New York: Random House, 1937) pp. lix, 651, 862, 71.

32. Most accounts of the decline of Rome are in this vein; for example, R. Latouche, *The Birth of Western Economy* (New York: Barnes and Noble, 1961).
33. See, for a summary of recent discussions on 'History of Climate', *The Journal of Interdisciplinary History*, vol. X, no. 4, Spring 1980.
34. See C. Quigley, *The Evolution of Civilizations* (Indianapolis: Liberty Press, 1979), p. 129. To Oswald Spengler, also, the 'culture' of earlier stages of civilisation gave way to the 'civilization' of the later stages in which character and energy were both weakened. Ibid., p. 130.
35. W. M. Flinders-Petrie, *The Revolutions of Civilization* (New York: Harper, 1911), pp. 123–5: 'The maximum of wealth must inevitably lead to the downfall.'
36. A point made long ago by C. E. Ayres (in *The Theory of Economic Progress*) and more recently by E. L. Jones (in *The European Miracle*).

7 The Growth of Mature Economies

W. A. LEWIS

What really constrains the rate of growth of a mature developed economy, defined as one where the proportion of the labour force in agriculture is down to less than 30 per cent? Japan claims to have been growing at ten to eleven per cent, whereas other developed market economies claim no more than five to six per cent, which is itself more than such economies could have claimed at any time before 1950.

The standard answers to this question are not satisfying – the savings ratio, the supply of labour, natural resources, foreign exchange, entrepreneurship and technology. I shall reflect on each of these, and argue eventually that the ultimate constraint is the ability of an industrial system to absorb change in orderly fashion.

I

The savings ratio is not an obstacle. It depends endogenously on the rate of growth: it is low when the growth rate is low, as in contemporary USA, and high when the growth rate is high, as in contemporary Japan. Besides it is not the total of savings and investment that 'determines' growth, but only that part which goes into productive industry, commerce and agriculture, which is less than 50 per cent of annual investment, when one has subtracted residential building, public service investment, and other aids to consumption rather than production. In a mature economy productive investment gets the first call on savings, in the sense that entrepreneurs can always raise the money needed to finance productive investment – from their own profits, from the banks, on the stock exchange and through private placement. As Phelps

Brown has suggested,[1] in a mature economy the supply of saving to business enterprise becomes infinitely elastic at some modest rate of return (say a real rate of around 12 per cent net of tax). If there is not enough saving for all the intended projects, public and private, it is the public sector that runs short. The country then borrows from abroad – fast growers can always borrow. Or it borrows from the banks (accounting for the slight correlation between fast growth and inflation). In any case fast growth changes the ratio of total savings by raising the relative share of profits, by increasing government receipts faster than government expenditure, and by mobilising personal saving that would otherwise not occur. 'Take care of investment and the savings ratio will take care of itself' is bad advice for poor countries, but is just about right for rich countries.

Keynes taught us to see the savings ratio as an obstacle to growth in the opposite sense, namely that it might be too high for the planned level of investment. Then we might also say that under-consumption is the constraint on growth. My question, however, presumes that there is no lack of willingness to invest. If this unwillingness exists, for any of the reasons yet to be explored, the growth rate of the economy will be constrained, and bouts of unemployment will show up as it shifts to a slower growth path. I count this, however, as a deficiency of investment rather than a surplus of savings.

II

The labour supply is also not an obstacle to growth. Up until around 1960 most developed countries had large reservoirs of cheap labour – in farming, domestic service, retailing, small scale transport and elsewhere – that could be transferred into high wage occupations and industries. As this supply diminished, it was replenished by importing cheap low-wage manufactures from developing countries. Also, low-wage industries were increasingly mechanised, or transformed by self-service. Then mechanisation of the home made it possible to bring great numbers of married women into the labour market. And finally these countries turned to immigration of unskilled labour. So labour was not a constraint on production – not even skilled labour, which seems to have been trained just about as rapidly as it was required.

Presumably there are physical limits to the speed at which people can be transferred from low-wage into high-wage industries. For one thing, this transfer frequently means migration into towns, and there must be physical limits to the speed with which towns can grow. During the nineteenth century urban populations grew in Germany and in the USA at around three per cent per annum. Several developing countries now have urbanisation rates exceeding five per cent, but the resulting urban chaos is not to be admired. There are also limits to the willingness of people to leave the countryside for the town, or the household for the factory job, an unwillingness which is sometimes advanced (along with the low birth rates) to explain the slow urbanisation of France at the end of the nineteenth century. Hence, even if the reservoir is full of cheap labour, the speed of transfer can be limited. Moreover the feasible speed may differ at different times. For example the willingness of married women living with their families to go into factory work is much greater now than it was a century ago. In general, labour is less of a constraint now than it was then.

What would happen if unskilled immigration ceased, if all the married women were at work, and all the labour reservoirs drained dry? Labour would then tend to be a constraint. According to Marx one would never reach this stage since the flow of labour-saving innovations would always be enough to maintain a large reservoir of unemployment. In practice up until now technological change has sustained an annual increase of two to three per cent of the labour force; immature countries with populations rising faster than this accumulate reservoirs of unemployed and low-productivity labour, whereas mature countries with slow population growth move up to labour scarcity. These quantitative relationships may change. Some economists fear that the new technology of the computer may severely reduce the demand for labour, in which case Marx's forecast will at last materialise. However, if we go only by historical experience, a mature country with five per cent per annum GNP growth must ultimately run into a labour constraint, unless it allows immigration.

To follow through: a scarcity of labour will presumably raise the share of wages in the national income. This will increase the attractiveness of foreign investment relatively to home investment. The savings ratio may not be affected in total (if wage earners save enough) but the ratio of domestic investment will decline, and so also will the rate of growth of commodity output. We are familiar with the combination of slow growth at home and heavy investment abroad (UK at the end of the nineteenth century, USA in the

1960s). It was not in the UK and US cases due to labour scarcity at home, since labour was abundant in both at the relevant times. But it remains a possible outcome of labour scarcity, say in Northwest Europe by 1990, if immigration is not resumed.

III

Natural resources may be a constraint on the development of this planet, considered as a single economic unit. This would have to be the case if technology were to stand still, but is not the case in so far as we learn to substitute cheaply one material for another. Our present purpose is not to discuss this global issue, but to consider the situation of a single country, open to imports, and free to purchase what it needs in a competitive market.

In such a situation natural resources may constrain the growth of a developing economy, but not of a mature economy. A poor country will not start to develop unless some part of it has special features that attract skills, capital and entrepreneurship. These special features are usually natural resources, including in that term advantages of location. At this level people move towards natural resources away from less favoured locations. However by the time that a country is well into industrialisation – has less than thirty per cent of its labour force in agriculture – what counts for further growth is not natural resources but skills, entrepreneurship, institutions and efficient management of the public sector and of public policy. At this stage the country is flexible enough to have a wide range of choice for specialisation. Ability to earn foreign exchange then substitutes for natural resources.

IV

Mature economies should be able to evade a foreign exchange constraint, but may not in fact succeed in doing so.

To say that foreign exchange is not a constraint is to say that, however fast the economy may grow, export income can grow as fast as the growth of imports may require. This may be taken for granted when dealing with small mature countries, but it is not so obvious for large ones, whose attempt to capture an increasing share of world trade may create resistance. Historic cases of fast growth of one's share of world trade in manufactures include UK in the 1830s, Germany in the 1880s, US in the 1890s, Japan in the 1930s and

Brazil at the end of the 1960s, all of which, except for the US case, provoked restrictive measures. The adverse repercussions need not be large. If a country which sells more also buys more to the same extent, the amount of trade available for its competitors diminishes only if supplies of what it is buying fail to expand appropriately. This turns the terms of trade against it and against its nearest competitors. World supplies have been pretty flexible over the past two centuries; changes in relative demand and supply for primary products have been reflected in changing terms of trade, most spectacularly in the British case over 1820 to 1860 but the orders of magnitude have never yet been such that the terms of trade have been a serious constraint on mature growth.

Mature countries should be able to produce goods for export and to sell them. They should not therefore be caught in the circumstances portrayed by the two-gap model as a menace to developing countries. This case turns on low elasticities; the country's low elasticity of demand for imports and its low elasticity of supply of exports (or alternatively its customers' low elasticity of demand for its exports) are such that devaluation does little to reduce the quantity of imports or increase the quantity exported. Mature economies should be sufficiently flexible to escape this fate.

They have, however, their own potential constraint on exports, namely a loss of technological leadership, such as occurred in Britain at the end of the nineteenth century, and is allegedly occurring in the USA today. We shall consider later the domestic effects of a slow down in innovation. Here we concentrate on the fact that as the technological gap closes, the leader loses the rent element in its terms of trade. The economy can retain its profitability only if the rate of growth of wages and other income is reduced, and these changes are difficult to accomplish, especially if foreign exchange rates are fixed and restrictive tariff and quota changes are prohibited by international or other agreement.

A third possible constraint, on developed and developing alike, is an overvalued currency. Policy is usually framed in the light of whether the balance of payments is in surplus or deficit, but this test is not adequate, unless it is coupled with equilibrium in the labour market. Given the level of exports, a country does not attain full employment unless its propensity to import is sufficiently low. With a too high propensity to import, the country will balance its payments, but will have less than full employment. In extreme cases we find countries where foreign exchange receipts seem to be enormous (from remunerative minerals or dividends or agricultural windfall prices), yet unemployment is widespread. Maybe the export industry earns large amounts of foreign exchange, but employs few people. Or maybe production for the domestic market cannot compete with imports, especially if rich export industries have set a level of wages which the domestic industries cannot match. Open unemployment reveals itself, but overvaluation as a source of disguised unemployment – excessive migration overseas, accumulation of labour in low wage occupations – may not be so obvious.

In the two preceding cases the emergence of unemployment turns on the downward inflexibility of wages and other incomes, combined with fixed exchange rates. Devaluation is supposed to remedy this, by reducing domestic prices relatively to international prices. But this will not happen if domestic prices rise *pari passu* with devaluation; in which case the country must use other means of reducing imports and promoting exports (quotas, tariffs, subsidies etc.) Economic control requires that the controllers be able to drive wedges between prices and costs. This can no longer be done in democratic countries simply by flipping general monetary or fiscal switches (interest rates, monetary reserves, exchange rates, budgetary surplus or deficits). Nowadays the price level has to be negotiated between labour, employers and the government. The more mature the country, the more powerful are the spokesmen of its private interests, and the more difficult it may be to agree on a combination of the price level and the foreign exchange rate that will enable the economy to succeed in international competition and to maintain profitability and high investment ratios at home.

V

Sociologists debate what is the elasticity of supply of domestic entrepreneurship over a period of say fifty years in a developing economy. Some think it to be rather low, on the ground that the supply of persons with the appropriate attitudes is controlled by slow-moving forces like religion, attitude to life, child rearing customs, class structure and historical experience; while others think that the combination of opportunity and high remuneration will call forth in a short time all the entrepreneurship that may be required.

Such arguments do not apply to mature economies. These

economies almost by definition have a long historical experience of entrepreneurship, and are unlikely to be deficient in this resource.

Another set of arguments has to do with the obsolescence of the entrepreneurial class as the economy matures. For example, British troubles at the end of the nineteenth century are sometimes attributed to family businesses passing into the hands of the third generation, presumed (without evidence) to be less stalwart than the first. And sometimes attributed to the formation of monopolies that stood in the path of new talent – which is unlikely, since British weakness was not in old established industries but in the new ones. Writers in the 1940s, including Schumpeter,[2] were impressed by the US capitalist's loss of confidence, in face of a depression whose magnitude and duration were beyond his comprehension, and also in face of irate criticism from all other social groups that had trusted in his leadership. These arguments are mounting again today.

Two facts run counter to these arguments. First, the concept of a shortage of entrepreneurship implies that profitable opportunities exist that are neglected. But when the alleged opportunities are examined they most often turn out to be unprofitable.[3] The second fact is that if profitable opportunities were being neglected by domestic entrepreneurs, foreign entrepreneurs would move in, since mature economies are usually wide open to foreign investors. If an economy is profitable it will not lack entrepreneurship. If a mature economy seems to lack entrepreneurship, the question to ask is why it lacks profitability. We have just sketched one possible answer to the question why it lacks profitability; that it is failing to compete in world trade. Another answer is that it has exhausted the technological possibilities. A third answer could be that the political climate is unfavourable. We will take the third first.

The political climate has many elements. The first is that the government maintain the public sector efficiently; that the telephones work, the planes run on time, the schools be adequate, the electrical supply not keep breaking down, and so on. Some mature economies have difficulty in passing this test (the postal system has inordinate delays or the telephone system is unhelpful) but in general this is not their problem.

The next level of the political climate is direct control of industry by means of licenses required for export, construction, and so on. This is a major problem in some developing countries, and is catching on in mature countries, but is not yet in the latter a serious constraint on private investment, except perhaps in electricity supply.

The third level is that of taxation. In theory, high taxation could constrain output by depleting saving, by reducing the net yield of investment, or by discouraging individual initiative. Saving we have already dismissed. The net yield of investment depends partly on whether the corporation tax is passed on to workers and consumers, and partly on its level. Looking back over a century the corporation tax seems to have been passed on, since the net return to capital is no lower now than it was when there was no corporation tax. As for its level, clearly a corporation tax of 100 per cent would bring corporate investment to a close, but the 50 per cent rate which was common in OECD countries in the 1950s and 1960s did not prevent us from having in those decades higher investment ratios than ever before. The same may be said of high marginal tax rates on individuals; they carried us through two booming decades. Besides, high taxes force some people to work harder while some work less, and the net effect is not certain.

In sum, the political climate could constrain growth. However, in mature economies the managerial class has substantial political influence, and the political climate is unlikely to become a major constraint on growth.

VI

We have established so far that the mature economy may have to slow down because it has run out of labour, or because it fails to compete in the world market; other constraints – saving, natural resources, entrepreneurship – are possible but unlikely. Our final question; can a mature economy which is not subject to any of the foregoing constraints nevertheless be restrained by running into a shortage of innovations in which to invest?

The question has two aspects. First, is there an upper bound to investment even in the presence of abundant technological opportunity? The answer is in the affirmative; the complexity of the economy – the interdependence of its parts – sets limits to the speed of its expansion. For example, during the 1950s and 1960s the output of steel in Japan doubled every five years. The demand for steel comes mainly from the construction and the engineering industries; these must have made plans to absorb steel at this rate. They in turn sell their machines to makers of all sorts of commodities, and these latter too must have made appropriate plans. A 'one-product' economy – such as an economy making steel only for armaments – does not have these problems of consistency and coordination. Neither does a young economy have such problems acutely, because it can adjust for surpluses and deficits by buying more or selling less abroad. An economy made up of state enterprises can hide the problems, and can continue unbalanced growth for an indefinite period; either accumulating stocks or disposing of them by fiat. But a mature, complex, private enterprise economy, dependent on profit making, has to grow in balance, and cannot do so at unlimited speed.

In fact, if we take growth of the labour force employed in industry as a proxy for the exploitation of technology we find that in mature economies (even in Japan) this rate has never exceeded four per cent per annum.

The second aspect of our question is whether entrepreneurs can run short of innovations before reaching this upper bound. This question applies only to the two or three countries leading in innovation; the followers cannot lack examples to modify and exploit.

One can only answer 'Yes' to the question whether it is possible. All theorists of long-run growth – classical, Marxist, neo-classical, Keynesian – have taken it for granted that profits will move towards zero and that growth will cease. This has not happened yet; new technology yielded as big a harvest as ever in the 1950s and 1960s; but it could of course happen at any time.

Schumpeter[4] did not believe that new technology was bound to dry up. He promoted instead the idea that innovation is bunched, and that investment therefore fluctuates over a long cycle, which he put at 50 years. This has not been established, and on current evidence seems implausible. There is some tendency in the United States for a decade of prosperity to be succeeded by a decade of recession, but this has been due to a building cycle rather than to a cycle in innovation.[5]

However, even assuming a constant flow of invention, the leadership in exploiting new possibilities may pass from one country to another, the individual country therefore showing spurts of relative growth lasting several decades, followed by decades of falling behind. One such transition occurred at the end of the eighteenth century, from France to Britain; another at the end of the nineteenth century, from Britain to the United States, and another may now be occurring from the United States to Germany or Japan. Loss of leadership does not necessarily imply a decline in the rate of growth. Other countries may grow faster, catch up in income per person, and move ahead, without any adverse consequence for the former leader. However the transitions of the last two centuries have not been of this innocuous kind. The economic signs have included, on the part of the former leader, deceleration of exports, unprofitability of domestic industry and an outburst of foreign investment.

Loss of leadership may reflect that the new technology requires attitudes and institutions (e.g., upgrading of applied science and technology in the educational system) which run counter to the national mores. Or it may result from the coming into play of one or more of the constraints we have already examined, which result in reduced domestic investment, especially failure to manage the balance of payments, or a worsening of the political climate. Sociologists and biologists could no doubt produce many reasons why a mature social system must lose its vigour, sooner or later.

VII

Finally, to sum up we consider the constraints on growth in two prosperous periods, 1900–13 and 1955–73. The analysis yields the following.

It is not clear what constrained US growth over 1900–13: most probably its capacity to absorb immigrants, who over this period averaged slightly over one per cent of population per annum. From 1955 to 1971 the dominant feature was the over-valuation of the dollar; imports of manufactures increased at thirteen per cent per annum, while exports of manufactures increased only at six per cent per annum. The economy was unprofitable most of the time, and had one of the lowest OECD investment ratios.

The UK was constrained over 1900–13 by failure to adapt to new inventions; net exports of manufactures grew slowly, and the country exported both people and capital at unprecedented rates. The 1960s found the UK still struggling with the same problem, each period of cyclical growth being aborted by too high a propensity to import manufactures coupled with too low a propensity to export.

German growth was well balanced in both periods. It probably grew about as fast as labour supply permitted.

France was accelerating over 1900 to 1913. Lack of coal and lack of modern entrepreneurship are advanced as constraints, but both are doubtful.[6] A constrained labour supply seems more probable – as also for 1955 to 1973.

Japan was not mature over 1900 to 1913. The economy seems almost to have had no constraints over the period 1955 to 1973 – which suggests that the principal constraint was the need of a complex system to grow in balance.

NOTES AND REFERENCES

1. E. H. Phelps Brown, *Pay and Profits* (Manchester University Press, 1968).
2. J. A. Schumpeter, *Capitalism, Socialism and Democracy* (New York: Harper, 1950).
3. The British case is discussed intensively in Chapter 5 of my *Growth and Fluctuations 1870–1913* (London: George Allen and Unwin, 1978).
4. J. A. Schumpeter, *Business Cycles* (New York: McGraw-Hill, 1939).
5. See my *Growth and Fluctuations*, op. cit., Chapters 2 and 3.
6. C. P. Kindleberger, *Economic Growth in France and Britain in 1851–1950* (Cambridge, Mass.: Harvard University Press, 1964) Chapter 6.

8 Stages of Economic Growth Revisited

E. S. MASON

The framework of Walt Rostow's stages of economic growth was originally published in an article in the *Economic Journal* in 1956[1] and elaborated in a series of lectures to Cambridge undergraduates in 1958. In this early formulation the process of economic growth was perceived to consist of three stages.

> In this argument the sequence of economic development is taken to consist of three periods; a long period (up to a century or conceivably more) when the preconditions for take-off are established; the take-off itself, defined within two or three decades; and a long period when growth becomes normal and relatively automatic.[2]

By the time these ideas had been expanded into a small book published in 1960[3] the three stages had become five; the traditional society, the preconditions for take-off, the take-off, the drive to technological maturity, and the age of high mass consumption. So far as the Western developed world is concerned the transition from the traditional society to the stage of the preconditions is roughly marked by the absorption of the Newtonian revolution in science and the expansion of rational habits of thought. The period of high mass consumption is characterised by the widespread use of services and of consumer durable goods, particularly the automobile. It is 'a phase from which Americans are beginning to emerge; whose not unequivocal joys Western Europe and Japan are beginning energetically to probe; and with which Soviet society is engaged in an uneasy flirtation'.[4] Beyond this 'it is impossible to predict' though Rostow, on occasion, joins other futurists in speculating what a diminishing marginal utility of goods might mean in a post-industrial society. We shall, however, along with other commentators, ignore the stages of traditional society and of mass consumption and concentrate attention on the preconditions, the take-off, and the drive to technological and economic maturity.

When these ideas were presented to the world in the late 1950s and early 1960s they were, in many quarters, given an enthusiastic reception. The *Economist* called them one of the most stimulating contributions made to economic and political thought since the war; the 'stages' was soon translated into numerous languages; and, as Goren Ohlin observed, the doctrine was accorded the compliment of an official refutation in Pravda.[5] Nor was the recognition limited to journalistic circles. The International Economic Association assembled a number of the leading economic historians and development economists in the world to a conference at Lake Konstanz in 1961 to discuss the *Stages of Growth* and later published an impressive volume of papers on the subject.[6] The criticism of the Stages by the assembled historians and economists was rather severe but Rostow had an opportunity to reply at length and later, in the second edition of the *Stages of Economic Growth* came to grips with his critics.[7] In the same year he published *Politics and the Stages of Growth* which discussed political as well as economic stages in the development process.[8] These ideas were reemphasised in subsequent writing including *How it all Began* which is a detailed examination of economic development in Great Britain.[9] In his latest writing on the subject, stages in the development process in some twenty countries come under scrutiny and the country experience related to global trends.[10] Although a few dates relating to the beginning and ends of economic stages in particular countries are changed, the theory remains essentially intact. In fact later examination of the evidence and the more or less continuous bombardment of the critics have not led Rostow to any serious revision of his views on economic development.

THE HISTORICAL EXPERIENCE

At the Lake Konstanz Conference most of the discussion was devoted to the course of development in the now developed world. But there is another area in which the theory has possible operational significance, i.e., in forecasting the development process in less developed countries. Rostow himself had and has a strong interest in these possibilities and this is the chief concern of this paper. Before going on to this subject, however, it will be useful to examine the main objections that have been levied against the notion of stages as a useful tool in analysing historical experience. At the Konstanz conference and in later discussion the central point of interest has been the concept of take-off. Rostow himself described it as 'the central proposition' and characterised the stage as follows:

> The take-off is defined as an industrial revolution tied directly to radical changes in methods of production, having their decisive consequences over a relatively short period of time . . . What this argument asserts is that the rapid growth of one or more new manufacturing sectors is a powerful and essential engine of economic transformation. Its power derives from the multiplicity of its given forms of impact, where a society is prepared to respond positively to this impact. Growth in such sectors, with new production functions of high productivity in itself tends to raise output per head; it places incomes in the hands of men who will not merely save a high proportion of an expanded income but who will plough it into highly productive investment; it sets up a drain of demand for other manufactured products; it sets up a requirement for enlarged urban areas, whose capital costs may be high but whose population and market organisation help to make industrialization an ongoing process; and, finally it opens up a range of external economy effects which, in the end, help to produce new leading sectors when the initial impulse of the take-off's leading sectors begins to wane.[11]

The take-off may be expected to raise savings and investment and to stimulate a growth in national incomes but these aggregate effects are not necessarily concentrated in the take-off period. The essence of the take-off is a sectoral expansion, a leading industry with sufficient forward and backward linkages and spread effects to influence the whole economy and to prepare the way for other industrial expansion before the impetus of this original leading sector fades. It is a discrete change in the process of development and it is accomplished in a relatively few years.

Other economic historians have tended to see the process of industrialisation from its beginnings in eighteenth century England as more or less continuous though interrupted by wars and depression; with striking uniformities in the process among countries but also with marked differences, occasioned by differences in timing, in natural resource endowments, in country size, in economic policies. And, in general they have been unable to detect the short periods in which leading sectors have set the process in motion. The similarities in the growth process among developed countries have probably been more significant than in the less developed world as a result of the relatively common culture in Western Europe and the areas of European settlement. In the less developed world, lacking that common culture, differences in the growth process among countries are more striking.

While there is considerable agreement among the critics that there are discontinuities in the development process, many of them resulting from large technological innovations, there is little consensus on the proposition that one particular set is responsible for a take-off into sustained growth. In Kuznets's opinion, shared by many others, 'the lines between the preconditions and the take-off period and between the take-off period and the move to maturity are blurred. What are described as characteristics of the take-off could be characteristics of either of the other periods.'[12] There are significant discontinuities in all periods.

In his most extensive reply to the critics Rostow concentrated on three major charges; that he conceives of the development process as automatic, a matter of historical necessity, not to be influenced by human volition; that he sees more uniformity in the process than in fact exists; and that he overemphasises one particular discontinuity in what is, in fact, a relatively continuous process although marked by many discontinuities.[13]

Myrdal is a chief exponent of the first line of criticism. In a lengthy discussion of Rostow and other 'stages' theorists he observes that

> This presentation of the stages of development – from 'lower' to 'higher' – renders the whole approach teleological. By a teleological approach is meant one in which a purpose, which is not explicitly intended by anyone, is fulfilled, while the process of fulfillment is presented as an inevitable sequence of events . . . The suggestion of *inevitability* gives the stream of historical forces a stickiness that reduces greatly the scope for manoeuvre, both in the past, ruling out hypothetical alternatives, and in the present ruling out planning.[14]

Man, in this interpretation, is in the hands of events; events that are sweeping him in a predetermined direction, to a foregone conclusion.

Looking backward, from the point of view of the developed nations, there is no denying that the process of growth in all countries has shown striking uniformities; uniformities that, in large part, have been the result of absorption from a common pool of technologies. Nor would economic historians who do not favour stage theories deny this. But they would assert that there have been differences in institutions and in policies that have deeply influenced the process of growth and that were not historically inevitable. And the question of inevitability comes much more to the fore when one considers the possibilities of prediction with respect to the growth process in less developed countries.

The charge that Rostow overemphasises the uniformities in development is closely related to that of historical inevitability. In Cairncross's words Rostow 'seems to me to have made the Muse of History lie on the bed of Procrustes'.[15] As Gerschenkron observes an overemphasis on uniformities can lead one to neglect the important role of the banks in German economic development and the Ministry of Finance in Russian growth. Again this is a question that assumes more importance in a study of the growth process in less developed countries where the absence of a common culture assumes significance.

We have already discussed the role of discontinuities. Here many economic historians would agree with Rostow's emphasis on discontinuities merely denying the reality of a particular discontinuity that leads to the take-off.

How much of the discussion on stages of growth is, in fact, a terminological dispute? Rostow admits in his latest writing on the subject that 'In terms of historical analysis, a good deal of the debate turned out to be a matter of vocabulary' while emphasising, correctly, the substantial agreement between himself and his critics on the timing of the entrance of various countries into sustained growth that might be called industrial revolution, the beginning of modern growth or take-off. There is some truth in David Landes's observation that the concept of stages 'rested on a new vocabulary and therefore inevitably presented an act of aggression against an established discipline'.[16] In particular this was true of the phrase 'take-off'. 'Nothing was so dangerous as a single, sharp image of a subtle nuanced phenomenon. No wonder that so much of the discussion had been devoted to demolishing Professor Rostow's vocabulary.'[17]

If one forgets about stages and views Professor Rostow's published work on the development process around the world it is impressive. Much of his thinking and extensive data collection has been brought together in *The World Economy*. Neglecting the concept of stages certain characteristics of his analyses are clear.

1. The stress on uniformities without much attention to diversity even in the less developed countries, leading to a sense of inevitability in the process. '. . . it is as sure as anything can be that, barring a global catastrophe, the societies of the underdeveloped areas will move through the transitional processes and establish the preconditions for take-off into economic growth and modernization. And they will then continue the process of sustained growth and move on to maturity; that is, to the stage when their societies are so structured that they can bring to bear on their resources the full capabilities of modern technology.'[18]

   Although Chenery also emphasises uniformities in structural change as per capita incomes increase he makes room for differences resulting from differences in social objectives and policies; differences in natural resource endowments; differences in country size; disparity in access to external capital; and changes in the uniform factors over time.[19] These differences and others which can have a significant effect on the process of growth over time are not given much attention by Rostow.
2. Emphasis on the growth of real inputs and the allocation of real resources as the primary sources of economic development to the relative neglect of cultural, social and psychological factors influencing human behaviour. Myrdal is particularly good on the attitudes and institutions lying deep in the culture that influence the growth process but that tend to be overlooked by 'structural' theories of development. '. . . certainly the main resistance to change in the social system stems from attitudes and institutions. They are part of an inherited culture and are not easily or rapidly moved in either direction. It will take time and endeavor for people to acquire discipline and habits of punctuality and cooperation, to want to improve their lot, to overcome their contempt for manual work, to become ready to experiment, and to take risks and accept change. And it will take time for the rigidities of an inegalitarian social stratification that

supports these attitudes to begin to wear down in response to higher income levels, to more and better facilities for education, and to greater mobility engendered by economic development.'[20]

3. Emphasis on supply considerations, mainly availability of inputs and technological changes rather than changing income elasticities of demand in explaining the changing structure of output and employment in the growth process. Rostow was rather late in introducing demand considerations to his analysis. But in *The World Economy* he agrees that 'The introduction and spread effects of new technology is not only influenced by effects on costs but by elasticities of demand for products that change with growth in per capita income.' He cites Chenery and Lance Taylor who differentiate early industries from middle and late industries in the form mainly of changing elasticities of demand with increase in per capita incomes.'Broadly speaking, Chenery and Taylor's "early industries" are similar to the typical leading sectors of take-off. Their "middle industries" embrace capital-deepening sectors typical of the drive to technological maturity. Their "late industries", including consumer durables (automobiles are subsumed in "metal products") embrace the sectors whose rapid expansion characterizes the stage of high mass-consumption.'[21]
4. Emphasis on the importance of discrete rather than continuous changes in the development process. Rostow's great movers in this process are the technological changes that come to fruition in the expansion of cotton textiles, railways and iron, steel, chemicals, electricity, automobiles. The discontinuous changes that accompany the rise and fall of these industrial sectors are exacerbated by tendencies in capital markets, both national and international, to over- and under-invest. 'If technological change takes place simply by "a large number of small advances over a wide front", then one can average the increase in productivity for an economy as a whole attributable to the absorption of new technology and stay at a theoretically and statistically high and comfortable level of aggregation. One can insert into conventional income analysis an overall variable measuring the rate of technological change and proceed with familiar neo-Keynesian manipulations.' But this is not Rostow's view of the development process. '(. . .) all inventions are not created equal . . .'.[22]

5. Closely related to the emphasis on discontinuity are Rostow's views on balanced versus unbalanced growth. Balanced growth theorists see economic development proceeding in response to changes in demand with investment continuously moving towards equality of marginal productivity in all resource uses. But Rostow along with Schumpeter, Hirschman, Streeten and others stress changes in supply conditions with significant forward and backward linkages and spread effects. The economy is viewed as in continuous disequilibrium with investment in and output of production; industries rising only to fall as other 'production functions' take ther place. In the 'drive to maturity' there is considerable resemblance between Rostow's successive production functions and Schumpeter's 'creative destruction'.
6. These characteristics of the Rostovian analysis, but particularly his emphasis on uniformities and his relative neglect of cultural and social influences lead to what seem to me to be excessively optimistic views on the prospects of both economic and political development in the now less developed countries. We have mentioned above his statement that '. . . it is as sure as anything that, barring global catastrophe' these countries will 'establish the preconditions' and then move on to 'sustained growth' and 'maturity'. I do not read the prospects that way for reasons that will be examined presently. And, like others, I fear that the argument of the inevitability of growth can lead to disappointment and frustration.[23]

POLITICAL STAGES

In his *Politics and the Stages of Growth* published in 1971 Rostow applies a stage theory to political development. The political stages do not quite conform to his economic stages – 'the rhythms of political life have a timing of their own' – but the process of economic change exerts a strong influence on the forms and purposes of government. He denies that he is proposing an economic interpretation of politics but, '. . . the "stages of growth" analysis, based on the notion of economies seeking to approximate optimum paths in production, is a congenial mate to the kind of dynamic political equilibrium analysis explored in this book'.[24]

During the period when the preconditions to take-off are being shaped the economic changes that occur facilitate, if they do not demand, appropriate changes in government. The development of communications, the growth of overhead capital, expansion of agricultural output, the emergence of inventors and entrepreneurs, the expansion of exports to pay for imports of needed industrial equipment and materials, all require a transition from local interests and forms of organisation to a broader framework.

> The balance of social and political power must then shift, in degree, from the village to the city, from the tasks and virtues of agricultural life to those of commerce, industry, and modern administration. The people must come to accept new forms for the organisation and for the transfer of political power. They must begin, in a process with many different stages, to judge politics and politicians in terms of policies rather than merely inherited statistics or even personality; and, if they are to emerge as democracies they must develop forms for granting and transferring power by registered consent.[25]

The stage of the economic preconditions is the stage of political nation building. During this period when emerging nationhood is threatened by foreign encroachment, security is the prime objective of government. 'It reflects the growth in national consciousness that is required for a central government to play its modernizing role. This was true even for Britain, the first to experience take-off'. The role of nationalism in shaping the internal politics and the external policies of the new states formed since the Second World War is a reflection of earlier experience in political development.

The stages of take-off and the drive to technological maturity build not only on the established economic preconditions but on the realisation of nationhood. Although economic analysis, according to Rostow, permits the two stages to be 'quite sharply distinguished', the 'rhythms of political life . . . render unrealistic excessively refined linkage of economic stages and political events'. The primary objectives of government shift from security to growth and welfare.

> Here the primary engine of change becomes internal rather than external. We are dealing with interactions among the economic, social, and political dimensions of society mainly initiated from within; rather than intrusion, pressure, or humiliation from without.[26]

Increasing real incomes makes possible the pursuit of welfare objectives, and urbanisation and industrialisation create pressures to allocate outputs in different ways.

The ultimate stage of political development is a 'constitutional order that enables government to provide justice, maintain public order, orderly change, and legitimate succession by some enforceable balance between public constraint and individual freedom . . . .[27] Presumably this constitutional order is democratically governed. But democracy need not wait until later stages of development. '. . . The possibilities for democracy increase when take-off emerges from the inherently contentious period of the preconditions . . .', though he warns that democracy is by no means a certain accompaniment of rapid growth.

Latin America presents a special problem 'because democracy continues there to labour under great difficulties although the bulk of the population lives in nations experiencing the drive to technological maturity'. He finds comfort in the thought that the union of democracy and effective government

> has occurred where large, but not monopolistic political parties – or coalitions – have emerged capable of conducting the ultimate function of political parties; that is to effect the compromises among various regional and other factional interests on the basis of which governments can conduct a reasonable orderly policy within the limits of their resources.

And he cites India with the Congress Party, Mexico with the PRI, Korea with Park's Democratic Republican Party, Malaysia through the Alliance Party, along with Colombia, Venezuela, Chile and Costa Rica.[28]

In some respects this seems a rather strange list even from the vantage point of 1971. Park Chung Kee was in the process of eliminating whatever elements of democracy existed in Korea; Chile was on the verge of yielding to the authoritarian government of Allende to be followed by the even more authoritarian government of Pinochet; the citizens of Malaysia were free to vote so long as the Malay party was kept in power; and in India the Congress Party was in process of dissolution.

Rostow seems to me to be even more optimistic, in terms of his values, in projecting political development than he is in dealing with economic prospects. 'Despite all its imperfections and the challenges to it, democracy is more than ever regarded as a touchstone of dignity and modernity.'[29] This may well be, but among the 130 odd countries that make up the less developed world it would be difficult to find more than half a dozen that could really be called democratic. Rostow counters by pointing out that, apart from Britain and the United States, parliamentary democracy came late in the economic development of the now developed countries and that there is no reason why this should not happen in the less developed countries (LDCs). This may be so but to date authoritarianism seems to have a firm grip in most of the Third World.

OBSTACLES TO DEVELOPMENT

As we indicated earlier, stages of growth can be used as a framework for the study of the development process in the now developed countries; it can also be used to forecast progress in countries early on in that process. It can be so used, that is, if it is thought that the uniformities observed in the early period will be duplicated in the later. Rostow clearly believes that this is so. It has been assumed

> that it is useful, as well as roughly accurate, to regard the process of development now going forward in Asia, the Middle East, Africa, and Latin America as analogous to the stages of preconditions and take-off of other societies in the late eighteenth, nineteenth, and early twentieth centuries.

Looking at the decade of the 1960s from the vantage point of 1970 Rostow has the feeling that

> there has been a fundamental breakthrough in human experience. . . .
>
> The list of success stories is quite impressive, even though some may still be fragile: South Korea, Taiwan, Malaysia, Pakistan, Iran, Turkey, Tunisia, Mexico, the Central American Common Market, Colombia, Venezuela, Paraguay: and, despite current vicissitudes, one can rightly add India, Brazil, Peru and Chile. . . .
>
> All face real and difficult problems in maintaining the momentum they have established. But the most important

demonstration of all has taken place; namely, that by their own efforts, with a margin of international support, they have the capacity to move into sustained growth and begin to fashion modern societies, capable of applying the best in contemporary science and technology, on terms which are consistent with their own history and culture and their own visions of the future.[30]

Ten years have passed since that judgement was offered and there have been significant changes in the prospects of many countries. Perhaps the most striking aspect of the present situation in the less developed world is the great disparity in rates of growth among countries. Korea, Taiwan, Singapore, Hongkong, (the gang of four) in East Asia, Brazil, Mexico, Malaysia, the oil-exporting countries as a group, and a few others have experienced a rapid increase in national income. In many more of the Third World countries development has been slow and stagnant and there have been a few countries with negative rates of growth. Even in the countries that have shown rapid growth it is difficult to discern the uniformities that were emphasised in the *Stages of Growth*. We shall come back to this question later.

The fact is there are significant differences in the environment and the prospects confronting most less developed countries from those faced by the now developed countries at early stages of growth. Rostow recognises this but, in my view, he minimises these differences. In one of the few passages I have been able to discover dealing with comparisons he lists the disadvantages and the advantages encountered by countries at early stages of development. By far the most serious disadvantage, in his view, is the high rate of population growth, accelerated by a rapid fall in the death rate. This rate is generally much higher than was the population growth rate in the early years of development in the now developed countries and, of course, it has a serious effect in slowing down the increase of per-capita incomes. Working in the same direction is the lack of opportunity for migration which in the nineteenth century greatly relieved the pressure of excess supplies in Western European labour markets. Partly as a result of rapid population growth and lack of opportunity to migrate he finds, as a second major disadvantage, much larger volumes of unemployment. Thirdly there are disadvantages inflicted by the Cold War: 'the pull and haul of Communist and non-Communist security interests diverts attention, talent and resources' away from the task of development.[31]

On the side of advantages Rostow cites in particular the existence of a pool of unapplied and relevant technology, and the availability of foreign aid.

This is an inadequate treatment of the subject and it minimises the disadvantages that most of the countries in the less developed world confront as compared with the now developed countries at early stages of their development. When industrialisation began in the late eighteenth and nineteenth centuries it emerged in societies that already had had several centuries of political, social and cultural development within the framework of nation-states. Governments, by and large, were capable of governing, adequate civil services had come into being, and – a most important consideration – governments were not called upon to perform the development tasks that have been assumed by governments in the now developing countries. Economic growth took place mainly through the market activities of the private sector and governments were not called on to manage public enterprises or to control by detailed regulation the operations of the private sector. Attitudes toward life and work, individual values and motivations, were definitely more amenable to organised economic activity than are those formed in most of the less developed countries of the world. These attitudes and values are slow to change and persist in impeding the structural shifts required for economic growth.

The technology available for import, though on the whole a distinct advantage to late comers, has been developed in economies in which capital is plentiful and labour scarce and is frequently ill adapted to surplus labour economies. Although these difficulties can be minimised by careful selection and adaptation the record indicates a penchant for capital and foreign exchange-intensive installations that contribute little to employment and are frequently monuments of inefficiency kept in operation by trade and foreign exchange policies that inflict their costs on the whole economy. When the foreign technology has been imported via foreign private investment it has sometimes led to enclaves with minimal spread effects to the domestic economy.

There is no denying that the availability of western technology and managerial policies can be a plus for late comers, and for a number of them has been, and that foreign assistance has provided advantages that early developers did not share but these advantages have been very unevenly exploited in the less developed world. In many if not most countries these advantages have been more than negated by the absence of institutions, attitudes, values and policies inimical to the development process.

Finally, in considering the advantages and disadvantages of late comers there is the question of climate. This is not discussed by Rostow and has been neglected by most writers on economic development. All of the now developed countries developed in the temperate zone and it is a striking fact that no country between the latitudes of Cancer and Capricorn, apart from certain oil exporters, stands high on the list of developing countries. The tropics are clearly not favourable to economic growth and it seems obvious that climate poses serious handicaps. Anyone who has spent a non-airconditioned summer in India, Pakistan, Egypt or other tropical countries knows how difficult it is to summon up the pretense of useful activity. Diseases both of man and beast are rampant and have an inevitable deleterious effect on productivity. Kamarck has illuminated the effect of some of these influences on productivity in Africa.[32] Some of the tropical handicaps can be overcome or at least alleviated; others will persist in making development difficult. No doubt too much can be made of impediments but most writers in economic development, including Rostow, do not seem to me to make enough.

DEVELOPMENT PROSPECTS

In the *World Economy*, published in 1978, Rostow provides a succinct analysis of the development experience and prospects in twenty countries. Ten of these are in the less developed world: Argentina, Turkey, Brazil, Mexico, Iran, India, China, Taiwan, Thailand, and South Korea. In all but one of them, Thailand, he judges that take-off has been completed and the countries well on their way to technological maturity. In a few, e.g. Argentina and Iran, although the drive to technological maturity has some way to go, per capita incomes are high enough to permit the beginning of high mass consumption.

The analysis is almost entirely on technological terms, the rise and subsequent relative decline of leading industries. There are, however, some striking differences in this experience from that of the now developed countries. Railway expansion which played a critical role in the take-offs in the United States, Canada and a number of western countries was not involved in take-offs in more recent development experience. In the larger countries where railways might have been expected to provide the necessary linkages and spread effects (India, China, Argentina, Brazil, Mexico) the railway networks were all but completed before the First World War while the beginnings of take-off are dated several decades later. In India the lack of a firm development purpose in the colonial government and a similar lack in the weak government of China together with the absorption of the energies of Indian and Chinese intelligence in political struggles explain the delay. 'In neither case is there serious doubt when sustained (if erratic) economic growth set in on a national basis'.[33] The take-off in India is dated from 1952–63 and in China from 1952–67.

In Argentina, Brazil and Mexico, railway expansion was merely one episode in the long process of establishing the preconditions for development. Why this Latin American experience should have been so different from the North American experience is susceptible to many explanations on which Rostow does not dwell at length. The take-off is dated for Argentina from 1933 to 1950; for Brazil from 1933 to 1950; and for Mexico from 1940 to 1960.

The succession of leading industries that characterise the take-off and drive to technological maturity is in the centre of Rostow's attention. There are close similarities in all the countries; first a group of consumer goods producers, usually favoured by high protection; then a series of intermediate and capital goods products (iron and steel, cement, fertilisers, chemicals); leading on to plastics, motor vehicles, electronics and durable consumer goods. Rostow traces the rise, and later decline (in relative terms) of these industries but it is difficult to see in this succession the clear dividing lines that separate preconditions from take-off, and take-off from the drive to technological maturity.

The analysis seems to me to minimise the influence of policy, of governmental organisation and culture on the development process. While he suggests, in Argentina, that neglect of agriculture leading to a shortage of foreign exchange, an excessively protectionist environment, and endemic inflation, led to a stagnant economy in the 1950s (the decade after the take-off had been accomplished), he considers that expansion of chemicals, metals, machinery and vehicles as evidence that the basis for sustained growth has been laid. The effect of highly protectionist policies in Turkey and India in producing price distortions in the economy and handicapping exports is apparently not deemed worthy of comment.

> Turkish development accelerated from 1961, moving forward on a more diversified basis with a range of industries leading the way which were typical of the early phase of the drive to technological maturity; steel, fertilizers, synthetic fibers.[34]

The current state of the Turkish economy must surely raise some doubts as to how healthy a drive is in process. India was supposed to have completed take-off in 1963 but the annual average rate of increase in per capita incomes since then of less than one per cent a year does not suggest a very vigorous drive to technological maturity.

Most economists who have given serious attention to the development process in Turkey and India are inclined to attribute a large measure of blame for stagnant economic growth to faulty development policies; excessive protection, overvalued currencies, subsidised public enterprises, industrial licensing, etc. Is it possible that the manufacturing sector may become more diversified, with new industries coming into being, and the economy still remain relatively stagnant? If little or no attention is paid to comparative advantage; if a country insists on producing everything it is technically capable of producing, regardless of costs; and its potential exports remain non-competitive in international markets, it seems quite possible that this should be so. The extraordinary differences in rates of growth in countries that have followed export oriented policies, such as South Korea and Taiwan, as compared with those, such as Turkey and India, that have followed autarchical policies, can hardly be ignored, but the effect of these differences on development prospects do not count for much in Rostow's analysis. One has the impression that, once the preconditions have been laid, technology takes over and the rise and fall of leading industries proceeds in an historically determined fashion almost untouched by human hands.

There is, in my opinion, a similar neglect of the importance of the structure and functioning of government in the development process. To be sure Rostow recognises that political instability can interrupt this process and that stable governments can promote it. He refers to 'political fragmentation and instability' in Argentina and their adverse effects on growth and to political stability in

Mexico and its positive effect. 'From 1940, Mexican growth continued for thirty-five years with a stability matched by few, if any, developing nations of the world'.[35] But there is more to the question than this. If a government is capable of formulating and implementing sensible development policies, what Rostow calls the take-off and drive to technological maturity are significantly facilitated; if not the obstacles may be serious.

Myrdal has a useful distinction between 'hard' and 'soft' states. Hard states are those that can put into effect policies necessary to development but contrary to the interests of particular groups, and enforce these policies. In soft states 'national governments require extraordinarily little of their citizens'.[36] It needs a strong government to put in place an effective tax system; devaluation, when necessary, will raise the price of imported goods and harm the interests of those with foreign debts; eliminating import controls will inflict injury on those holding scarce import licenses; and, of course, land reform will be opposed by land lords. It is unlikely that soft states will be able to undertake measures such as this, however necessary to development. If sensible policies are to be effective they must also be implemented and as Nehru, speaking of India, once said, 'I fear we are better at planning than we are at implementing plans'. In Myrdal's opinion, India is a soft state and this has had a lot to do with its lagging economic growth.

Among the ten less developed countries discussed by Rostow only two, India and Turkey, could properly be called democracies. Mexico might be added if one includes single party states. South Korea since independence had organised political parties and held elections, though rigged, during the personal authoritarianism of Syngman Rhee and, after a revolution in 1960 and a *coup d'état* in 1961, again enjoyed a democracy of sorts until Park Chung Hee put an end to it with the constitutional revisions of 1972. During most of the period since the Second World War most of these ten countries have lived under authoritarian governments of one sort or another. Has this had anything to do with the course of their economic development? It is clear that it takes more than authoritarian government to stimulate economic growth, witness Ghana under Nkruma and Indonesia under Sukarno. Among our ten countries authoritarian government in Argentina has not been spectacularly successful. Still it is worthy of note that among the rapidly growing countries in this list only Mexico can escape the stigma of authoritarianism and this judgement is subject to some doubt. Korea, Taiwan, Brazil and

Iran, during their periods of rapid growth, have all been subject to highly centralised and authoritarian rule.

In Korea and Iran erstwhile dictators have recently 'come a cropper' and it may well be that this is to be the fate of all authoritarian governments in the Third World; *sic semper tyrannis*. It is, however, a little early to say what kinds of government will follow these tyrants. Rostow, writing well before recent events in Iran commented on its 'ebullient, perhaps excessively ebullient growth' and went on perspicaciously to observe,

> It is by no means clear that Iran's absorptive capacity can match the flow of resources from abroad; agriculture appears still to be ominously neglected; and it is possible that the profligate effort is creating considerable social tension marked by an accentuation rather than a narrowing of income differentials.[37]

All that is being suggested here is that at certain stages of development, the transition from traditional to modern economies is not likely to be accomplished effectively without some of the trappings of a hard state and hard states usually exhibit some of the characteristics of authoritarian rule. Whether economic growth is worth a sacrifice of the civil liberties that usually flourish under democracy is a different question. This seems to be a continuing enigma in Latin America, and not only in Latin America; is it necessary to have the Pinochets of Chile or the generals in Brazil to administer the 'shock treatments' that may be necessary to get economic growth under way? In any case this question of the relation of the structure and functioning of government to the development process is an important issue and one that is relatively neglected in Rostow's analysis.

So also is that social mix of habit, values, motivations and institutional arrangements that fall under the heading of culture. There are vast differences in this respect among less developed countries and these differences have a good deal to do with economic development. How is one to explain the rapid growth of Korea, Taiwan, Hongkong and Singapore without significant reference to the great East Asian culture all have inherited? Everywhere the Chinese have penetrated; in Indonesia, Malaysia, Thailand and, to a less extent, the Philippines, they are in the forefront of business activity. There are strong racial overtones in Lee Yuan Kew's remark that you can't expect rapid economic growth in a 'Sarong culture' but, racial or not, there is something in it. It is too much to say that South Korea has grown because it is occupied by Koreans but the individual and social discipline, work habits, passion for education, and desire for personal and family advancement that characterise that population have had a lot to do with it.

Speaking of India in particular and South Asia in general Myrdal observes,

> The prevailing attitudes and patterns of individual performance in life and at work are from the development point of view deficient in various respects; low levels of work discipline, punctuality and orderliness; superstitious beliefs and irrational outlook; lack of alertness, adaptability, ambition, and the general readiness for change and experiment; contempt for manual work; submissiveness to authority and exploitation; low aptitude for cooperation; low standards of personal hygiene; and so on.[38]

These characteristics may not prevent the emergence of a succession of industries based on imported technology that Rostow emphasises in his *Stages* but they certainly lessen the increase in productivity and growth in per capita income that he anticipates from such technological change. There is something more to economic development than technological progress and structural change.

THE STAGES AS PROGNOSTICATORS

To what extent can the concept of stages of growth be used operationally to predict future developments? It is certainly true that with growth in per capita incomes there are striking uniformities among countries in the expansion of inputs and their allocation among sectors of the economy. Chenery and his collaborators have cultivated this area thoroughly, analysing not only the uniformities but also variations.[39] This approach in effect looks back from realised per capita growth to the changes in inputs and sectoral structure that accompany growth, explaining structural changes mainly by changes in the income elasticities of demand for various groups of products (Engels effects). The realisation of these structural changes presupposes, of course, technological changes necessary to produce the altered output mix and the increase in savings and investment and improvements in the work force associated with increased per capita incomes and changes in resource allocation. Also associated are urbanisation, development communications, improvements in health, increase in education, etc. But it essentially is a backward-looking analysis explaining what has happened after it has happened. It does not lend itself easily to forecasts and predictions.

The Harrod–Domar analysis begins at the other end with an assumed increase in capital investment, sweeping all other influences on productivity under the mat of the capital-output ratio. This is a forward-looking approach, advanced as a theory of how development takes place and it has been used in innumerable planning exercises. Rostow accepts the increase in capital investment as a lesser but important stimulant to growth but concentrates the primary explanation of increases in productivity on the technological changes that produce a succession of leading industries. It is also a forward-looking theory of growth. With respect to the role of increase in savings and investment he finds support for his thesis in the cross-country calculations of Chenery and Syrquin of the relation of per capita incomes and investment.[40] These figures appear to indicate, in US 1964 dollars, that

> The great rise in the investment rate comes between countries under $100 per capita and those in the $200 per capita category. After that point the average investment rate rises more slowly, levelling off at $1 000 per capita. . . . We can somewhat arbitrarily relate [these] figures to stages of growth as follows:
> Under $100–$200 per capita – Take off.
> $200–$500 per capita – Drive to technological maturity.
> $500 per capita and over – High mass consumption.[41]

But again this approaches the development process looking backward from realised per capita income to rates of savings and investment generation by the rise in per capita incomes and changes in its distribution. For the prime causes of these increases in per capita income one has to look to the emergence of leading sectors with significant linkages and nation-wide real effects. Changes in savings rates generally follow after.

Is it possible so to specify the preconditions of growth that a take-off becomes inevitable and is it possible to specify the characteristics of take-off with sufficient precision to be able to predict a drive to technological maturity? Although Rostow frequently urges caution and surrounds his thesis with safeguards the general thrust of his argument is certainly in this direction. In various discussions of the preconditions Rostow emphasises the building up of social overhead capital (including education); an increase in agricultural output, reorganisation of land tenure and the diversion of net flows to more modern sectors of the economy; generation of a capacity to earn foreign exchange; emergence of a group of capable entrepreneurs.[42] I think I would have to agree with Habakkuk that

> Most of what are termed preconditions turn out to be essential manifestations of growth. . . . The factors favorable to development are so varied and have historically combined in so many different ways that I see no possibility of isolating a small number of crucial variables.[43]

Take the case of Pakistan where, according to Rostow, take-off has already taken place and a drive to maturity is in progress. Although Pakistan inherited a certain amount of capital overhead from undivided India it was sorely deficient in roads, communication and good port facilities. In the first years of independence the country paid little attention to education. The two principal earners of foreign exchange, jute and cotton, were handicapped by export taxes and the very high prices of heavily protected manufactured goods turned the terms of trade heavily against agriculture. It is difficult indeed to distinguish preconditions from take-off in Pakistan if take-off, indeed, has occurred. What happened to shake Pakistan out of early lethargy was the cut-off of imports from India which had formerly supplied over three-quarters of the shipments of manufactured goods into what became Pakistan. This, plus high tariff barriers to imports from other countries, gave an unlimited degree of protection to Pakistan manufactures and this, plus an influx of entrepreneurs and capital from Bombay, set in motion manufactures of consumer goods at profit rates of 100 per cent or more per annum. Manufactured output grew at a rate of 16 per cent a year during the 1950s while per capita income remained stagnant. Cotton textiles was far and away the leading industry but did its expansion occur in the preconditions period or in the take-off? Economic development in the sense of a sustained growth of per capita income did not appear until the 1960s under the relatively stable and authoritarian regime of Ayub Kahn. It was greatly facilitated by policy changes that improved the terms of trade for agriculture, turned manufactures toward lines of comparative advantage, and laid the basis for export expansion. Whether Pakistan is now formally embarked on a drive to technological maturity is at best subject to doubt.

The difficulties of distinguishing take-off from the drive to technical maturity and predicting the course of the latter are at least as great. I think I would have to agree with Fishlow that the concept is non-operational.

> To talk knowingly of countries in the world today as in the pre-conditions phase or in the midst of take-off is sheer guesswork, unrelated to the theory itself. This is why it is possible (so far) to be right with the assessment of Mexico but wrong with Argentina.[44]

Take the case of Egypt which, according to Rostow, has also completed its take-off and is in the midst of a drive to technological maturity. When the so-called Free Officers took control in 1952 Egypt already had a sizeable manufacturing sector largely in the hands of foreigners. The Suez crisis of 1956 led to the nationalising of foreign holdings and, in 1960 and 1961, the acquisition by the state of all large-scale private enterprises, made Egypt by far the most socialised and centrally controlled economy in the non-communist world. During the 1960s new state-controlled enterprises continued to come into being but one would hardly call what happened a process of 'creative destruction'. Little account was taken of comparative advantage and many of the new enterprises continued to exist only by grace of government subsidy. By 1973, when President Sadat announced his 'Open Door' policy, the manufacturing sector in Egypt accounted for nearly a quarter of value added in the economy. But, during the previous decade per capita income in Egypt had grown at about one per cent a year. Three quarters of manufactured output was in the public sector. It was and is a highly bureaucratic public sector sharing the disadvantages of both socialism and capitalism. It is essentially unplanned and subject to administrative rather than market decision-making. It is difficult to see how a further drive to technological maturity can spring from this source.

There is little doubt that per capita incomes will continue to increase in the rest of the less developed countries of the world. Capital investment will increase and discernible uniformities will occur in the changes in the structures of production and employment. But irregularities in the impact of change, the influence of policies favourable and unfavourable to economic growth, the instability of governments, and, in many countries, the retarding effects of traditional mores and customs, make the stages of growth a less than satisfactory prognosticator.

CONCLUSION

Rostow is a leader among those economic historians who, during the last few decades, have turned the rather dry subject of economic history into a much more exciting examination of the process of economic development. His contributions have been large and these contributions have been brought together in his magisterial volume *The World Economy: History and Prospect*. This is really a study of the industrial revolution and its sweep around the globe during the last two centuries, with a venturesome peep into the future. I am sure he will forgive an old admirer his inability to discern in this history the sharp demarcations which are celebrated in the *Stages of Growth*.

NOTES AND REFERENCES

1. W. W. Rostow, 'The Take-Off into Self-Sustained Growth' *Economic Journal* (March 1956).
2. Ibid., p. 27.
3. W. W. Rostow, *The Stages of Economic Growth; A Non-Communist Manifesto* (London: Cambridge University Press, 1960).
4. Ibid. p. 10.
5. Goren Ohlin, 'Reflections on the Rostow Doctrine', *Economic Development and Cultural Change* (July 1961).
6. W. W. Rostow (ed.), *The Economics of the Take-Off into Sustained Growth; Proceedings of a Conference held by the International Economics Association* (New York: St Martin's, 1963). This is hereafter referred to as the Konstanz Volume.
7. W. W. Rostow, *The Stages of Economic Growth*, 2nd edn Appendix B, 'The Critics and the Evidence' (London: Cambridge University Press, 1971).
8. W. W. Rostow, *Politics and the Stages of Growth* (London: Cambridge University Press, 1971).
9. W. W. Rostow, *How it All Began* (New York: McGraw-Hill, 1975).

10. W. W. Rostow, *The World Economy* (London: Macmillan, 1978).
11. Konstanz Volume, Introduction and Epilogue, p. XVII, 1963.
12. Simon Kuznets, 'Notes on the Take-Off', in the Konstanz Volume, p. 34.
13. W. W. Rostow, *The Stages of Growth*, 2nd edn, Appendix B.
14. Gunnar Myrdal, *Asian Drama; An Inquiry into the Poverty of Nations* (New York: Twentieth Century Fund, 1968) p. 1851.
15. A. K. Cairncross, 'Essays in Bibliography and Criticism. XLV. The Stages of Economic Growth', *Economic History Review*, second series, vol. XIII, no. 3 (1961).
16. W. W. Rostow, *The World Economy*, p. 365–6.
17. Konstanz Volume, p. 391.
18. W. W. Rostow, *The United States in the World Arena* (New York: Harper and Row, 1960) p. 412. Quoted by Myrdal, op. cit. p. 1854.
19. Hollis B. Chenery *et al.*, *Structural Change and Development Policy* (New York: Oxford University Press for the World Bank, 1979) pp. 6–7.
20. Myrdal, op. cit. p. 1873.
21. W. W. Rostow, *The World Economy*, pp. 369–70. The reference is to Hollis B. Chenery and Lance Taylor, 'Development Patterns; Among Countries and Over Time', *Review of Economics and Statistics* (November 1968).
22. W. W. Rostow, *The World Economy*, op. cit., p. 367. The quotation is from Donald F. Gordon which reads in full, 'Economic growth has not been the result of a small number of spectacular inventions and leading sector industries, but rather it appears as a result of a large number of small advances over a wide front'. From a review of *How It All Began*, in *Business Week* (19 May 1975) p. 23.
23. Cf. David Wrightman, 'The Stages of Economic Growth'; in *El Politico*, Vol. XXVI, no. 1, University of Pavia (1961) p. 134. 'To say, as Rostow does, that India is in the take-off stage may be very encouraging to those who are moved by magical phrases. But what if it proves to be wrong: What frustrations and disillusionments might follow?', quoted by Myrdal, op. cit., p. 1854, note 1.
24. W. W. Rostow, *Politics and the Stages of Growth*, p. 21.
25. Ibid., p. 59.
26. Ibid., p. 98.
27. Ibid., p. 12.
28. Ibid., p. 272.
29. W. W. Rostow, *The Stages of Growth*, 2nd edn, p. 139.
30. W. W. Rostow, *Politics and the Stages of Growth*, op. cit., pp. 316–17.
31. W. W. Rostow, *The Stages of Growth*, 2nd edn, p. 139.
32. Andrew M. Kamarck, *The Tropics and Economic Development* (Baltimore: Johns Hopkins Press, 1976).
33. W. W. Rostow, *The World Economy*, p. 532.
34. Ibid., p. 476.
35. Ibid., p. 492.
36. Myrdal, *Asian Drama*, p. 896.
37. W. W. Rostow, *The World Economy*, p. 506.
38. Myrdal, *Asian Drama*, p. 1862.
39. This work is summarised in Chenery *et al.*, *Structural Change and Development Policy*, op. cit.

40. Hollis B. Chenery and Moises Syrquin, with the assistance of Hazel Elkinton, *Patterns of Development 1950–1970* (London: Oxford University Press, 1975) pp. 20–1.
41. W. W. Rostow, *The World Economy*, pp. 58–9.
42. Ibid., p. 561. 'The rule is not, of course universal (. . .) more than economic problems are involved in this transformation, and history offers no guarantee that this acceleration of growth will happen'.
43. H. G. Habakkuk, 'Historical Experience of Economic Development', in E. A. G. Robinson (ed.), *Proceedings Conference of International Association* (London: Macmillan, 1965) pp. 118–19.
44. A. Fishlow, 'Empty Economic Stages', *Economic Journal* (March 1965) p. 112.

9 Take-off and Breakdown: Vicissitudes of the Developing Countries

R. DE OLIVEIRA CAMPOS

Economic science with all its severity of mien, is particularly vulnerable to the shifting winds of fashion: economic jargon, to begin with. In the aftermath of the Second World War, when interest was rekindled in international cooperation for economic development, the non-industrialised countries were labelled 'poor countries', reflecting a static, almost fatalistic vision of underdevelopment. Subsequently, as we moved on to an era of 'dynamic pessimism', the epithet was changed to 'backward countries' (which at least implied the possibility of rebound and advancement), and later to 'underdeveloped and less developed countries'. More recently we have reached a phase of dynamic optimism, where the expression in vogue is 'developing countries'. As social dynamics has also swept into fashion, we now talk about expectant countries, stirred by the revolution of rising expectations.

Another irresistible vagary of fashion was the 'take-off theory', imaginatively formulated by Walt Rostow as a response to the obsolete phraseology of the Communist Manifesto. Instead of an evolution from feudalism to bourgeois mercantilism, industrial capitalism, socialism and communism, we would have, with a much more generic application, irrespective of ideological systems, a transmutation of the traditional society into a transitional society, characterised by the 'take-off' process. This would usher in the industrial society and finally the high consumption society.

The economic requirements for the 'take-off' would seem to be primarily the creation of an infrastructure, chiefly in the transportation sectors; secondly, an upsurge of agricultural production capable of financing industrialisation; thirdly, a minimal level of savings of 10 per cent to 12 per cent per annum; fourthly, the existence of capacity to import, fostered either by exports or by the inflow of capital, to acquire industrial equipment and raw materials; fifthly, the emergence of 'vanguard sectors' that trigger the modernising process. It is presupposed that there exists an entrepreneurial cluster capable of absorbing technology. In certain situations, the take-off can also be stimulated by a reactive nationalism, when the population acquires cohesion and solidarity under the impulsion of a foreign menace.

The advantage of Rostow's growth stages over the Marxist formulation is that the former admits and incorporates non-economic variables, whereas in the Marxist model class interests and ideologies are strictly a function of production techniques.

The driving force of Western development in the last two hundred years has been the 'individualistic and utilitarian' creed. But as Myrdal, Robbins and Rostow himself have noted, this creed did not concentrate exclusively on the promotion of profit motivation and defense of private ownership, as the Marxists maintain. With the passage of time, the individualistic and utilitarian creed evolved in the direction of defense of political freedom and the universal suffrage, monopolies were brought under control, together with social legislation that moderated the profit incentive and conferred respectability, if not predominance, to welfare motivations; and finally with the introduction of progressive income tax, a powerful instrument was forged to redistribute surplus value and moderate its absorption by the capitalist.

Several objections have been interposed to the 'take-off theory'. The historical evidence seems inconclusive. The stages are held to be inaccurately defined, the facts less than cogent, and in various cases the dates assigned by Rostow to the 'critical threshold of take-off' seem questionable, indicating a more or less continuous growth process rather than a dramatic 'take-off'. There is, however, no doubt that, for breadth of conception and characterisation of the development process as an overall societal process, contrasting with the narrow Marxist emphasis on production techniques, the 'take-off theory' merits an outstanding place in modern economic thinking. In many quarters it has indeed become something of a fad.

Incautious handling of the Rostow theory is not, however,

without peril, amongst which stress should be laid on the analogical treatment and the linear hypothesis. While Rostow did admit noneconomic motivations, there was a presumption of universality of economic motivations underlying his idea. But bizarre cases can be cited where civilisations systematically degrade economic motivation. An extreme example is that of Burma, which professes an anti-industrial ideology. And, despite its Marxian roots it is curious to see that the Maoist motivation is based far more massively on the Chinese prudential philosophy of the five guarantees – to the effect that the government must provide every citizen with food, clothing and adequate housing, satisfactory medical assistance and a decent funeral – than on the socialistic 'maximization' of production. Mao's 'cultural revolution' was a much clearer reflection of concern with ideological purity than with economic efficiency.

No less questionable is the linear hypothesis, i.e. that the 'take-off' leads to cumulative and continuous economic development by the wondrous mechanics of compound interest. In reality, history records numerous cases of 'relapse'. And these examples are particularly frequent in South America. By the outbreak of the Second World War, Argentina, for instance, had reached an income level capable of giving it self-propelling velocity. It was the first country in Latin America to be provided with telephones and electric energy, and in 1913 Buenos Aires built its first underground railway. In the twenties, its agricultural productivity rivalled that of the United States. Political instability, however, resulting from the scission of the political body between Peronism and the traditional parties, engendered ten years of stagnation, followed by a degree of growth that is still hesitant and uncertain. On a lesser scale, Uruguay and Chile would seem to have overcome the barriers of underdevelopment, only to sink, the former into regression and the latter into stagnation, by the late sixties and early seventies. And through the recurrence of political turmoil in the early sixties, Brazil also lost the developmental impetus it displayed in the fifties, and only now appears to have resumed a firm onward trend of growth.

It would seem therefore apposite to construct, parallel to the 'take-off' hypothesis, a theory of the 'collapse', a sort of pedestrian and sectorial version of Toynbee's apocalyptic vision of the breakdown of civilisations. This theory would find its roots in the blind alleys and vicious circles peculiar to underdevelopment. It is not so much a question of economic variables as of the political and social context in which society operates.

Far from being a constant rectilinear process, development appears to be an adventure threatened with deadlocks. In the following subsections it is intended to discuss the savings deadlock, the managerial deadlock and the political deadlock.

THE DILEMMAS IN MOBILISING RESOURCES

The possibility of a deadlock in the mobilisation of adequate savings for purposes of economic development resides mainly in three factors: the population trap, the rivalry between welfare aspirations and the exactions of accumulation, and the conflict between inflation and development.

The extensive literature on the population explosion makes it wearisome to go over the analysis once again. The facts are common knowledge. The more rapid decline in the death rate than in fertility has boosted the rate of endogenous population growth in most of the underdeveloped countries. This makes it necessary to channel a high proportion of the scarce savings available, to the so-called 'demographic investments', which are only indirectly productive or of slow productivity, thus retarding either the rhythm of economic development (rise in the capital stock per inhabitant) or social development (improvement in the standard of living of the existing population). The only consolation is that the 'Malthusian demon', i.e. the spectre of hunger as punishment for the demographic explosion, seems to be less relevant than in earlier times on account of the enormous revolutionary advance in agricultural productivity in the last two decades. But other demons have emerged: unemployment, building up of social stresses, urban overcrowding, political stresses, pollution, erosion of the quality of living, and the emulous unrest of the masses seduced by the image of the prosperity of other peoples who benefit from a more satisfactory relationship between population, natural resources and saving capacity.

The second source of deadlocks is the dilemma between well-being and accumulation. The level of consumer aspirations and demands, particularly of the urban classes in the less developed countries, is almost always vastly superior to what the economic effort can supply, without falling prey to price inflation or stagnation of investment. The truth is that the 'demonstration effect', stimulated by the instruments of mass communication, is profoundly asymmetrical: consumption habits are transmitted swiftly, while production techniques filter in only slowly. Numerous are the examples of countries where premature distributivism (characterised above all by extremely ambitious social legislation) has helped to throttle down the development take-off: Uruguay, Chile, Argentina, are cases of this kind. Among the young (decolonised) nations of Africa and Asia, Ghana and Sri Lanka are perhaps the best examples.

The third conflicting element lies in the interaction of inflation with development. The vast and, up to a certain point, inconclusive literature on the subject inclines one to brevity. It is known that moderate, discontinuous and short-lived inflations can be used to distribute resources in the direction of investment, besides encouraging entrepreneurial daring. It is also known that chronic inflation amounts to a bloodless civil war, sterile from the viewpoint of extracting savings and fertile in social conflicts and economic distortions. The inflationary dilemma of developing countries is that the social pressures of consumption and aspiration for grandiose development projects tend to exceed what can be financed by the level of domestic savings and the inflow of foreign resources. When this happens, it is a presage of more or less chronic inflation, the usual effect of which is: a) to discourage the forms of savings most useful for development; b) to deflect the normal course of investments; c) to unsettle the balance of payments; d) to exacerbate social friction.

The various deadlocks described above may interrupt the development take-off, triggering crises of stagnation and regression that disrupt the linearity of the Rostovian setting.

THE MANAGEMENT DEADLOCK

Let us now turn to another series of obstacles to development: obstacles of a managerial and administrative nature. The three topics to be considered are the gap between motivation and understanding, the contrast between planning and implementation, and finally what might be termed the 'uncomfortable parallelism'.

In the developing countries, the gap between motivation to solve problems and the capacity to understand them and formulate adequate solutions is abnormally wide. Motivation is frequently emulous: an attempt is made to imitate achievements attained in other countries. But the concrete ability to solve problems is lacking by reason of the low level of technical training and administrative education. In the developed countries of today, the evolution was gradual and there was no great lag between the problems that had to be faced and the means available for solving them. Economic problems were incremental rather than escalating.

Borrowing from the language of Albert Hirschman we might say that in the backward countries on the road to development there exists a strong tendency for 'motivation' to advance more rapidly than 'understanding'.[1] A gap therefore develops between 'want formation' and 'want satisfaction', as Huntington puts it.[2]

This produces not only economic inefficiency, but also social frustration and not infrequently political instability. This frustration arouses increasing impatience with remedial or palliative solutions and kindles enthusiasm for ideological or radical cure-alls. In the semantics of developing countries, the term 'revolution', without any evaluation of the enormous social cost of true revolutions, is far more current, and accepted more unreservedly, than the more meaningful concept of 'reform'.

A cognate problem is the gap between planning and implementation. In the developing countries, planning has greater importance than in the mature economies, whose growth has become more or less automatic. There are various reasons for this. First, the need to rationalise and coordinate government action, fixing priority objectives and defining development policies, whether of the 'centralist' type (as under socialist regimes) or of the 'indicative' type (for guidance of the private sector in nonsocialistic regimes). Secondly, the manipulation of planning as an instrument of social motivation for attaining predetermined targets related to production and income growth.

The difficulty that usually arises is that the plans are formulated by a technocratic elite of the 'Weberian' type, oriented towards accomplishment, whereas their execution falls to the lot of a 'prismatic bureaucracy', essentially traditionalist, but concerned with social status and personal promotion.[3]

It should be added that the plans tend to be technocratic lucubrations, thought up in the rarefied atmosphere of research departments; assuming the best, they may entail a commitment of the Executive Power, but are rarely transformed into a political platform (for the very reason of the instability of political institutions), or into a source of populist motivation.

Another problem might be termed the 'embarrassing parallelism'. The socialising and statist tendency so often observed in developing countries is frequently explained in terms of inadequacy and entrepreneurial weakness of the private sector. But the insufficiency of the latter reflects a whole interlocking series of social and cultural conditions that have likewise a negative influence on the level of efficiency of the public sector. The indubitable advantage of the State as economic agent of development stems from: a) its capacity to gather and conglomerate savings in the form of taxation, and b) its capacity for long-term investment, irrespective of current market stimuli. But merely to transfer activities from the private to the public sector is not a magic formula for development. It does not correct inefficiency and perhaps achieves no more than a concentration of errors. There is an awkward parallelism between the shortage of business entrepreneurship and that of public administration élites.

THE CONTRADICTIONS OF MODERNISATION

By far the most important factor of discontinuity in the development process, and the main case of breakdowns after take-off, is political instability. As Huntington has observed, there is no constant relationship between the level of economic development and political stability, but rather a variable relationship dependent on the level of development: '. . . the relation between the rate of economic growth and political instability varies with the level of economic development. At low levels, a positive relation exists, at medium levels no significant relation, and at high levels, a negative relationship'.[4]

Another way of looking at the problem, again according to Huntington, is to distinguish between 'modernization' and 'modernity'. Modernity brings stability, but the modernisation process kindles instability. In primitive and traditional societies, there is a certain passivity of aspirations and a corresponding inability to voice them. Primitive, undifferentiated regimes of a hierarchical and authoritarian type tend to be stable. With the start of the modernising process, pressures begin to build up, generally originating in the fact of social mobilisation being out of step with political participation. These pressures inflame political instability that only simmers down in the higher stages of modernisation, with the achievement of a reasonable degree of rationalisation of authority, differentiation of structure and political participation.[5]

It is now possible to delimit the field of discussion with greater accuracy. The three crucial concepts are social mobilisation, economic development and political participation. Social mobilisation, according to Deutsch, is the process by which 'major clusters of old social, economic and psychological commitments are eroded or broken and people become available for new patterns of socialization and behavior'.[6] The principal vehicles of mobilisation are urbanisation, which brings greater geographical and occupational mobility, literacy, education and development of mass communication media. The concept of economic development is better known: we are dealing here with a quantitative increase in the level of production of a society, accompanied by qualitative structural transformations. Economic development is commonly gauged by the level of income per inhabitant, rate of industrialisation and level of well being, evidenced by life expectancy, level of education, diet and social assistance. As Huntington aptly expresses it, 'Social mobilization involves changes in the aspirations of individuals, groups, and societies; economic development involves changes in their capabilities. Modernization requires both'.[7]

As to political modernisation, it includes rationalisation of authority, differentiation of political functions and, finally, expansion of political participation. Rationalisation of authority requires primarily a certain concentration of power, formerly dispersed among tribal, religious, familial, and ethnic groupings, so as to form a national political authority. And, secondly, assertion of the national power against the world abroad and of the central power against regional powers. Differentiation of functions means the creation of differentiated structures with specific areas of competence such as administrative, legislative, juridical and military, while, on a par, recruitment tends increasingly to be based on achievement rather than on ascription. Political modernisation would involve of course increased participation in politics by the various social groups. There is, however, a crucial distinction between political participation and political institutionalisation, and a lag between them leads inevitably to instability. A high level of political participation is reached when, in addition to the traditional bureaucratic élite, the middle class becomes politically activist and, finally, the masses are incorporated in political activities. But political participation only enables the individual to mobilise his aspirations and his demands. Adequate political institutions must be available to express, filter and satisfy those aspirations (or to form symbols – charismatic or ideological – to replace them). When the level of participation rises above the level of institutionalisation, instability results, with extreme oscillations between massocracy (the 'mass society' of Kornhauser's theory) and autocracy (the Praetorian State, as Rapoport calls it).

It is easy to understand why the modernisation process can temporarily exacerbate political instability instead of attenuating it. On the one hand, social mobilisation, and particularly urbanisation, trigger an escalation of demands and aspirations. On the other hand, economic development on its own initially causes the gap to widen between income levels, in favour of the more dynamic groups and regions. When swift development is accompanied by inflation in a context of explosive increases of population, wages are liable to rise less than prices, accentuating inequalities. Inasmuch as the most efficient instrument for correcting inequalities is government power, social mobilisation in quest of a better distribution of income frequently involves attempts to take over the reins of government by political rebellion. As is rightly stressed by Huntington: 'Economic development increases economic inequality at the same time that social mobilization decreases the legitimacy of that inequality. Both aspects of modernization combine to produce political instability.'[8]

A recently observed, and bizarre, reaction to modernisation processes is 'religious repristination', as occurred in Iran after the downfall of the Pahlavi regime. The swift redistribution of economic power in favour of a 'new class' of industrialists, merchants, and technocrats, met with strong resistance from traditional strata – the clergy and the bazaar – and was more than could be absorbed by a rather primitive political system devoid of mechanisms for diffusion of power and redressment of grievances. There was a 'systemic frustration', which led people (including, strangely enough, revolutionary students) to hark back to religious fundamentalism and traditional social institutions, despite the low capability level of those systems to deal with the complexities of a modernising economy.[9]

Political instability, perhaps the greatest obstacle to economic development, is therefore the result of complex interrelations. Particularly vulnerable are the societies in rapid process of modernisation, when 1) the rhythm of social mobilisation exceeds the rhythm of economic development, inducing social frustration, 2) this social frustration is transformed into activist political demands on the part of not only the élites and the middle class, but also the masses, and 3) when political institutions, and particularly political parties – as instruments for channelling aspirations, articulating interests and formulating programmes – are unable to absorb, moderate, coordinate and satisfy those aspirations, or create substitute symbols, reducing social frustrations to a tolerable level.

It is also easy to understand why, in societies where the process of modernisation is well advanced, political stability is more readily obtained and consequently more prevalent. On the one hand, the gap between social and economic development is not unbearably serious; on the other, the unbalancing effect of the high level of political participation is absorbed by the high degree of political institutionalisation, either in the form of political parties, in the Western polities and in Japan, or by the predominance of a sole party, manipulating a mobilising ideology to ensure continuity of power (as in socialist states). Even so, threats to the stability of the regime may take shape when certain sectors (or ethnical and religious groups) begin to feel that their desire for political participation is not accepted by the system of values practiced by existing political institutions.

In the developing and modernising countries, political stability is the exception rather than the rule. It may, moreover, occur as much where the rate of development is rising sharply, as in Mexico, or relatively slowly, as in India. But in either case, there was a high level of political institutionalisation – in the former through the Mexican Institutional Revolutionary Party, (*Partido Revolucionario Institucional*) which coordinated aspirations and created an efficient mechanism of leadership substitution, and in India, through the Congress Party, heir to the British parliamentary tradition and possessed of a solidarity built up in the struggles for independence – contrasting with a low level of political participation. A reverse example is to be found in Argentina, where a high level of political participation (thanks to intense urbanisation and the standard of education) is not paralleled with a satisfactory degree of political institutionalisation, fostering government instability and stunting the growth process. Brazil occupies an intermediate position: an only average degree of political participation and institutionalisation alike. In 1964, this precarious balance was overturned. While populist participation in the political process had been actively encouraged, often by methods of demagogic mobilisation, the institutions weakened under the impact of ideological radicalisation. Since 1964, a reasonable degree of political stability has been maintained, not so much by improvement in the institutions as by temporarily cutting back the degree of participation.

It may safely be said that, in the Latin American context, the major problem is not the organisation of economic development, but definitely the preservation of a tolerable level of political stability. The determinant variables of economic development are reasonably well understood and readily manipulated. It is much more difficult to organise and maintain an adequate political and social context, for, as has been pointed out, the very pressures of modernisation hamper the achievement of political stability. A great deal more is known about the mechanics of development than about the social engineering of political institutions.

The two basic problems that must be solved if the 'Rostovian take-off' is to be assured of continuity, centre on 1) social motivation for the savings effort and 2) achievement of a reasonable degree of political stability, to allow for sufficient administrative continuity and inspire confidence in medium- to long-term investment planning.

THE VARIOUS MOTIVATIONS

The problem of social motivation involves various aspects, such as how to extract savings from relatively poor communities, moderate aspirations to well-being, and intensify the productive effort. There is historical evidence of a number of motivations acting separately or jointly to promote the onsurge of development. They may be classified in three broad groups:

political motivations
ideological motivations
economic motivations

Among the political motivations may be grouped the stimulus of lost wars, canalising energy to avenge humiliations and restore national power; threats to survival, which create a sense of solidarity and facilitate the making of reforms; and finally imperial motivation, which inspires the conquest of new frontiers (continental expansion) or the subjugation of other countries (imperialistic expansion). The threat to survival was present, for instance, in the upswing of Japan after the Meiji Restoration – which constituted an effort of modernisation to survive the cultural and economic challenge of the West – and also in the dramatic Japanese reconstruction and expansion after the Second World War. Another instance is perhaps the present impulsion of Chinese communism, inspired in a profound resurrection of national pride, wounded by centuries of colonial humiliation, but also nurturing itself by resentment over the territorial mutilation imposed by the so-called 'unjust treaties'.

Among the ideological motivations, two of the utmost importance may be cited: Marxism and nationalism.

Marxism may exert a strong modernising influence in three ways: by overthrowing ancient feudal and patriarchal structures; by promoting industrialisation; and by establishing governments that are politically stable, even though violently repressive. Nevertheless, it is not in the field of economic development that it exerts the strongest influence, for, under certain aspects, the economic efficiency of the Marxist model is essentially unequal, being much more efficient in heavy industry than in light industry, farming and services. 'The strength of communism', as Huntington observes, 'is found not in its economics – which is hopelessly antiquated – nor in its character as a secular religion, where it can be easily outclassed by the appeals of nationalism. Its most relevant characteristic is its political theory and practice, not its Marxism but its Leninism'.[10] It was, indeed, Lenin that transformed Marxism from a frustrated theory of social evolution into a successful theory of political action.

The role of nationalism, as a factor of political mobilisation, is well known. Its maximal utility is found in the formative period of a national political conscience, as an agglutinating element of scattered tribal, regional or religious segments, and to overcome colonial ties. This type of reactive nationalism strongly contributes to government cohesion, mobilisation of savings, and formation of a native entrepreneurship. However, the political efficacy of nationalism is probably greater than its economic efficacy. It tends to discourage absorption of technology and imports of capital which would be useful to speed up the investment effort. The constant need to create mobilising symbols interferes, moreover, with rationality in allocating investment resources. Its effect as a mobilising ideology is, therefore, to a large extent ambivalent, and its importance is greater in societies in formation, which lack social cohesion, than in societies that are more politically mature and increasingly interconnected by trade, investments and the spread of technology. In short, the utility of nationalism as a factor of cohesion is unquestionable; in the initial stages of development it can help to mobilise savings and discipline the national effort; it grows less and less useful as the country advances along the road to development, for it tends to impair the rationality of resource allocation and interfere with the absorption of the capital and technology needed to hasten progress.

This brings us to the third group of possible motivations: economic motivation. This involves the deliberate intention of preserving a propitious economic and social context for economic development. This type of ideological construction is particularly useful in Latin America. It would be absurd to suggest exposing those countries to the stimulus of lost wars or challenges to survival, simply to create developmental motivations. On the other hand, only one or two of the larger countries – Brazil, Argentina or perhaps Mexico – can take advantage of the 'imperial' stimulus, afforded by the conquest of inland territory, occupying virgin soil and unfurling the banner of 'national integration'.

For lack of spontaneous motivation, Latin America has to construct motivating symbols, among which two main types can be distinguished: emulative ideology and futurist ideology.

Emulative ideology aims essentially at mobilising the population for the purpose of reaching the level of development of other countries – the prototype countries – spanning the gap and eliminating backwardness. This is the so-called 'gap ideology'. Exploiting this sentiment is not a practice confined to underdeveloped countries. It will be readily recalled that Khrushchev proposed to do so when he suggested, as motivation for Soviet planning, that the United States level be attained and surpassed in the seventies.

Gap ideology is expressed in various development plans designed to narrow the 'income per capita' gap or the 'industrialization coefficient' gap.

The futurist ideology models follow much the same line of reasoning; a symbolic date – say, the year 2000 – is chosen to mark the definitive incorporation to the industrial society and to complete the modernisation process. This enables the objectives or 'targets' to be scheduled successively, and constantly reviewed in the light of achievement, allowing sufficient length of time for the vast transformations of modernisation, without however placing them so far ahead as to lack relevance for the present generation.

The disadvantage of fabricated motivations of the economic type as compared with political and ideological motivation lies in their lesser mobilising capacity. Their advantage resides in allowing a higher level of rationality to obtain in the allocation of resources.

ECONOMIC TAKE-OFF OR POLITICAL BREAKDOWN?

When contemplating the political instability now prevailing in the Third World, with periodical interruptions of the economic development process, it is hard to elude the conclusion that we are facing a problem not so much of 'economic take-off' as of 'political breakdown'. Various slogans, such as 'economic development guarantees social peace', or 'the new name for development is peace', as Pope Paul VI suggested, are attractive but unfortunately not supported by historical evidence. Political stability and the absence of violence are relatively easy to find at either end of the spectrum, i.e., in either traditional or modern societies – but rarely a feature of societies in the process of modernisation, a phase common to nearly all of present-day Latin America, which for that very reason is perhaps the least stable continent, excluding Central and West Africa.[11]

Curiously enough the frequency of insurrections is greater in the relatively rich countries, in more rapid transformation, than in the poorer countries. From a study conducted by the World Bank, it appears that at the beginning of 1966, amongst the twenty countries of Latin America, five of the richest (or least poor), and only one of the most backward were troubled by insurrections. In the last decade of the seventies, countries with a relatively high income level such as Chile, Uruguay and Argentina (the last two enjoying also a high level of literacy and university education), traversed periods of acute political turmoil.

A much broader sample, encompassing 84 countries for the period 1948–65, examined by Ivo Feierabend, Rosalind Feierabend and Betty Nesvold, musters additional empirical evidence on the same theme. Of 24 countries classified as modern, only four experienced political instability. The ratio was higher for the traditional countries (13 classified as unstable out of 23). But the maximum level of instability was found among the transitional countries. In those, political instability predominated by the striking ratio of 2:1 (25 unstable out of 37)![12]

It would then appear that the period of 'economic take-off', involving structural adjustments and burgeoning aspirations, is a period of both economic promise and political vulnerability. In fact, the pitfalls of the economic transition to modernity are not altogether unlike those of the 'Tocqueville effect', arising from political reforms in politically backward societies. It may be recalled that when analysing the transition from the *Ancien Régime* to pluralistic societies, Alexis de Tocqueville notes that 'the most dangerous moment for a bad government is generally that in which it sets about to reform'. For at that moment, he adds 'the evil, it is true, has become less, but sensibility to it has become more acute' . . ..[13]

Much more progress has been made in understanding the mechanics of economic development than in the construction of feasible political models. Meanwhile, the most urgent and challenging issue for the developing world, be it in Latin America or elsewhere, is 'how to concentrate authority, differentiate functions and broaden political participation'. Without a parallel effort of political modernisation, economic modernisation will continue to suffer political breakdowns, and promising outbursts of development will not become self-supporting.

Discarding motivations of a catastrophic nature – such as misfortunes of war and challenges to survival – or radical ideologies (whose social cost would probably exceed their yield), Third World countries, particularly those of Latin America which are at a somewhat higher state of development, would do well to seek motivations of a more rational type and institutionalise them by political party commitments. Those solutions are certainly not dramatic, but they are the only ones compatible with the attainment of important (and lasting) democratic values.

NOTES AND REFERENCES

1. A. Hirschman, *Journeys Toward Progress* (New York: Twentieth Century Fund, 1963) p. 237.
2. Samuel P. Huntington, *Political Order in Changing Societies* (Yale University Press, 1968) p. 54.
3. Robert T. Daland, *Brazilian Planning* (University of North Carolina Press, 1967) p. 143.
4. Samuel P. Huntington, op. cit., p. 53. Huntington's book inspired a considerable part of the political analysis in this article.
5. Huntington, op. cit., pp. 34–5.
6. Karl Deutsch, 'Social Mobilization and Political Development', *American Political Science Review* (September 1961) p. 494.
7. Huntington, op. cit., p. 34.
8. Huntington, op. cit., pp. 58–9.
9. For an elaborate definition of 'systemic frustration', see Ivo K. Feierabend, Rosalind L. Feierabend and Betty A. Nesvold, 'Social change and political violence: cross national patterns', in Jason L. Finkle and Richard W. Gable (eds), *Political Development and Social Change*, 2nd edn (New York and London: John Wiley, 1971) p. 571.
10. Huntington, op. cit., p. 336.
11. See Ivo Feierabend, *et al.*, op. cit., p. 579: 'Highly modern and truly traditional nations should experience less systemic frustration – in the modern nations, because of their ability to provide a high level of attainment commensurate with modern aspirations; in the traditional nations, unexposed to aspirations, because modern aspirations are still lacking'.
12. See Ivo Feierabend *et al.*, op. cit., Table 3, p. 586.
13. Alexis de Tocqueville, *L'Ancien Régime*, trans. M. W. Patterson (Oxford: Basil Blackwell, 1947) p. 186.

10 Some First Thoughts on Rural Development[1]

E. A. G. ROBINSON

THE PROBLEMS

There is today a wide-spread tendency among developing countries to abandon the industrialisation-led strategies of the past and to put the emphasis on rural development, by implication changing over to an agriculture-led strategy.

It is not difficult to make a useful list of ways in which agricultural productivity might be increased or social welfare in rural areas improved. It is very much more difficult to envisage a dynamic for an agriculture-led development which will provide a continuing incentive to expand and grow. One must always remember that Shakespeare's farmer hung himself in the expectation of plenty.

Thus any agriculture-led strategy must, if it is to be continuously effective, be made up of two elements:

1. measures that will progressively increase productivity;
2. measures that will prevent the farmers from collectively hanging themselves.

Price elasticities and income elasticities for food products being what they are, the emergence of surpluses as the result of measures to increase productivity unaccompanied by measures to affect the market will simply result in re-contraction of output. No lasting progress will have been achieved. The farmer will merely retreat again into minimum-risk farming as dictated by the vagaries of the market.

North American and European farming went through these difficulties in the 1930s. The great majority of these countries emerged with some variation or other of a system of guaranteed prices or of price support. It is very easy to criticise some of these national schemes in detail, to find oneself resistant to the excessive strength of farm-lobbies, and allergic to the over-readiness of farmers to squeal when under pressure. It remains that the subsequent forty years have seen the most tremendous upsurge in agricultural productivities, efficiency and output and also in average real farm incomes. At the same time technical progress in agriculture is now in a number of countries more rapid than technical progress in industry.

Are there lessons here for third world agriculture? I think there are. But before we come to these, there is one very important point that needs to be made. The developing countries differ greatly. Some are ostensibly socialist; some are ostensibly capitalist. But all of them are, in reality, in different degrees mixed economies. In almost all of them, agriculture is in the private sector, in the sense that the individual farmer decides what he shall grow, what inputs he shall use, how much he shall sell and how much he shall consume himself. He can be urged, exhorted and cajoled. But he makes his decisions largely in the light of price-incentives. If the price incentives are right, he may listen to the exhortations. But if the incentives are wrong, all experience seems to show that exhortations are ineffective and output targets are irrelevant.

Thus I suggest that the economic problems that are posed by rural development are these:

1. How can we initially increase farm incomes? What parts in this process should be played by (a) increased productivity; (b) more favourable rural/urban terms of trade; (c) assurance of markets and removal of market-price-risks from the farmer onto the state or some other organisation capable of averaging good years and bad.
2. If increased food production is (as it must be) a large element in (1.), how shall it (a) be purchased, stored and marketed; (b) how shall it be used for export or for other internal purposes of development? How shall these processes be financed?
3. How can we make use of the multiplier effects of initial larger farm incomes so that they filter down into increased production and activity in village industries, in smaller towns and, where appropriate, in the big cities, and so that each of these progressively (a) provides a larger market in its turn for the

increased food and other agricultural output and (b) at the same time gradually draws increasing numbers of workers out of the agricultural population? This must be the ultimate objective of the whole operation.

THE REASONS FOR THE FAILURE OF INDUSTRY-LED DEVELOPMENT

If we are to foresee the probable difficulties of agriculture-led development, it is well to understand as clearly as we can why industry-led development failed to deliver the results expected from it.

The original strategy for industry-led development, though it was seldom thought out and formulated with sufficient clarity, may be summarised as follows:

1. Invest (a) in infra-structure, (b) in machine-building industries and (c) in import-saving consumer industries.
2. By so doing you will
   a. increase employment;
   b. increase urban incomes;
   c. make it possible, with more adequate infra-structure, for private enterprise to push further with import-saving investment;
   d. reduce the import-content of investment, and thus reduce the extent of the foreign-exchange constraint on all investment;
   e. reduce the import-content of consumption, and thus increase the local multiplier effects of any given expansion and reduce the leaks out of the system;
   f. create additional markets for food (which represents a large part of consumer expenditure) and thus increase rural incomes and rural expenditures;
   g. as result of (a) manpower will progressively be attracted to urban industrial and other employment, and, following a pattern familiar in all developed countries, the manpower in agriculture will contract and income per head in agriculture will rise with growing productivity per head in agriculture.

Inevitably the reasons why this strategy has not worked out have differed from country to country and the degree of failure has differed from country to country. But a generalised account, applicable to many countries in Africa and Asia, would emphasise the following points:

1. In most developing countries (leaving out the OPEC countries) the most powerful limiting factors have been, and continue to be, (a) shortage of savings and potential capital investment (b) shortage of foreign earnings associated with a high import-content of capital investment. When development has reached the limits imposed by foreign resources and reasonably non-inflationary savings the brake is inevitably applied.
2. Attempts to 'modernise' industry, using Western technologies, made very heavy demands both on the available savings and on the available foreign resources; relatively few jobs were created on the basis of large use of these limiting resources.
3. The higher earnings of those employed in the modernised industries were largely devoted to consumer goods which had to be imported or, if locally manufactured, had a high import-content of materials and components and a high required import of equipment.
4. Thus relatively little of the added expenditure filtered down to increase agricultural incomes.
5. At the same time, failures to improve the channels for collection and marketing of food and agricultural products, associated with crop failures and with fears of inflation, led governments to welcome food imports, and particularly aid in the form of food imports, so that the big cities have been fed increasingly by imports, and so that such effect as there has been under (4) on agricultural incomes has been greatly reduced.
6. The rapid growth of population in these countries, and especially in their rural areas, meant that, in sharp contrast with what happened in Europe and North America at the similar stage (it happened before the medical revolution and before modern increases of population growth), industrial development in the developing countries did not reduce the rural population and draw it increasingly into new activities, leaving fewer people to live off agriculture; on the contrary the slow increase of urban jobs and of industrial employment has left increasing numbers to live, with increasing under-employment, off the proceeds of agriculture.
7. Because the farm incomes and rural incomes generally were not

increasing significantly there was hesitation on the part of entrepreneurs to invest in the production of the desirable mass-production consumer goods to the extent that was necessary to give the whole strategy a dynamic.

8. Thus the breakdown of the industry-led strategy came:
   a. because the domestic incomes and demand that were created in the rural areas through the expenditures generated in the urban areas were inadequate to create the necessary expectations of markets for the potential products;
   b. because the income distribution that resulted from it was inequitable and politically unacceptable;
   c. because without the creation of mass-consumption by the large rural populations, the strategy had no continuing dynamic or clear objective.

Despite the increasing signs of breakdown, many governments have tried to go ahead with particular measures that will, if an agriculture-led development can be successfully adopted, ultimately be necessary ingredients of it:

1. Village industries. In a number of countries great efforts have been put into developing village industries. In most cases they have had very little success, mainly because the rural markets they were best suited to serve could offer little demand, whereas, if they were to compete for the more sophisticated demands of the big cities, where the benefits of industrialisation were concentrated, they had to meet the competition in those markets of imported goods, while bearing the higher distribution costs necessary to reach those markets. Nevertheless in a number of countries an initial structure of village industries already exists and an organisation is there to develop them further when the market is there.
2. Appropriate technologies. The general concepts of appropriate technologies and the applied research that has flowed from it are ultimately concerned with two separate questions. First, if a policy of industrialisation and creation of infrastructure is to continue, need it absorb such a very large proportion of national savings and foreign exchange to produce its results? If Western technology is in fact the most capital-saving as regards the essential core of certain projects, can the peripheral and service activities be made substantially less capital-intensive? Second, if

one starts with an agriculture-led development, can the expenditures generated in agriculture be satisfied, consistently with the tastes of the rural communities, more nearly as they were half a century ago by small-scale industries in the villages and small towns, if these are suitably equipped with appropriate technologies? Again valuable work has been done. But it fails to find an outlet because of lack of rural effective demand.

While this represents, I believe, a faithful picture of a great many developing countries – I would say a considerable majority of them – there are a few notable and exciting exceptions where a combination of improved agricultural methods or crops and an adequate local market have combined to create an atmosphere of agricultural prosperity and high rural incomes spent on new goods. One notable example has been the cultivation of the new high yield varieties of wheat in the Indian Punjab. There is no doubt there of the agricultural prosperity. Certain local service activities have unquestionably benefited. But there are different accounts of the pattern of expenditures and of the beneficiaries from it. My own impression is that a greater proportion of expenditure has gone to the products of the big cities than would be welcomed by anyone anxious to see the spill-over benefiting the small industries of the small towns.

AN AGRICULTURE-LED STRATEGY

How then does one envisage an agriculture-led strategy? Again in very summary form it can be formulated as follows:

1. Devise a sufficient group of measures to increase agricultural productivity;
2. (and simultaneously) devise a set of measures for purchase of agricultural output and support of farm prices;
3. take steps, as may be appropriate, to turn the rural/urban terms of trade more favourable to rural areas and make them more consistently favourable; improve greatly the channels for purchase, transport and marketing of rural produce;
4. devise measures to export so much of any surplus as can find export markets;

5. devise measures to use internally such surplus as remains after (3) and (4);
6. devise measures to promote village industries to the maximum extent possible to meet (a) increased farm inputs, (b) increased expenditure of rural incomes;
7. while giving all reasonable preference to (6) be prepared to give big-city production a sufficient preference over import of consumption goods;
8. give vigorous support to all research and development which will (a) increase agricultural yields, (b) assist village or small town industries to compete with big city or imported products;
9. encourage rather than discourage a shift within the rural areas from agriculture into other occupations and from strictly rural areas into productive occupations in small towns;
10. encourage an adequate filtering down of the benefits of greater productivity to those engaged in urban industry so that their demand increasingly absorbs the growing output of agriculture.

THE VULNERABILITY OF SUCH A STRATEGY: FOOD SURPLUSES

Can such a strategy work? Where is it vulnerable? Will it collapse in the same sort of way that the industry-led strategy did?

First, it must be asked, is it a certain recipe for cereals-mountains that will out-top the butter-mountains and the wine-mountains of the EEC as tremendously as the Himalayas out-top the Alps? The answer obviously depends on whether the strategy can include nation-building uses for potential increases of output of cereals. I believe that a workable strategy can and should include such uses.

It must be remembered that many of these developing countries have become importers of cereals for the first time within the past two or three decades, chiefly as a consequence of growing urban populations. At the same time these countries have been dependent for their foreign earnings largely on exports of a limited range of 'colonial' type products which are difficult to expand. Thus the claims of food imports have imposed an increasingly powerful constraint on their power to import capital equipment for development and have made development increasingly dependent on the receipt of aid. If increased cereal production can diminish the need for imports, that represents an immediate relaxation of one of the two principal constraints on growth.

Apart from replacement of imports, increased cereal outputs can also, within limits, find export markets. While an increase of cereal exports cannot simultaneously provide a solution for all the countries of the world, there are likely to be individual countries that can find regional markets in other countries that will continue to import and which wish to find, in another developing country to which it is easier to make payment, a more continued source of supply than is afforded by food aid.

It must, at the same time, be borne in mind that FAO estimates suggest that at present food supplies in the Far East, taken as a whole, fall short of estimated nutritional requirements by seven per cent or thereabouts and in individual Far Eastern countries by well over ten per cent; in Africa as a whole they are estimated to fall short of nutritional requirements by nine per cent and again in a number of individual African countries by over ten per cent. There is no lack of ability to consume but rather of effective demand to buy.

The agricultural sector and the rural community in general in most developing countries are in effect performing at present two functions. They represent the industry providing the food and other agricultural outputs for the nation. They provide at the same time a major part of the social services of the country, maintaining not only the great majority of the aged but also a large part of those who are at present unemployed or underemployed. If agriculture is to be made efficient and prosperous and capable of providing a market for industrial output, it is desirable, on economic grounds as well as those of social welfare and equity, that some of the burden of these social services should be taken off the backs of the agricultural industry and become to a greater extent a responsibility of the state, through the provision of useful work that can contribute to rural and national development.

Thus I suggest that one important element in an agriculture-led strategy should be rural investment, organised on a large scale on a 'food for work' basis; this should be designed among other things for the following purposes:

1. to improve agricultural productivity through minor as well as major farm improvements, irrigation facilities, including on-the-farm facilities, land drainage, wells and pumps, tanks, fishponds;

2. to provide for land reclamation, terracing and similar improvements where appropriate;
3. to improve common pastures and grassland, provide water facilities for cattle and similar improvements;
4. to create facilities for the production of organic fertilisers;
5. to provide facilities that will increase the productivity of fisheries or improve the marketing of fish;
6. to improve rural as well as long-distance roads and communications;
7. to provide facilities for rural bus services and rural lorry services;
8. to improve water transport facilities, especially where this will help to integrate rural development into overall national development;
9. to provide facilities for the storage and handling of agricultural crops;
10. to provide facilities for the processing of agricultural crops or products in rural areas;
11. to construct the buildings and facilities required for rural education, health and other social and community services;
12. to construct the buildings and facilities required for agricultural extension, demonstration, research and education;
13. to assist in construction of facilities in rural areas required for the carrying out of such a programme of works (e.g. local facilities for brick-making, cement, saw-mills, etc.).

These represent some of the activities that might be covered by such a programme. Most of these are activities which, in advanced as well as backward countries, are frequently subsidised to a greater or lesser extent by governments. Many of these things are already being done–often in a half-hearted way–by individual developing countries.

I envisage the programme as primarily a public works programme, in the sense that the amount of such works would depend on the extent of local unemployment and underemployment rather than on a strict comparison of the benefits conferred by projects when completed. Within any area, however, strict account should be taken of the comparative benefits of alternative projects in terms of increased productivity or greater social welfare. For on-the-farm improvements the land-owner should make an appropriate small contribution, possibly being asked to cover non-labour inputs.

I envisage the programme also as varying in scale at different times of the year and taking account of the seasonal demands of agriculture.

So far as possible all non-labour inputs should be drawn from local rural sources. Unless wholly unavoidable, the grain supplies for 'food for work' should be purchased in the local area and not imported from outside.

The aggregate scale in any one year would depend on:

1. the current estimated extent of unemployment and underemployment;
2. the amount of grain it is thought to be desirable to purchase to support the grain price;
3. the amount of grain successfully exported.

At any time, having regard to the objective of agriculture-led development, it would be desirable to purchase enough grain to create a continuing incentive to increase output. It is at least thinkable that in some circumstances it might be proper to import grain for urban consumption while purchasing grain in rural areas for public works that were justified by the employment situation. If more grain were purchased than was immediately required for public works it would be stored and released in some later year.

In the initial stages, before grain surpluses had been stimulated, it might be necessary to start the policy with somewhat less procurement than would be dictated by the employment situation alone. It would, however, be a mistake to provide a greater scale of initial operation through imports of food at the cost of removing the incentive to expand domestic agriculture.

THE VULNERABILITY OF SUCH A STRATEGY: FAILURE TO FILTER DOWN

It is necessary now to look at other ways in which an agriculture-led strategy might be vulnerable. It was argued earlier that the industry-led strategy failed in part at least because it failed to filter down from the industrial development, where it started, to demand for food products and thus stimulation to agriculture. Is there a danger that, in reverse, an agriculture-led development would fail to filter down and provide a stimulus to adequate industrial development?

To that, there are, I suggest, two answers. First, the failure to filter down was especially serious in the industry-led development because the important ultimate desired destination represented by the cure of poverty was at the bottom end of the filtering process, so that unless benefit filtered down, it failed to reach the desired beneficiaries. An agriculture-led development starts with the most desired beneficiaries. Its chief benefits will be achieved even if the filtering process is imperfect.

Second, there is much less doubt in this case about the process of filtering down. At present the rural community is provided with food, not, it is true, to the point that its desirable nutritional requirements are fully met, but to a point perhaps some ten per cent lower. If rural incomes increase, the increases will be spent with little doubt largely on manufactures and thus on urban-produced goods. At present one's fears are that the rural expenditures will filter faster and more directly to the city industries than maximum benefit to the smaller towns would suggest is desirable. It may indeed prove necessary, as some countries have already attempted, to reserve certain products for rural-town production and thus restrict the filtering process. But in more general terms the agriculture-led development is likely to be more directed to domestic city-made goods than to the imported goods to which much of the industrial incomes were directed and which thereby increased the leaks in the expansionary system and diminished the multiplier effects.

THE VULNERABILITY OF SUCH A STRATEGY: POPULATION GROWTH

The failure of the industry-led strategy was in part due to the effects of population growth. With industry-led growth the immediate beneficiaries formed a small and only very slowly growing proportion of the total population and spent their added incomes principally on products that came either from the group itself or from imports. With an agriculture-led development the immediate beneficiaries will immediately include the largest growing sector of the population, and population growth will be principally within the group of immediate beneficiaries and not outside it.

Thus it would appear that the principal reasons for the failure of the industry-led strategy apply with much less force in the case of an agriculture-led strategy.

It remains to ask whether an agriculture-led strategy has different and equally powerful difficulties and constraints of its own.

DOES AN AGRICULTURE-LED STRATEGY PRESENT OVERWHELMING ADMINISTRATIVE DIFFICULTIES?

It may be argued that an agriculture-led strategy is inevitably very decentralised, requiring the intelligent co-operation of a very large number of individuals in the districts and local administration units who will be difficult to co-ordinate, and additionally that a large-scale and widely distributed 'public works' programme will present great opportunities for ambitious local politicians to distribute favours and acquire power, while at the same time making vulnerable the politicians and administrators at the centre, where the essential co-ordination must be strong and effective.

It cannot be denied that such a strategy will be capable of abuse, or that, as happened in Europe under fascist governments, local political favours may be granted. It is doubtful, however, whether any development strategy can be wholly proof against such abuse.

It is necessary, however, to be clear what elements in an agriculture-led strategy must be operated as well as supervised and controlled by the government. Clearly there must be overall control in aggregate of the 'food for work' policy and the public works organised under it. Clearly the total of food to be acquired for distribution through 'food for work' must be centrally determined and financed, though the purchase can be made either through local government agencies or from merchants, where there is a reasonably satisfactory and honest body of traders. If the market for grain is to be supported by stock-building or export, the government is again free itself to build stocks or purchase for export directly, or it may use the merchants and traders to deliver into central warehouses and silos. If a government for practical or ideological reasons wishes to minimise its direct involvement in the local small-scale operations of purchase and transport, it is possible for it to perform the essential functions and make the essential decisions without great involvement, though it must have a general responsibility for the efficiency and honesty of the system.

Are there insuperable difficulties – it must be asked – in fixing a satisfactory buying or support price in a third world developing country? Was the successful operation of the support or marketing-board system in Europe and North America due to the fact that the differences of yield between year and year in those countries were relatively small as compared with the cataclysmic differences between years that are encountered in Asian and African countries? Can any thinkable guaranteed purchase price for grain both be appropriate in a good year and capable of removing part of the risk from the farmer in a bad year?

In this context it is important to distinguish two different systems which have been operated in different countries in Europe and North America. The marketing-board system establishes a monopolist buying agency which buys all of the product from the grower and sells it on the market. In a year of big crops the farmer has an assured market. In a year of bad crops the farmer might do better in an unregulated market. The support-price system leaves the farmer to benefit in a bad year or a tight market. It prevents a glut from causing a very low price in a good year. The first is a two way regulation of the market; the second is a one-way regulation.

If the principal objective of the agriculture-led strategy is to give an incentive to the farmer to expand output without fear of a collapse of the market, it is price-support in the good year which alone is really needed. Thus the difficulty of foreseeing and fixing a price which will be satisfactory however large or small the crop need not, and should not, exist. One can confine attention in this respect to the problem of fixing a suitable support-price for the good year. This is difficult but not insuperably difficult. If the strategy is to succeed one must be prepared to turn the rural/urban terms of trade appreciably in favour of the rural areas and be prepared to provide an incentive to expand that is strong enough to work.

The problem of the bad year cannot, however, be forgotten. The central government of most developing countries has a major responsibility for grain imports. It has at the same time a responsibility for the prevention of famine and the control of inflation. In a year of crop failure it is faced by the exceedingly difficult dilemma of how to protect the urban populations against famine and at the same time protect the agricultural population against the financial consequences of a collapse of incomes and mounting debts. In this situation the question of how much the price of grain rises depends on the volume of imports. In a very bad year the duty of the government to prevent famine must be paramount. But in a year that is only moderately bad, the choice will be between more inflation, accompanied by more benefit to the farmer, and less inflation and less incentive to the farmer. It is arguable that over-concern with inflation and over-generous provision of food-aid have considerably diminished the incentives for agricultural expansion in developing countries. If agriculture-led development is the strategy, a somewhat conservative policy over grain imports is a corollary.

A conservative policy over imports is, however, only possible if there is reasonably good assurance that domestic supplies will reach the cities. In a number of developing countries it would appear to be increasingly true that the big cities have been fed by imported grain. In some countries a careful examination and drastic overhaul of the grain trading system and all the associated problems of terms of purchase, credit for agricultural inputs, transport and storage facilities is overdue. It must always be borne in mind that the rural/urban terms of trade that it is desirable to improve are the 'farm-gate' terms of trade: the terms on which the actual producer exchanges his own products, which he might well consume himself, for other consumer or capital goods that he wishes to buy, with all the various handling charges added to the latter. These terms of trade are very different from the rural/urban wholesale terms of trade in a big-city market.

THE COST AND FINANCE OF AN AGRICULTURE-LED STRATEGY

It is not easy to estimate, even for one country, what might be the cost of such an agriculture-led policy or to envisage in detail the problems of financing it. One can do no more than try to see some of the possible orders of magnitude. Some of the cost, if one thinks for the moment in terms of what will be transferred to the agricultural community, will represent in fact an internal re-distribution of income as between more affluent middle-class recipients and poor farmers, which will be achieved through market prices and which will not involve any government financing.

The main elements in the strategy envisaged in this note which will require government financing are:

the 'food for work' public works scheme;
the subsidy, if that should prove necessary for any grain exports sold at less than the domestic support-price.

If the 'food for work' scheme were operated at a level sufficient to raise the national nutritional level of an African or Far Eastern country, to about the level represented by the estimated nutritional 'requirements', that would need an addition of roughly ten per cent of food supply and a not widely different addition to agricultural output. If one were content initially to close a half rather than the whole of the gap, it would represent roughly five per cent of agricultural output. If agricultural production is typically about 50 per cent of GDP, the value of the food to be acquired would be equivalent in the five per cent case to 2.5 per cent of GDP. If the non-food inputs (such as cement, fuel for brick-making, timber, steel if necessary) of the public works were about half the labour inputs, they would bring the total public works cost to about four per cent of GDP. For a typical developing country this represents about one-third to a one-quarter of total gross capital formation. It is of a possible order of magnitude. The more ambitious ten per cent case would represent a half to two-thirds of total gross investment. A not inconsiderable part of present investment is, it must be remembered, already included in the rural public works.

It is difficult to make an accurate guess of possible expenditure on support and subsidisation. It is improbable that added exports would exceed five per cent of agricultural output. A subsidy as large as 20 per cent to make good any difference between the support price and the export price would represent one per cent of the value of agricultural output, or about 0.5 per cent of GDP. This probably greatly overestimates the cost, which would arise only in years of exceptional crops. Such a cost would again appear to be well within national resources.

POSSIBLE EFFECTS ON MACROECONOMIC CONSTRAINTS

One must finally ask how the principal macroeconomic indicators and constraints might be affected, and their probable repercussions on economic growth. The two constraints that it is most important to consider are those represented by savings and by the foreign balance.

It is easy to begin by arguing that any proposed agriculture-led strategy will involve – is indeed designed to involve – a redistribution of income from richer to poorer, and thus (it is inferred) from a potentially saving group to a potentially consuming group. That naive picture of the socio-economics of saving and spending is, however, increasingly suspect. The intended redistribution will at the same time be a redistribution from passive receivers of profits, interest and dividends to active producers and the middlemen associated with agricultural marketing. There is good reason to think that such people can and do save to finance their own investment (one has seen it at Comilla). That apart, some at least of the agricultural investment required is likely to be covered by extra effort and extra working time on the part of farmers improving their own holdings.

It is very difficult to guess the amount of agricultural investment that is needed. If one thinks in terms of an annual growth of six per cent in agricultural output (too high a figure for most Far Eastern and African countries) and a capital/output ratio of 1.0 (which is higher than most agricultural investment), the required agricultural investment would be equivalent, if one still assumes that agricultural production is 50 per cent of GDP, to 3.0 per cent of GDP. There is some duplication between this purely agricultural investment and the assumed 'public works' much of which will, however, be devoted to social welfare, communications and other non-agricultural projects. If one quarter of the 'public works' investment (estimated above at four per cent of GDP) is in reality agricultural investment (irrigation etc.), the two together would amount to 3.0 + 1.0 (= 4.0 per cent) of GDP. That represents about one-third of national investment. The remaining two-thirds would be available to provide for the infrastructure, industrial and service growths which would filter down from the increasing rural welfare.

This would obviously imply some slowing down of present infrastructure investment. It is consistent with a six per cent industrial growth if that growth can be achieved with appropriate technologies and a capital/output ratio of the order of four to one or less. This is in any case desirable and an essential part of an agriculture-led strategy.

What would be the effects of such a strategy on aid? Would it inhibit aid, and thus diminish investment to the point that the benefits of a more desirable and more appropriate strategy were lost through lower resources for growth? My own order of magnitude calculations suggest that is not the case. If one looks at the very broad issues, one is devising a strategy which makes considerably more use of the national manpower, and of the national resources, for investment through public works, while possibly losing foreign resources equivalent to about 3 per cent of GDP which are somewhat wastefully applied in non-appropriate technology. The overall balance of gain or loss would not be large. I myself believe there to be an over-all gain, even if aid were entirely lost, which is unlikely.

What would be the effects of an agriculture-led strategy on the foreign balance? Again there are possible gains and possible losses. They may be summarised as follows:

1. the import-content of investment is clearly reduced;
2. the import-content of food consumption is clearly reduced;
3. the direct import-content of non-food consumption is almost certainly reduced;
4. the indirect import-content of non food consumption (imported materials, components, etc.) may perhaps be increased;
5. petroleum imports will be reduced rather than increased provided that agricultural development is labour intensive and animal-intensive;
6. fertiliser imports, or feed-stocks for fertilisers, will almost certainly need to be increased, even if there is emphasis on use of natural fertilisers;
7. agricultural (non-food) exports should be increased if expansion of food production does not unduly conflict (as may happen) with the export crops;
8. food grain exports may be increased, at least in good years.

In general terms it seems likely that an agriculture-led development is less likely to be limited by the constraint of foreign exchange shortage than the present pattern of development. Putting this another way, it will be somewhat easier to finance needed imports for development without having to depend to an undesirable extent on aid.

FINAL CONSIDERATIONS

This paper has been wholly concerned with some of the peculiarly economic problems of creating and operating an agriculture-led strategy. It raises, I think, some points that need careful thought in any consideration that FAO may be giving in future to the planning of rural development. I have been particularly worried that so little thought, and that such poor thought, has been given to how rural incomes, and particularly agricultural incomes, can be increased and maintained at increased levels. Unless that can be done most of the beautiful lists of sociological desiderata are pure pie in the sky.

I have deliberately refrained from any discussion of the technical agricultural content of an agriculture-led strategy. That is a matter regarding which agricultural scientists are far more expert than I can hope to be. It is a matter also that will differ between country and country, and between region and region.

There are, however, certain economic generalities that it will be important to have in mind. The principal limiting-factor on expansion of agriculture throughout the Far East is the limit of available land. This is less true in Africa and Latin America generally, but true enough in certain parts. Any technical plan for agriculture, if it is to succeed in such countries, must have a large element of 'land-saving' measures. Such measures include:

measures to increase yields per hectare by increased use of high-yield varieties, fertilisers, pesticides and multi-cropping;
active research policies to develop such improved varieties, and to make yields more consistent;
measures to increase irrigation, so as to permit multi-cropping in seasons of inadequate rainfall;
measures to concentrate production so far as possible on those crops and branches of agriculture which have a high product in value terms per hectare;
measures to reclaim land for agricultural use which can be made productive with moderate capital investment;
measures to identify and introduce generally all practices that result in increased yields;
measures to modify land tenures in ways that will lead to increased production per hectare; in general the smaller the holding, the greater the yield per hectare.

The second general consideration that requires to be borne in mind in preparing any national agricultural strategy is that the most gravely under-utilised resource in almost all these countries is rural manpower. There is value in creating work and providing income for these impoverished landless labourers or underemployed small holders quite apart from any strictly economic analysis of whether it does or does not pay to employ them rather than to use labour-saving machinery. It is very rarely that the relative market prices for a day's work of a man and for a day's work of a machine are such that even a strictly economic decision to substitute machinery will be rightly made. In general all agricultural plans should be as labour-intensive as is practicable. If more machinery is to be used, it should require some exceptional justification – the need to lighten work rather than to save hours, the need to speed harvesting and cultivation in order to permit multi-cropping, the need to increase irrigation at particular times, to take a few examples. The temptation to ape the technologies of the North American prairies, with their huge acreage per worker, and to regard this alone as agricultural progress – a temptation felt by every foreign trained expert – must be resisted.

Quite apart from more general aspects of improving agriculture and increasing agricultural productivity, there remains the importance of ensuring that the benefits of rural development shall be spread as evenly as may be possible over all the members of the rural community and not confined to the fortunate owners of land or others in a privileged position. The problems of the poor landless labourers may in part be alleviated by a public works policy. But this should be in essentials a temporary, seasonal, and pump-priming operation, while the rural unemployed are increasingly absorbed into other more permanent occupations. Part of this absorption may need in many countries to take the form of revisions of land-holdings and land-tenures.

While food production is of primary importance, many of these developing countries depend on agricultural exports to meet their needs for imports. In a world in which man-made fibres, synthetic plastics and rubber, and other artificial materials have increasingly been substituted for the natural products which were the basis of the 'colonial' exports of the past, it has been increasingly difficult for many developing countries to find and retain profitable exports which will grow at all correspondingly with their economic growth.

After a period in which such substitute materials were inferior to the natural products, the artificial products are now in very many cases regarded as superior, so that natural wool, natural cotton, natural jute, natural rubber are at a discount. A corollary of a successful agriculture-led development is the greatest possible effort to discover a new generation of natural products which will permit developing countries to diversify their exports and at the same time diversify their diets and food consumption.

But one element in a successful agriculture-led strategy should be a very thorough survey of a nation's natural resources and of the natural fibres and other industrial materials that it might potentially produce for itself, so that part of a successful growth would take the form of adjusting consumption patterns, in respect of diet, housing construction, clothing materials and all else, as perfectly as possible to the potential output of the national environment. Not a few of the problems of developing countries result from over-zealous pursuit of inappropriate products and exogenous consumption patterns.

It is not claimed that the suggestions made in this note represent the only possible solution of the problems of rural development. But I am convinced that any solution that is to be successful must have, as one of its essential ingredients, a solution of the problem of how agricultural incomes are to be increased, maintained and made to grow continuously. Any scheme which fails to provide for that will have no continuing dynamic.

May I attempt finally to set my suggested strategy in a broader perspective? My suggestions have a three-fold but essentially complementary purpose:

1. They are designed as a pump-priming operation with the intention of creating opportunities for employment for the rural unemployed and underemployed in the only forms in which they can quickly and easily be drawn into employment.
2. They are designed to create in the short term a higher level of effective demand in those geographical areas and in the possession of those people who may be expected to possess this effective demand in a longer period if a successful agriculture-led development is achieved.
3. Thus the suggested strategy may be expected to generate expenditures both on those types of goods and in those geographical areas in which in the longer term similar, though

larger expenditures are to be expected, as and when these workers become absorbed into long-term employment in new activities.

Thus such a strategy will begin to create the necessary incentives to develop those industries and activities which will become necessary in rural and urban areas as activity increases towards the full employment level, including those industries in smaller and larger cities which will meet the full-employment effective demand in due course. Among the activities which will greatly benefit from this higher effective demand are the agricultural producers of foodstuffs themselves.

These suggestions represent in effect, that is to say, a pump-priming operation. Theoretically, if the whole national system has, after a period, been made to develop, with filtering down of expenditures, investment in construction of new rural and urban enterprises, absorption of labour into them, and progressive reduction of the population dependent on agriculture, the immediate need for further pump-priming may come to an end. Theoretically the public works pump-priming organisation can then be terminated. In practice its continued existence will do no possible harm, may serve at intervals to restore a dynamic when needed, and at the same time provide an instrument for rural investment on a changing basis.

NOTES

1. This chapter was written while I was holding for a few weeks a short-period consultancy in FAO in Rome at a time when rural development was very much under discussion. It inevitably draws heavily on ideas of others who were working in FAO at the time. But the responsibility for any policy suggestions is wholly my own. It was written argumentatively in order to provoke argument. I make it my contribution to a book in honour of Walt Rostow in the hope that it may provoke others to a small fraction of the extent to which I myself have been stimulated by Walt Rostow's writings.

11 Trade and Growth in the Industrial Revolution

R. FINDLAY

The Industrial Revolution of the eighteenth century in England is the central event of modern economic history. In spite of Ranke's dictum that every moment is 'equidistant from God' much of the research on earlier periods has been devoted to seeking its origins and antecedents. The experience of the last two centuries can be interpreted as the diffusion of the mechanism of continuous technical progress from Britain, where in the evocative title of David Landes's book Prometheus was first unbound, to Western Europe and the United States, then to Russia and Japan and in our own time, with varying degrees of success, to the developing countries. The sequence of Walt Rostow's seminal works has reflected this very same movement, beginning with the British economy of the nineteenth century and moving outwards in space and time to encompass the contemporary world.

International trade is assigned a major role in the genesis of the Industrial Revolution in every major school of thought in our discipline. The Adam Smith tradition sees international trade as being responsible for the expansion of the market that widens the scope for the division of labour. It cheapens food and raises the rate of profit and capital accumulation in the Ricardian system. Marxists stress the role of plunder and colonial exploitation in the 'primitive accumulation' that was a necessary precursor of industrialisation in England. Keynesians are wont to see the stimulating role of exports on a slack domestic economy and of trade surpluses in lowering the rate of interest. The writings of economic historians have reflected all of these streams of thought so one would expect that they should all have contributed to a clear understanding of the place of international trade in the Industrial Revolution.

Yet in spite, or perhaps because of this very abundance of intellectual riches the exact mechanism whereby international trade was associated with the Industrial Revolution is far from clear and a subject of considerable controversy. Hartwell (1967, p. 54) refers to the role of international trade as 'untested dogma, still to be investigated thoroughly'. Deane and Habakkuk (1963, p. 80) in one of the very few quantitative assessments of the subject, conclude that 'the precise mechanism by which it became an "engine of growth" or a "leading sector" has still to be explored'. The purpose of the present essay is to attempt to shed some light on this difficult question by an application of the modern theory of trade and growth to some of the 'stylized facts' of the British economy in the period 1783–1802 within which Rostow located the first 'take-off'.

I

In his evergreen classic Paul Mantoux (1961) presents a graph, the only one in the book, of English foreign trade from 1700 to 1800. On his arithmetical scale the curves explode almost vertically upwards after 1780 in what he calls a 'giddy ascent'. He notes that the importance of the movement has been disputed by those who point out that trade represented only about a fifteenth of domestic output. He goes on to say (p. 103) however, that 'only a negligible quantity of ferment is needed to effect a radical change in a considerable volume of matter', a refreshing contrast to the relentlessly arithmetical approach, expressed once again in our own time, for example, by Hartwell (p. 75). The indispensable quantitative study by Deane and Cole (1969) provides much more valuable detail, while leaving Mantoux's impression of dramatic change essentially unaltered. They present indices of export volume which indicate an increase of about 2.2 times between 1780 and 1800. Their index of output in export industries goes from 246 in 1780 to 544 in 1800, with 123 and 152 being the corresponding figures for home industries, while total real output goes from 167 to 251 between the same dates.

This spectacular growth in the over-all volume of exports was accompanied by an even more significant structural shift in the composition of exports. Woollen cloth, which had dominated English exports since the Middle Ages, yielded first place to cotton fabrics in 1802, as Mantoux pointed out in a footnote to the page next to his graph. In 1772 woollens were 42 per cent of exports and cotton goods less than 3 per cent, while even in 1790 woollens were over a third of total exports while cotton had risen to 10 per cent. In the first decade of the nineteenth century cotton textiles had become 39 per cent of exports while woollens had fallen to only 24 per cent. The role of leading sector in the first take-off is assigned by Rostow (1960) to the cotton textile industry. The rather meager statistics that he presents to support his 1783–1802 dating of the British take-off are confined largely to figures on import of raw cotton, showing a huge 320 per cent increase for the decade of the 1780s followed by a further 67 per cent increase to the end of the century.

In their investigation of the take-off in Britain Deane and Habakkuk do not find evidence of a sharp acceleration in population or income growth or in the ratio of productive investment to national income in the last two decades of the eighteenth century. Spectacular expansion of the cotton textile industry is granted but the weight of the industry in the economy as a whole is regarded as being too small to be of decisive significance. The one aspect of the British economy that did undergo a significant alteration, in their view, was international trade. They agree with an article by Berrill (1960) that the explanation for the acceleration of British growth that became unmistakable in the first half of the nineteenth century is to be sought in the opportunities opened up by the expansion of overseas markets, particularly the former colonies of North America. The authors appear to vacillate, however, on whether the foreign trade expansion of the late eighteenth century was due to genuine structural factors such as technological change, or to the influence of war in disrupting the channels of commerce, giving an edge to Britain because of the command of the seas by the Royal Navy. It is at this point that they make their statement, quoted earlier, about the precise nature of the links between trade and growth in this period needing to be explored.

Habakkuk and Deane, in common with many other British economic historians, for example Flinn (1966, Chapter 4), appear to think instinctively in terms of a Keynesian model in connection with the problem of trade and growth. It is an exogenous increase in exports raising domestic income through the operation of the foreign trade multiplier that they seem to have in mind. This Keynesian model however assumes idle productive capacity and open unemployment that do not appear to be appropriate assumptions for the case at hand. The lack of congruence between the theoretical model and historical experience thus tends to lead either to a denial of the importance of foreign trade as a factor in the acceleration of growth or to a feeling that there is some puzzle or anomaly involved in the situation. My own view is that they are using the wrong model. Kindleberger (1961) has pointed out that there are a variety of possible channels linking growth and trade that may even be mutually contradictory, so that it is always necessary to be explicit about what model one is using in making any statements about the influence of trade on growth in any historical context.

The next section develops a very simple model, based on the neoclassical theory of trade and growth that, in my opinion, is a more helpful framework for the analysis of the British experience during this crucial period than the Keynesian or other models that have been used, mostly implicitly, in the literature in the subject. This type of model is a standard one in the theory of international trade but it has been neglected by economic historians, except for some applications to the United States in the nineteenth century by younger members of the 'cliometric' school. The reader is referred to Findlay and Grubert (1959) and Johnson (1962, Chapter 4) for a more complete presentation of the structure and properties of the model. Only the barest essentials will be derived here.

II

The economy is assumed to be divided into two sectors, one of which is identified as 'manufacturing'. There is a constant return to scale production function for each of the two sectors which, together with given factor supplies determine a transformation or production-possibilities curve showing the combinations of the two outputs that are obtainable at any instant of time. This curve is concave to the origin: with perfectly competitive markets the quantity of each good supplied will be determined by the equality of marginal cost with whatever relative price-ratio the producers confront, with marginal cost determined as the slope of the transformation curve which varies as an increasing function of the level of either output. The intersection of either one of these supply curves with a demand curve for the corresponding type of output, determines the equilibrium price-ratio and quantity demanded and supplied of that good and hence of the other good as well by Walras' Law. The incomes of consumers determining the position of the demand curve are derived from their participation in production, rewards being determined by marginal productivity.

Consider the same economy after the passage of a certain amount of time. Factor supplies are augmented, technology has improved. The production-possibilities curve shifts outward and consequently the supply curves shift to the right, as do the demand curves on account of the higher incomes reflecting the factor augmentation and technical improvement. Suppose we choose the market for manufactures in which to conduct our analysis. Both the supply and the demand curves will shift to the right at each price-ratio and hence at the original equilibrium price-ratio as well. What can we say about the new equilibrium price-ratio? It will rise or fall depending upon whether the increase in demand exceeds or falls short of the increase in supply at the original price-ratio. The extent of the former shift depends upon the increase in income and the income-elasticity of demand for manufactures and that of the latter on the effect, at *constant relative prices*, of the factor augmentation and technological progress on the supply of manufactures. If supply exceeds demand the relative price of manufactures will decline until demand increases and supply decreases just enough to clear the market. International trade can be introduced simply by adding the foreign demand for imports of manufactures to the domestic demand. Export earnings of the home country are spent on imports from the foreign country so equilibrium in the market for manufactured goods is consistent with a zero balance of trade (assuming no net international lending).

It will now be convenient to express these relationships in a more formal, but nevertheless straightforward way. Equilibrium in the market for manufactures (and hence for our entire two-sector economy by Walras' Law) requires that

$$S(p, \alpha) = D(p, y) + I^*(p, y^*) \qquad (1)$$

in which S and D denote the home supply and demand for manufacturers, p the price of manufactures relative to other goods, y and y^* the domestic and foreign incomes, I^* the import of manufactures by the rest of the world and α a shift parameter.

Differentiating equation (1) totally we obtain, with a little manipulation

$$\hat{p} = \frac{h\varepsilon\hat{y} + (1-h)\varepsilon^*\hat{y}^* - X\hat{\alpha}}{[\sigma + h\eta + (1-h)\eta^*]} \qquad (2).$$

in which

$$h \equiv \frac{D}{(D+I^*)} \quad \frac{D}{S}; \quad X \equiv \frac{\alpha}{S}\frac{\partial S}{\partial \hat{\alpha}}$$

A circumflex or 'hat' above a variable denotes its relative rate of change, σ is the price-elasticity of domestic supply of manufactures, η is the price-elasticity of domestic demand for manufactures, η^* is the price-elasticity of foreign demand for imports, ε is the income-elasticity of domestic demand for manufactures, and ε^* the foreign income-elasticity of demand for imports.

Under 'normal' conditions σ, η and η^* will all be positive so that the direction in which the relative price of manufactures changes will depend upon the sign of the numerator. The numerator is made up of three exogenous changes, the first two giving the increase in demand at a constant relative price and the last the increase in supply of manufactures arising from factor growth and technological change, also at constant relative prices. The relative price will therefore rise if there is excess demand or fall if there is excess supply to an extent depending upon the magnitude of the three elasticities in the denominator, the higher these elasticities the smaller the change in relative prices necessary to clear the market.

Inspection of equation (2) indicates that all the variables and parameters entering it are directly measurable, such as h, $\hat{p}$, $\hat{y}$ and $\hat{y}^*$, or capable of being estimated by econometric methods, such as the various elasticities. The one term that immediately appears as a problem is the 'supply shift at constant relative prices' $X\hat{\alpha}$. However we can turn equation (2) around to obtain

$$X\hat{\alpha} = h\varepsilon\hat{y} + (1-h)\varepsilon^*\hat{y}^* - [\sigma + h\eta + (1-h)\eta^*]\hat{p} \qquad (3)$$

in which $X\hat{\alpha}$ can be determined from the measured values of $\hat{y}$, $\hat{y}^*$ and $\hat{p}$ and the coefficients of these variables on the right hand side.

A further and trickier problem that remains would be breaking up $X\hat{\alpha}$ between the influence of factor growth and technological change.

III

We now turn to consider the British economy from 1780 to 1800 in the light of this model. For convenience, the relevant figures from the study by Deane and Cole are presented in the form of Table 11.1, with a page reference to their book for each line of the table. The reader is warned that Deane and Cole regard most of the data that they present for the eighteenth century as being extremely subjective and tentative in nature. They are not of course responsible for the heavy-handed use of their work by a trade theorist whose only training in economic history consisted of a single course with Professor Rostow at MIT in the spring of 1957.

TABLE 11.1. *Figures on the British Economy, 1780 and 1800*

	1780	1800
Population (millions) (Table 3, p. 8)	13.0	15.9
Average real output (1700 = 100) (Table 19, p. 78)	129	160
Total real output (1700 = 100) (Table 19, p. 78)	167	251
Total industry output (1700 = 100) (Table 19, p. 78)	197	387
Export industries output (1700 = 100) (Table 19, p. 78)	246	544
Domestic exports (thousands of pounds sterling) (Table 14, p. 48)	9 246	21 933
Gross barter terms of trade (1700 = 100) (Table 85, p. 321)	106	141
Ratio of wheat to other prices (Table 23, p. 91)	122	170

SOURCE Deane and Cole, *British Economic growth 1688–1959* (Cambridge University Press, 1969).

The 'manufacturing' sector of the model can be identified for present purposes with the 'total industry and commerce' of Dean and Cole's Table 19 (p. 78) which had a weight of 30 per cent in total output in 1800. The price variable p of the model, the price of manufactures relative to that of other goods, is proxied here by two different measures, the Gross Barter Terms of Trade (ratio of index of export volume to import volume) and the price of wheat relative to prices of other goods, both of which should in principle have a strong negative correlation with the relative price of manufactures.

Table 11.1. indicates that population and per capita output both increased by about 23 per cent over the period. With an income-elasticity of demand for manufactures slightly larger than unity this would come to say a 50 per cent expansion of domestic demand for manufactures at constant relative prices. Foreign demand may have grown faster than this in the former American colonies, responsible for about half the market, but probably slower in Europe and the other colonies such as India and the West Indies. With the relative importance of external and internal market expansion a matter of some dispute between historians let us assume that both grew equally fast so that 50 per cent represents the over-all growth of the market. That the 'supply shift' at constant prices exceeded 50 per cent is implied by the decline in the relative price of manufactures by about a third, as measured by the terms of trade, and of about 40 per cent as measured by the price of wheat relative to other prices. Industrial output almost exactly doubled, implying a price-elasticity of total demand of between 1.25 and 1.50 since 50 per cent of this expansion was attributed to growth of population and per capita incomes at home and abroad, the decline in the relative price-ratio accounting for the other half of the total growth in demand. The 'supply shift' at constant prices is 100 per cent if the price-elasticity of supply in zero and $[100 + \sigma\ (33\text{–}40)]$ per cent in general. With the relatively low requirements of physical and human capital in the key cotton industry, a relative abundance of female labour for spinning and initial excess capacity in weaving one would imagine the elasticity of supply to be quite high in this the most dynamic component of the manufacturing sector, though lower elsewhere.

With a supply-elasticity of unity the 'supply shift' at constant prices would be 135 per cent or so, of which about 25 per cent could be attributed simply to the growth of population, assuming no significant changes in per capita endowment of capital and land. This leaves about 110 per cent as the order of magnitude of technical progress, most of it undoubtedly concentrated in the manufacturing sector itself, particularly of course in cotton. In terms of our model this would seem to be the major exogenous factor influencing the pattern of growth, trade and relative prices in the British economy from 1780 to 1800.

This interpretation is in conformity with that of Deane and Cole, who stress the inverse relation between export expansion and the terms of trade during the eighteenth century. On the other hand, as noted earlier, Deane and Habakkuk stress the influence of war-time disruption of navigation in giving Britain an edge due to her naval superiority. If this factor were the dominant one for the 1780–1800 period as a whole, however, we would expect it to be reflected in an improvement, rather than a worsening of the terms of trade. It may well be true that these conditions made the terms of trade more favourable for Britain than they would have been in their absence but this certainly does not mean that war was more important than technological change in accounting for the remarkable growth of British trade during this period. As Crouzet (1964) has emphasised the effect of the Napoleonic Wars was to protect French industry, particularly cotton textiles, which would have been wiped out under free trade conditions. Tariff protection was necessary after 1815.

The Keynesian analysis alluded to earlier in terms of the foreign trade multiplier effect cannot account satisfactorily for the adverse movement of the terms of trade associated with the expansion, and also for the structural change in the composition of output which accompanied it. Another authority much cited by economic historians is Adam Smith, whose name is generally invoked in connection with fuzzy observations on the role of market expansion in promoting specialisation and cost reductions in view of his celebrated dictum that 'the division of labor is limited by the extent of the market'. One way in which this proposition can be interpreted is that there is a falling long-run marginal cost curve, perhaps with a discontinuity at a certain critical level. On this view it is the shift of demand over time that results in expanding exports with deteriorating terms of trade as the economy is driven along the negatively sloped supply curve that remains fixed throughout. This 'increasing returns' model does not seem very applicable to what we know of the relatively small scale of plant and the competitive market structure of the Lancashire cotton industry in this period. It also does not explain why Britain and not France, with a larger home market and a faster growth of foreign trade in the eighteenth century, should have been first in the Industrial Revolution. As Crouzet (1967) points out, it was only the technological breakthrough of the last decades of the eighteenth century that put Britain decisively ahead of France.

IV

The analysis of the trade-growth nexus in the formative period of the Industrial Revolution given here seems to imply that the causal arrow runs from growth (in the form of technological change in the manufacturing sector) to trade rather than in the reverse direction that the literature appears to have emphasised. However, the 'manna from heaven' nature of technical progress as it appears in simple formal models needs to be supplemented with common sense.

To begin with imagine that the doubling of efficiency in the manufacturing sector that we arrived at in the previous section took place in a closed economy. Relative prices would have turned much more sharply against manufactures than the 33–40 per cent that it apparently did, and the actual expansion of manufacturing output would have been smaller to an extent depending upon the price-elasticity of supply. Deane and Cole (1969, p. 42) estimate that up to about one-third of manufacturing was exported so the decline in price would have been of the order of at least another third or worse. Under these circumstances it is difficult to imagine the crucial innovations being diffused as rapidly and pervasively as they were, particularly since the dynamic cotton textile industry was much more export-oriented than any other. In 1781–83 the gross value of cotton industry output was £54 million and exports were 0.9 million, according to Deane and Cole (Table 42, p. 185). By 1801–3 output had risen to 15.0 million while exports rose to 9.3 million, a 'marginal propensity to export' of about seven-eighth's.

The development of the English cotton industry, as Mantoux (1961, p. 203) says 'is a clear example of the influence of commercial on industrial development. The new industry was a child of the East Indian Trade'. The industry in England apparently owed its origin to, of all things, the infamous 'Spanish Fury' of 1576, the sack of Antwerp by the mercenaries of Philip II during the revolt of the Netherlands. As with so many other instances it was the Protestant refugees fleeing from this atrocity who carried out the 'transfer of technology' of cotton spinning and weaving from the continent to England. The industry did not prosper since the Lancashire operative lacked 'the supple fingers and the extraordinary skill of the Indian workmen'. The old established woollen industry, however, succeeded in imposing a prohibition on the import of cotton piece goods from India in 1700 against the strenuous opposition of the East India Company, eventually to be hoist on its own petard as a result of the protection this measure afforded to the fledgling domestic cotton industry, a nice illustration of Hegelian *List der Vernunft*. Colonies and trade were crucial at the raw material end as well, in this case on the other side of the world.

Contemporary development economists could find no better case history of 'import substitution' leading to 'export diversification' than this classic example. Unlike the great pioneers of the carrying trade – Venice and Holland – Britain was able to replace an exotic oriental commodity, in this case the Indian calicoes, with a domestically manufactured commodity. The market and distribution channels for the new manufactures had already been created by the older trading system, which of course benefited mightily from the aggressive colonial policy and naval supremacy established during the eighteenth century. Trade and growth, like trade and the flag, are inextricably intertwined in the first take-off.

REFERENCES

Berrill, K., 'International Trade and the Rate of Economic Growth', *Economic History Review* (December 1960).

Crouzet, F., 'Wars, Blockade and Economic Change in Europe 1792–1815', *Journal of Economic History* (December 1964).

Crouzet, F., 'England and France in the Eighteenth Century: A Comparative Analysis of Two Economic Growths', Chap. 7 of R. M. Hartwell (ed.), *The Causes of the Industrial Revolution* (London: Methuen, 1967).

Deane, P. and Cole, W. A., *British Economic Growth 1688–1959* (Cambridge University Press, 1969).

Deane, P. and Habakkuk, H. J., 'The Take-Off in Britain', in W. W. Rostow (ed.), *The Economics of Take-Off into Sustained Growth* (London: Macmillan, 1963).

Findlay, R. and Grubert, H., 'Factor Intensities, Technological Progress and the Terms of Trade', *Oxford Economic Papers* (February 1959).

Flinn, M. W., *Origins of the Industrial Revolution* (London: Longmans, 1966).

Hartwell, R. M., 'The Causes of the Industrial Revolution: An Essay in Methodoloy', in R. M. Hartwell (ed.), *The Causes of the Industrial Revolution* (London: Methuen, 1967).

Johnson, H. G., *Money, Trade and Economic Growth* (London: Allen and Unwin, 1962).

Kindleberger, C. P., 'Foreign Trade and Economic Growth: Lessons from Britain and France, 1850–1913', *Economic History Review* (December 1961).

Mantoux, P., *The Industrial Revolution in the Eighteenth Century* (London: Jonathan Cape, 1961).

Rostow, W. W., *The Stages of Economic Growth* (Cambridge University Press, 1960).

12 The New Terms of Trade Problem: Economic Rents in International Exchange

C. W. REYNOLDS

The Post-OPEC petroleum economy permits one to apply Professor Rostow's leading and lagging sectors approach to growth at the global level. He saw the process of economic change as one of overlapping patterns of sectoral growth, in which some industries led while others lagged.[1] When leading sectors moved forward in a group, as during the epoch of British textile and steam power development at the beginning of the nineteenth century, their yields permitted new levels of accumulation. Entrepreneurs were then enabled to acquire financial capital and invest in lagging sectors in response to the opportunities provided by induced demand and technological change. The process of progressive alteration of values by market forces and government policy, generating a succession of sectoral surpluses, was seen by Rostow, in the great Schumpeterian tradition, to be essential to sustained economic growth. This paper examines the effect of recent improvements in the energy terms of trade on the pattern of international economic rents. It raises questions about the role of these changes, including the inducement of energy import-competing sectors, for the development of rich, poor, and middle-income countries.

Following the recovery of Europe and Japan after the Second World War, the principal global economic problem was seen by many in the industrial countries to be one of assisting the developing regions to achieve sustained economic growth. The Cold War brought with it a fear that if development of the emerging countries did not occur fast enough, those nations would fall prey to political doctrines which promised both growth and a radical redistribution of wealth. The Soviet Union would take advantage of third world ambitions by offering ideological solidarity, military assistance, and economic aid. Hence the perception from the perspective of the industrial countries was that political links between third world development and their own security were greater than those of economic interdependence.Most western observers saw their own development as economically separable from that of the third world. Trade, foreign investment, and aid would assist the emerging nations to grow in ways that would not adversely affect the already industrialised countries.

It was from the third world, and particularly Latin America, that the most articulate challenges to this separability assumption came. A growing number of self-appointed spokesmen for the developing countries argued that growth of the industrial 'centre' was fundamentally linked to underdevelopment of the 'periphery'. They saw the latter as being inhibited from the realisation of its potential through the draining of resource rents, profits, and manpower to favour a domestic and foreign elite. Technology, tastes, and attitudes were distorted in the process, to prevent the mass of the population from achieving its rightful political and economic destiny. Their focus was as much on questions of value and distribution as on production, with value flows reflecting an unequal structure of power at the expense of social welfare. Economists in the two regions tended to talk past each other, the science of one being the subjectivity of the other.

It was not until the 1970s that aspects of the doctrine of dependence were felt in the industrial centre. Suddenly, after OPEC, the vulnerability of its economies to sharp changes in the petroleum terms of trade became evident. Separability no longer made sense as a viewpoint, when the petroleum lifeline was threatened, and the tastes and behaviour of a few small Moslem states could affect the West in a manner not thought possible since the Crusades. Dependence took on new meaning, once it was perceived to be a two-way procees, and it became appropriate to examine some of the basic issues of development economics, including the relations between value, distribution, structure, and growth, in a new light.

THE NEW TERMS OF TRADE PROBLEM

In the 1950s a major area of debate focused on the so-called Singer-Prebisch doctrine that the underdeveloped raw material and primary product exporting economies faced inevitable secular declines in the terms of trade for their exports.[2] Relatively high elasticities of demand for manufactured goods, set against low elasticities of demand for food and raw materials, meant that if such economies were successful in raising the supply of exports and per capita incomes, both factors would push the terms of trade against them, at least until they diversified production away from traditional commodity exports.[3] In their haste to sponsor new 'import-substituting industries', many of these countries brought about declining internal terms of trade on their own, through policies which taxed traditional exports, subsidised the new industries, distorted the exchange rate, and withheld infrastructure from agriculture and mining. The effect of these policies on the profitability of commodity exports tended to worsen export earnings, though this was offset somewhat by market and policy-induced increases in the national share of value added of raw-material and primary-product exports, particularly in those cases where foreign investors had previously extracted large amounts of economic rent. Hence the 'returned value terms of trade' (the share of unit value of exports retained by nationals of the exporting country, divided by the unit value of imports) tended to move upward even as the net barter terms of trade (unit value of exports divided by unit value of imports) declined.[4]

While there is legitimate room for debate over the long-time trend in terms of trade for raw materials versus manufactured goods, another element in the Singer–Prebisch doctrine was the sensitivity such exports caused in developing countries to fluctuations in the world market, as transmitted through export prices. There is little question of the high degree of instability in international commodity prices or of its adverse consequences on the stability of exporting nations' 'returned value' (domestic share of the value of export earnings) and domestic income. Indeed the historical trend toward increasing domestic shares of resource rent has exacerbated the vulnerability of export economies to world trade cycles, since the residual rent share of value added of their exports is particularly susceptible to price fluctuations. Hence even without its secular component, the Singer–Prebisch doctrine held important elements of truth for economies in which commodity trade, rather than investment, was seen to be the major source of instability.

In an epoch dominated by Keynesian 'full employment' economics, it is not surprising that economic policy makers of the third world were preoccupied with questions of income stability and that this preoccupation led to a bias against traditional rent-generating exports of raw materials and primary products. Unfortunately this tended to cause their policies to work against the most logical source of potential economic surplus, that of resource rents, which could be mobilised to provide savings for further investment and economic diversification. Their answer was to industrialise as rapidly as possible so as to reduce their external dependence. The fact that the new import-substituting industries, with their voracious demand for imported capital and intermediate goods, made these economies more trade-dependent than ever was not accepted as a refutation of the initial premise on which the industrialisation strategy was founded.

In the 1970s the tables were turned. The international dollar price of petroleum exports rose ten-fold, and while not all raw-material and primary-product prices have risen with those of energy exports, there is a perceptible upward trend in both agricultural and industrial raw-material values relative to those of manufactured goods. The developing countries are returning to focus on primary-product exports and import-substituting raw material production, as an important adjunct to their industrialisation policies, and even these are pursued with an eye to exports and competitive pricing. Meanwhile the advanced industrial countries, for the first time in years, are perceiving a 'terms of trade' problem of their own, focusing on energy imports. This has been all the more surprising, since the terms of trade for petroleum had actually been declining before 1973. Rapid expansion in oil production was partly responsible for this decline, but another likely factor was that the major oil companies found it profitable to let the price of oil lag at the well-head, now that exporting countries demanded a greater share of the rents, permitting rents to be shifted downstream to industry-controlled refining, processing, and distribution.

With the advent of OPEC the process was abruptly reversed. The Organisation of Petroleum Exporting Countries has learned from the domestic practices of the United States petroleum industry and even patterned itself somewhat on the model of the Texas Railway Commission. As such it was able to impose the first significant supply restraints on the industry since the heyday of John D. Rockefeller's Standard Oil Trust, but this time at the well-head rather than at the refinery. It can be argued that OPEC merely restored the price to what would have prevailed under more competitive conditions in the industry and more far-sighted conservation policies. If so, one would need evidence of collusion on the demand side before 1973, or of unwise extraction policies given producers' long term interests. Such an argument is made for copper, an industry in which some allege that the world price is depressed by countries with state ownership of the mines which are said to be selling the metal below marginal cost to earn scarce foreign exchange for the payment of previous indebtedness and essential imports. Indeed a declining price before 1973, if perceived to be a trend, might have actually encouraged further extraction, following the rule that it is advisable to mine exhaustible resources if the expected future price rises by less than the rate of interest on international financial assets.

Whatever the reasons for the abrupt OPEC price increase in the 1970s, most observers predict that the petroleum terms of trade will continue to improve in the foreseeable future, as steady increases in world demand are brought to bear against increasing costs of supply even under the most optimistic projections about new reserve finds. Given such a trend, the resource rents accruing to those infra-marginal suppliers who enjoy abundant low-cost reserves are certain to increase as well. So great has been the shift in the level and distribution of petroleum rents already, and so sensitive have the industrial countries and non-petroleum developing countries become to loss of control over their energy lifeline, that this new terms-of-trade problem takes on unprecedented proportions. Oil exports of 26 million barrels a day mean gross sales of over $280 billion dollars a year. This makes oil exports account for 23 per cent of world exports, assuming that they amount to $1.2 trillion or 15 per cent of global GNP ($8 trillion dollars in 1980, including the Socialist countries). If petroleum export rents average one third of gross sales, they add up to ten per cent of total non-petroleum exports, constituting a monumental transfer problem for all trading countries, rich and poor. Indeed it could be argued that the petroleum terms of trade problem for the industrial countries is greater than was the Singer–Prebisch problem for the developing nations.

The new terms of trade problem is aggravated for the industrial countries since their share of resource rents is decreasing. Tax policies, royalties, and outright expropriation are being used by commodity-exporting countries to assure maximum retention of resource rents that in earlier times might well have accrued to foreign investors. Just as the exporting countries' 'returned value terms of trade' improve with every increase in the national share of export unit values, by the same token the industrial centre experiences an increase in the amount of goods and services it must export in exchange for a unit of commodity imports. (Conventional terms of trade measures fail to capture this effect, since they are confined to gross values of commodity trade uncorrected for return flows of profits, interest, and rent.)

THE CHANGING PATTERN OF INTERNATIONAL ECONOMIC RENT

One would expect that the shift in commodity terms of trade against the advanced industrial countries would lead to a rise in resource rents favouring the commodity-exporting countries. By the same token, the international profile of resource wealth, representing the discounted stream of future rents, would also alter in favour of the resource-rich countries, many of which are in the third world. These rents constitute a form of surplus value, in the sense that by definition they are not a return to any man-made factor of production. (It is assumed that returns to the latter fall under the categories of wages, returns to capital, and rents of other factors than land and natural resources.) Hence this form of wealth is particularly suitable for saving and investment. While resource rents may well be the readiest source of accumulation, history reveals that most of such rents have, in fact, been consumed rather than invested. If development gives rise to new resource rents, and if they are not immediately invested in the expansion of productive capacity, under conditions of full employment, then for their effect to be noninflationary other factor incomes must decline by the same amount, whether they be profits, interest, wages, or other forms of rent.

In addition to resource rents (or Ricardian rents) on land and other natural resources, there are two other principal forms of rent. One form represents the return to market imperfections, due to natural or artificial barriers to entry, including both monopoly and monopsony profits. These may be called protection rents. Some, if not all, of the profits of industries established behind protective barriers to trade are in fact protection rents, since they would not be earned under competitive conditions. The share of wages gained through threats or actual restrictions to labour supply also constitute a form of protection rent, including the effect of immigration barriers on wages, since such incomes would not be earned under purely competitive labour-market conditions. Profits resulting from the monopsonistic power of employers over workers, permitting them to depress wages below their marginal product, are also a form of protection rents. Clearly a significant share of factor income in most countries constitutes one or another kind of economic rent. This is as true of the returns to capital in protected industries as it is to the wages of labour in economies subject to immigration barriers.

Economists who challenge such rental incomes often appear to be politically naive, since the beneficiaries of protection rents are likely to use the same power employed to gain them in order to preserve them. We have seen how developing countries pursued policies in the interest of reduced dependency on traditional exports which diverted resource rents into protection rents. As the latter are returns based on restraints on production and trade rather than the dynamic forces of competitive growth, they tend to hamper further development rather than incentivate it. The political forces used to gain the rents operate to prevent competition. A nonpecuniary type of protection rent may also accrue to those who acquire power by their ability to place obstacles in the process of production and exchange. Because protection rents may take the form of power or prestige, governments are common vehicles for their acquisition. It is common for governments to impose costly controls on the economic process even when the protection rents they generate are not received in monetary form (such as bribes) but in terms of the ability of officials to grant or withhold privileges. Hence the attractiveness to potential power brokers of highly-centralised political systems where a large bureaucracy provides ample opportunities to offer patronage and distribute protection rents.

The third and most important type of economic rent, from the viewpoint of development, is the return to entrepreneurship or innovation rent. This is the reward focused on by Schumpeter in *The Theory of Economic Development*,[5] which attracts individuals into the creative process that matches innovations with marketing and finance to raise economies to higher levels of production and society to improved welfare. The source of Schumpeter's insights included a visit to Great Britain shortly after receiving his degree in economics from the University of Vienna at the beginning of this century. He was immediately overwhelmed with the evidence of the creative vitality of British enterprise in that period, especially when viewed against the bureaucratic backdrop of late Imperial Austria, hemmed about as it was with restrictions, regulations, customs, and social convention. He wrote his treatise on development in the form of a series of lectures as a young professor. While the model it presents has never been surpassed in clarity and succinctness, neither Schumpeter in his subsequent career nor anyone else has been able to identify those psychological attributes (which Rostow calls 'propensities') that make an entrepreneur and hence generate innovation rent.

Yet historically that portion of the world's rents most responsible for productivity growth has almost certainly been innovation rents, appearing statistically in the form of returns to capital in excess of the going international rate of interest, capital gains, entrepreneurial salaries, and royalty payments on patents. Often innovation rents are disguised in the capital structure of enterprise, taking the form of assets acquired through excess profits retained by the firm or as the capitalisation of entrepreneurial rents, in cases where the original entrepreneurs sell out all or part of their equity, accepting innovation rents in the form of capital gains. According to the Schumpeterian long view, but making use of the concepts introduced above, if economies which earn resource rents are to develop, they must channel that surplus into innovation rents. This is especially true where resource rents derive from non-renewable resources such as oil, copper, and other minerals. A second-best approach would be to use savings from resource rents to reproduce industries that have profitably innovated elsewhere, paying for the privilege through patents and royalty fees, and earning a normal return on capital. Since competition, according to Schumpeter, will eventually reduce innovation rents to zero, such fees will eventually be unnecessary, though of course the surplus to innovation will also disappear for both the initiator and the borrower. Only as a poor third best approach should resource rents be used to subsidise the earning of protection rents, since the latter place a dead weight cost on the economy at least until the protected enterprises grow up into fully competitive firms capable of their own innovation.

MEASURING INTERNATIONAL ECONOMIC RENTS

In order to examine the effect of recent oil price rises and improvements in mineral terms of trade on the pattern of international rents, the following section makes some extremely rough estimates of the international functional distribution of income by four main classes of countries for 1972 and 1976, years which bracket the first major oil price increases. The country classifications used (low income, mineral exporters, other middle income, and industrial countries) are based on those presented in the World Bank *World Development Report, 1979*. Data on functional income distribution used as a basis for estimating the rent share of income are taken from the United Nations *Yearbook of National Accounts Statistics* for the relevant years. A sample of countries was used for the estimates in each group, which includes 58 to 70 per cent of GNP in that group, with the exception of mineral exporters for which a sample of only 24 per cent was obtainable owing to the limited information on functional income shares for those countries.[6] While the figures are subject to significant margins of error, they are nevertheless suggestive of some important trends which bear on the points raised in the preceding section.

As a first step factor shares for labour and capital (including rents) were obtained for each group of countries based on national factor income distribution figures for the selected years. Factor income of each country is supplemented by 'other income' in the form of depreciation, indirect taxes, and (−) subsidies to total GNP (see Table 12.1). The United Nations figures on 'compensation of employees' and 'operating surplus' of enterprise comprise total factor income, and these categories are summed over all economic sectors for each country to determine labour and capital income (including rents) for that country. Country GNPs and factor shares were aggregated by group using World Bank implicit conversion rates for transforming domestic currency values into current dollars. The factor shares of the combined group GNP were then averaged to obtain the figures in Table 12.1.

TABLE 12.1 *Functional distribution of GNP by group of countries*

	1972			1976		
	Rents and returns to capital	Labour income	Other*	Rents and returns to capital	Labour income	Other*
Low-income countries	.158	.690	.162	.152	.686	.172
Mineral exporters	.528	.367	.105	.667	.286	.047
Other middle-income countries	.436	.409	.155	.410	.435	.155
Industrial countries	.221	.589	.190	.196	.594	.210

Note Low-income countries represent those with per capita GNP of $300 or less. The sample used for this study includes Burma, India and Kenya, totalling 65 per cent of GNP in the group according to the World Bank, *World Development Report, 1979*. Mineral exporters in the sample include Gabon, Jamaica, Saudi Arabia and Venezuela, totalling 24 per cent of group GNP; other middle income countries sampled included Brazil, Egypt, Korea, Mexico, Spain and Thailand, totalling 58 per cent of group GNP; industrial countries in the sample are Germany, Japan, United Kingdom and the United States, representing 70 per cent of that group's GNP.

* *Other* includes depreciation, indirect taxes, and (–) subsidies. 1975 percentages are used for India.

Table 12.1 shows that the labour share of GNP is large and growing in both very low and very high-income countries, low but rising still faster for other middle-income countries, and low and falling for mineral exporters. In low-income countries, the smallness and possible misallocation of the capital stock due to the limited development of capital markets help to explain the high labour share, together with the fact that the proximity of per capita income of such economies to a subsistence floor leaves little scope for profits and rents. In the high-income industrial countries a low observed rate of return on capital (negative in real terms), political development and strong union bargaining power help to account for the high and rising share of labour. The capital and rent shares are falling, notwithstanding the fact that some of the largest corporations in the industrial countries have participated substantially in energy resource rents, although the rate of profits on sales is much higher for the middle-income countries than for the largest industrial countries.

In middle-income countries where labour is still unable to bargain for major increases in their share of profits and resource rents, the latter show a much higher share of GNP, although that share fell significantly between 1972 and 1976. Whatever the adverse effect of energy terms of trade shifts during the 1970s on middle-income and industrial countries, it has not been sufficient to offset rising wage shares. This indicates that the 'surplus' from profits and rents available for investment in new industries, including those substituting for energy imports and growth, has fallen as a share of GNP for those very economies whose dependence on energy imports has increased. This would suggest that a trade-off has occurred between energy-related resource rents and other forms of economic rent in the world economy, something which is supported by the rent estimates in Table 12.4.

The next step in determining the share of economic rents in GNP is to calculate a hypothetical normal return on capital for each group of countries and deduct this figure from the combined rent and returns to capital ('operating surplus') share of GNP presented in Table 12.1. Normal profits are estimated on the assumption that a normal flow of profits would flow to capital in each country under conditions of pure competition, and that an excess over that amount reflects a share of economic rent to the owners of enterprise. The capital stock base used for these calculations derives from the application of assumed capital-output ratios to GNP of each country group as presented in Table 12.2. The capital-output ratios are built up from physical capital stock estimates by country averaged for the group. In cases where capital stock figures were unavailable, they were estimated at twenty times the annual depreciation allowances in GNP which assumes an average asset life of 20 years and straight-line depreciation. In all groups the capital-output ratios showed a slight increase, indicating progressive capital deepening during the period 1972 to 1976. The industrial countries, as might be expected, showed capital-output ratios three times as

TABLE 12.2 *Average capital-output ratios by group of countries for 1972, 1976*

	1972	1976
Low-income countries	1.0	1.1
Mineral exporters	1.9	2.1
Other middle-income countries	1.6	1.8
Industrial countries	3.0	3.1

Note The ratios above are an average of physical capital stock divided by GNP for the same year for all countries in the group sample. (See Table 12.1.) Data were based on the UN *Yearbook of National Account Statistics* plus the author's estimates and are extremely crude.

high as the low-income countries, while mineral exporters had relatively high capital requirements.

To arrive at normal profit income flows for each income group, the capital-output ratio based on the figures in Table 12.2. was multiplied by a hypothetical 'normal rate of return' on capital for the group, as presented in Table 12.3. This resulting competitive rate of return on capital in the form of normal profits plus non-compensated depreciation was deducted from the profit and rent share based on Table 12.1. The remaining figure, representing economic rent in the capital share of GNP, is the weakest of all the estimates, being a residual of an already-crude estimate of normal profits. Nevertheless the results in Table 12.4. are very suggestive, justifying the roughness of the procedure used as a tentative first step in the calculation of all-important rental income flows, since these are assumed to be essential to the analysis of the relationship between changing international values, distribution, and growth.

TABLE 12.3 *Hypothetical normal rates of return on capital by group of countries in 1972 and 1976 (in percentages)*

Low-income countries	10
Mineral exporters	15
Other middle-income countries	15
Industrial countries	6

Note These rates of return include an estimated return to noncompensated depreciation. While they are based on reasonable assumptions, the reader is welcome to use alternative estimates as a basis for calculating the economic rent residual in Table 12.4.

The normal rate of return assumption needs some justification. The returns hypothesised in Table 12.3. include discounts for political and economic risk, both at the enterprise level and for the economy as a whole. For this reason a higher return is posited for the low-income countries than for the industrial countries, despite their lack of evident high yields on physical capital. The middle-income countries have the highest posited normal return, owing to the combination of high productivity of assets, imperfect capital markets, and significant degree of risk. Normal profits, following Schumpeterian analysis, are assumed to be the rate of return on capital essential to elicit the replacement of existing assets in equilibrium. This follows from the assumption that net growth requires a return on capital above the normal rate of interest in the form of economic rents. The existence of well-developed capital markets with freely-traded international financial assets permits us to assume that for the industrial countries the normal return is lowest, with additional assumption that life-cyle and other non-interest determinants of savings may operate with some degree of independence from the domestic productivity of investment, equilibrium being established through international financial flows. While the rate of return on capital posited for the industrial countries might appear to be low in Table 12.3., a glance ahead to Table 12.4. reveals that any higher return than six per cent would lead to negative rents to capital for the industrial countries, especially in 1976.[7]

Finally in Table 12.4. estimates are made of the rent residual for each country group. While the results are extremely tentative, owing to a process of averaging which glosses over wide disparities among industries and countries, because of incomplete reporting of profits, and due to the speculative nature of the concept of normal returns on which the rent residual is based, the results are nevertheless revealing. They indicate that the rental share of GNP is highly uneven among groups of countries, with mineral exporters well ahead, followed by other middle-income countries, in which protection rents play an important role. Low-income countries are surprisingly ahead of the industrial countries, where according to Schumpeter innovation rents once led to growth.

TABLE 12.4 *The economic rent share of GNP by country group (in percentages)*

Group of Countries	1972	1976
Low-income countries	5.8	4.2
Mineral exporters	24.3	35.2
Other middle-income countries	19.6	14.0
Industrial countries	4.1	1.0

Note The economic rent share (not including rent in the wage bill) is a residual obtained by deducting our estimate of the 'normal' return to capital from the capital and rent share in Table 12.1. The normal return to capital was estimated by multiplying the group capital-output ratios in Table 12.2 by the assumed rates of return in Table 12.3. Since the rent residual varies inversely with the estimates in Tables 12.2. and 12.3. it is sensitive to those estimates and should be used with caveats.

The rent shares appear to have fallen in all country groups between 1972 and 1976, except for the mineral exporters where the share rose by 11 percentage points. While the latter group's shares are based on only a 24 per cent sample, by GNP, they confirm the suspicion that mineral rents, led by petroleum and other hydrocarbons, have grown disproportionately. In addition Table 12.4. indicates that mineral rents may well have risen at the expense of other forms of economic rent, including innovation rents in non-energy sectors. The fall in rent shares is steepest for other middle-income countries, yet so rapid was their growth during the period covered that absolute rents actually rose while falling for the industrial countries and low-income countries. It should be stressed that the shares above do not include rent in the wage bill. The industrial countries are particularly subject to wage rents through higher levels of education and skill-training, unionisation, and protection against the migration of low-cost foreign labour. Rental incomes affect all income groups of wage earners in the industrial countries, whereas they are most likely to appear in the upper portions of the wage strata in low and middle-income countries where those with scarce education and access to jobs constitute a 'labor elite'.

Since the estimates in Table 12.4. omit rent in the wage bill they understate total rental income (or surplus) which economies receive, especially for the middle-income and industrial countries. The capital-rich countries are politically vulnerable to competition from low-wage labour, either through trade or migration, which will tend to reduce the rental share in the wage bill. This could happen even when the wage share is rising, as in the industrial countries between 1972 and 1976, if the effect of a declining rent share is offset by increased employment. For example in the United States while real wages for lower skilled workers declined during the period, higher participation by women and young people in the work force caused household wage income to rise in real terms. This could account for a rising wage share in GNP despite the lagging performance of real wages. At the top end of the salary spectrum, management salaries have risen much more rapidly than GNP.

Based on our sample, the total increase in rents of mineral exporting countries was $98 billion dollars, while the total rents of industrial countries declined by $56 billion. Rents in the rapidly growing other middle-income group rose by an estimated $31 billion (offsetting the fall in relative rent shares of GNP) and rents of the low income countries remained virtually unchanged. The total net growth in world rents by these calculations was $73 billion dollars. This increase amounted to 40 per cent in nominal dollars and six per cent in constant dollars. Total rent flows of the non-Socialist countries amounted to about $182 billion dollars in 1972 and $255 billion in 1976. Increases in the petroleum terms of trade in the early 1970s were associated with a major shift in economic rents from the industrial to the middle-income countries and not only to the mineral exporters.

Resource rents lend themselves to financial intermediation, especially where the return to non-renewable resources (such as oil) calls for investments in new rent-generating activities, in order to insure sustained income flows even after the reserves are depleted. Even before the appearance of OPEC the establishment of an international Eurodollar market allowed the world banking community vastly to expand its intermediation among all groups of countries, rich and poor. In the 1960s, for the first time since the bond market boom of the 1920s, international financial intermediation began to operate on a global scale. Ready finance at reasonable rates of interest stimulated trade, permitting middle-income countries with significant growth potential and capital scarcity to overcome long-standing balance of payments constraints to import producers' goods, technology, and intermediate products. After the OPEC-induced 1973 oil price increase, and given the limited absorptive capacity of the oil-exporting nations, additional resource rents became available for intermediation by the international banking institutions providing substantial opportunities for profits on the provision of financial services. Hence if petroleum was a leading sector of the 1970s, banking followed soon after, permitting resources to flow to those regions of the world offering the best combinations of risk and return on capital.

It is quite likely that the rapid expansion of middle-income country borrowing in the 1970s permitted their economic rents to expand rapidly, even as their share of rents in GNP declined, through rapid growth. The pattern was different for the industrial countries. While their capital markets were more attractive to OPEC-surplus countries, they failed to use the increased transfers for growth. One may ask to what extent the financial system played a Schumpeterian role in transferring resource rents into activities which generated innovation rents. While this may have occurred in the middle-income countries it was by no means the case in the industrial countries where unusually low and declining rent shares indicate just the opposite, as does the decline in the rental income received between 1972 and 1976.

Instead rising petroleum rents seemed to have reduced innovation rents for the rich countries, forcing them to pursue policies of income maintenance, in which labour was channeled toward lower productivity occupations and government transfer payments rose as a share of GNP. Foreign borrowing by the United States was used to sustain the importation of consumer goods and fuel, while the rate of investment fell. In Germany, Switzerland, and Japan specie and foreign exchange were accumulated, while employment and growth lagged. If resource rents are to be used to generate additional innovation rents, which are essential to world development, the evidence suggests that two simultaneous strategies should be followed. The first is to increase the role of financial intermediation in the direction of the innovation-prone countries, regions, and economic activities. The second is to reduce the barriers to innovation rents in all groups of countries, and most clearly in the industrial countries. Otherwise the steady increase in resource rents (over $100 billion a year in petroleum rents alone, during the 1980s) will lead to a swamping of international liquidity, inflation, and stagnation for both industrial and developing countries.

PETROLEUM AND PROFITS AMONG THE WORLD'S LARGEST CORPORATIONS

An industry becomes a leading sector through a relatively rapid expansion in sales with a disproportionately large increase in profits. By both measures the international petroleum industry is the leading sector of today's global economy, reflecting the upward trend in petroleum terms of trade during the 1970s. A recent survey by *Business Week* magazine of 1200 United States and 770 corporations from 55 other countries, indicated that total net profits of petroleum related enterprises and other fuel related natural resource industries in the United States in 1979 amounted to $43 billion dollars, or one fourth of the profits of all major international enterprises surveyed.[8] Petroleum company sales totalled $663 billion dollars, or 17 per cent of total world sales of $3905 billion, while petroleum profits were 24 per cent of the total among companies surveyed. Hence, petroleum returned 6.5 per cent earnings on sales while the return of the world's largest non-petroleum companies was 4.2 per cent. Net profits in the petroleum industry tend to understate total earnings since they do not include allowance for depletion and other write-offs. On the other hand the rent share must be calculated after taking into consideration the high capital costs and significant element of risk in petroleum exploration and development.

In terms of corporate rankings, 1970s oil price increases, translated into profits and sales, caused petroleum firms to move into the top ranks of world corporate enterprise. In 1979 the world leader in earnings was the Royal Dutch/Shell Group, with net profits of $6.8 billion dollars on sales of $62 billion, giving a return on sales of 10.9 per cent. EXXON led the world in sales with $84.3 billion dollars, and among United States corporations it was second in profits in 1979 only to American Telephone and Telegraph ($4.3 and $5.6 billion respectively), earning a 5.1 per cent return on sales. Among the top 25 corporate giants in the United States in 1979, 13 were petroleum companies in terms of profits and 9 in terms of sales. Among the 20 non-United States giants, in terms of sales, seven were petroleum companies, including the top two. This actually understates the true situation, since no non-European state petroleum enterprises were included in the sample except Petroleos de Venezuela which earned $2.9 billion profits on $14.1 billion sales or a return of 20.6 per cent and the Mexican PEMEX corporation which did not report its profits on 1979 sales of $4.4 billion. The National Iranian Oil Company, which held the world's record for profits in 1977 with $19.4 billion earnings on $22.4 billion in sales (a return of 87 per cent on sales!) has not reported since that year, and its sales and profit picture must remain conjectural.

The 20 per cent growth in profits of the largest United States companies during 1979 is misleading. The performance was extremely mixed, in direct relation to the importance of petroleum in the supply or demand for the firms involved. For example, the OPEC-related oil price increases in 1979 produced record profits not only for the top petroleum corporations but also for non-ferrous metals and mining, railroads and containers, and foreign manufacturers of fuel-efficient automobiles. Declining profits or losses were posted for fuel-intensive trucking (earnings down 11 per cent), automobile production (down 26 per cent), airlines (down 59 per cent) and steel (39 per cent). In the fourth quarter of 1979, net losses were posted for both airlines and steel, and Chrysler corporation showed an historical record loss of $1 billion for the whole year. In short the positions of individual firms support the aggregate findings of the earlier section, that increased resource rents to petroleum and related industries displaced the profits (including rents) of other major industries in the industrial countries. Meanwhile the opportunities for increased financial intermediation which resource rents provide have helped banking profits to grow disproportionately; the top 25 United States banks increased their operating profits by 22 per cent in 1979 and averaged a 15 per cent return on equity and 0.66 per cent on assets. As seen below this increased intermediation has not led to higher rates of investment and innovation in the industrial countries, though there is some evidence that it may well have assisted in the rapid growth of non-OPEC middle-income countries.

CONCLUSIONS

The recent rise in petroleum prices, accompanied by the actual or potential increase in prices of food and other basic commodities, relative to manufactures, poses a new terms of trade problem. Professor Rostow has compared this watershed in international values to those in previous periods, and takes the relatively optimistic view that greater attention to 'supply side' economic policies, and a higher rate of investment in import-substituting energy resource industries and energy-conserving innovations, will permit the industrial countries to follow the natural forces of the latest 'long cycle' of growth into a new upswing. The present recession, associated with positive rents in energy-supplying and negative rents in energy-using sectors, simply needs some stimuli from tax incentives and subsidies for recovery and sustained growth. However our estimates of the trends in the distribution of international rents call into question any optimism that might arise from a partial structuralism that does not take fully into consideration recent transformations in the global economy. The surplus available for productive investment in the industrial countries is rapidly diminishing. Innovations will be needed simply to provide substitutes for mineral imports and are unlikely to spur additional productivity growth. Instead we face the spectre of protection rents, rather than innovation rents, as the industrial countries seek to reduce their international vulnerability.

Meanwhile the world rent pattern is shifting toward middle-income countries, where abundant labour and natural resources are available for combination with technology, much of which was developed in the industrial countries but is being brought into production in the developing world. The financial resources made available by the petroleum price rise and associated rents have facilitated this internationalisation of the production process, with its potential for factor price equalisation. However, an increase in the wages of workers in the middle and low-income countries is likely to occur at the same time that the rent component of real wages of competing workers in the industrial countries declines. This may be offset for a time, through increased labour participation rates, but eventually an 'iron law of factor price equalization' is likely to operate, whereby improvement in the level and share of wages of the poorer countries is associated with a declining level and share of wages in the industrial countries. Rent in the wage bill of the latter will fall, as resource and innovation rents in the developing countries increase.

It is perhaps ironic that Ricardian growth in resource rents, led by petroleum, may lead to improved economic equality among the world's workers and to a parallel decline in the returns to international capital. However, it is also possible that the surplus from resource rents will not be adequately recycled toward innovative enterprises but to asset transfers, protection rents, and consumption subsidies. If so, then the historical process of development on which the work of Schumpeter and Rostow is based will be choked off. Attempts may even be made, perhaps through military means, to reverse the resource terms of trade despite the forces of supply and demand, and to ration scarce commodities for the benefit of the most powerful industrial countries. Suppliers of raw materials, on the other hand, may wish to avoid the risks to recycled investments in distant lands, attempting to maximise the liquidity of their portfolio and restrict their exports. The pattern of the 1970s was not ideal in this regard, despite the impressive performance of middle-income countries. It will take a major political as well as economic awakening on the part of all countries to accept the challenge of increased interdependence of the 1980s. The industrial countries must accept that the process of innovation, entrepreneurship, and finance are leading to irreversible changes in world economic structure, in response to an unprecedented shift in international values.

NOTES

I acknowledge with gratitude the research assistance of Robert McCleery and the comments of William O. Jones.

1. The concept of leading and lagging sectors which appears throughout Professor Rostow's writings on development is stated most succinctly in 'Trends in the Allocation of Resources in Secular Growth', in Leon H. Dupriez (ed.), *Economic Progress*, Papers and Proceedings of a Round Table held by the International Economic Association, Louvain, 1955, pp. 367–82.
2. The classical articles beginning this controversy were Raul Prebisch, 'The Economic Development of Latin America and Its Principal Problems', *Economic Bulletin for Latin America*, vol. VII, (Feb 1962) no. 1, pp. 1–22 (the article first appeared in May, 1950); H. W. Singer, 'The Distribution of Gains between Investing and Borrowing Countries', *American Economic Review*, (May 1950) (paper presented at the annual meeting of the American Economic Association, 1949). A useful discussion of the controversy at the time appeared in C. P. Kindleberger, *Economic Development* (New York: McGraw-Hill, 1958) pp. 246–9. Both writers have subsequently substantially modified their views. An example is H. W. Singer, 'The Distribution of Gains from Trade and Investment – Revisited', *Journal of Development Studies* (October 1975).
3. This is in contrast to the viewpoint put forward by Lord Keynes in 1912 concerning the deterioration of Britain's terms of trade *vis-à-vis* primary product exporters:

   > The deterioration – from the point of view of this country . . . is due, of course, to the operation of the law of diminishing returns for raw products which, after a temporary lull, has been setting in sharply in quite recent years. There is now again a steady tendency for a given unit of manufactured product to purchase year by year a diminishing quantity of raw product. The comparative advantage is moving sharply against the industrial countries.

   J. M. Keynes, *Economic Journal*, 22 (1912); 630, as quoted in Lloyd G. Reynolds, *Image and Reality in Economic Development*, (New Haven: Yale University Press, 1977) p. 174. Professor Rostow has also referred to the importance of 'long cycles' in terms of trade in *The World Economy. History and Prospect*, (Austin: University of Texas Press, 1978) with the 1970s as a new turning point.
4. The concept 'returned value' and 'returned value terms of trade' appears in C. W. Reynolds, 'Development Problems of an Export Economy: the Case of Chile and Copper', in Mamalakis and Reynolds (eds), *Essays on the Chilean Economy* (Homewood, Illinois: Irwin, 1965) pp. 273–287; and in C. W. Reynolds, 'Domestic Consequences of Export Instability', *American Economic Review* (May 1963) pp. 93–102.
5. Joseph A. Schumpeter, *The Theory of Economic Development*, transl. by Redvers Opie (Cambridge: Harvard University Press 1955) (first published in German, 1911).
6. The mineral exporting countries as defined by the World Bank in its *1979 World Development Report* include: Algeria, Bolivia, Chile, Ecuador, Indonesia, Iran,

Iraq, Jamaica, Kuwait, Liberia, Libya, Mauritania, Nigeria, Peru, Saudi Arabia, Sierra Leone, Syria, Togo, Trinidad–Tobago, Venezuela, Zaire, and Zambia. Those with populations under one million include Bahrain, Botswana, Gabon, Guyana, Oman, Qatar, and the United Arab Emirates.

7. Simon Kuznets shows a zero return on 'entrepreneurial equity' for the United States in the period 1954–60, falling from 2 per cent for the period 1899 through 1928. This is calculated as a share of total income from assets which was 19 per cent of national income for the US in the same period 1954–60. Simon Kuznets, *Modern Economic Growth*, (New Haven: Yale University Press, 1966) p. 169.
8. 'Oil Profits Lead the Pack Again', *Business Week* (21 July 1980) pp. 118–150; 'How 1200 Companies Performed in 1979', ibid. (17 March 1980) pp. 81–119; 'How the Top 200 Banks Performed in 1979', ibid. (21 April 1980) pp. 105–118.

REFERENCES

Business Week, 1980, selected issues.

International Bank for Reconstruction and Development (World Bank), *World Bank Atlas, 1974; 1978*, Washington DC.

Kindleberger, C. P. *Economic Development*, (New York: McGraw-Hill, 1958).

Kuznets, Simon, *Modern Economic Growth*, (New Haven: Yale University Press, 1966).

Mamalakis, Markos and C. W. Reynolds (eds), *Essays on the Chilean Economy* (Homewood, Illinois: Irwin, 1965).

Prebisch, Raul, 'The Economic Development of Latin America and Its Principal Problems', *Economic Bulletin for Latin America*, vol. VII (Feb 1962) no. 1.

Reynolds, C. W. 'Domestic Consequences of Export Instability', *American Economic Review* (May 1963) pp. 93–102.

Reynolds, Lloyd G., *Image and Reality in Economic Development*, (New Haven: Yale University Press 1977).

Rostow, W. W., *The World Economy. History and Prospect* (Austin: University of Texas Press, 1978).

Rostow, W. W., 'Trends in the Allocation of Resources in Secular Growth', in Leon H. Dupriez (ed.), *Economic Progress*, (Louvain: International Economic Association, 1955).

Schumpeter, Joseph A., *The Theory of Economic Development* (Cambridge: Harvard University Press, 1955).

Singer, H. W., 'The Distribution of Gains between Investing and Borrowing Countries', *American Economic Review* (May 1950).

Singer, H. W., 'The Distribution of Gains from Trade and Investment – Revisited', *Journal of Development Studies* (Oct 1975).

United Nations Statistical Office, *Statistical Yearbook* (New York, 1977).

United Nations Statistical Office, *Yearbook of National Accounts Statistics*, vol. I, (New York, 1979).

World Bank, *World Development Report, 1979*, (Washington DC: Oxford University Press, 1979).

13 The Economics of the Frontier

GUIDO DI TELLA*

This work analyses some peculiarities of the economic expansion of the frontier and of the process of growth based on it. First, rather succinctly, it examines some of the main frontier expansions, so as to understand the nature of the historical processes which have given rise to our kind of questions. It then proceeds to the analysis of two different concepts of the frontier.

The first, the more neo-classical, considers the frontier as being in a state of equilibrium –even if moving. The other, much less neo-classical, takes the frontier to be in a state of disequilibrium, which is more relevant for the interpretation of the expansionary processes in question. An analysis is then considered of the theoretical consequences of the two different conceptions of frontier expansion on the possible growth path.

Not only are there reasons why the disequilibrium type of expansion may be more dynamic but there are also reasons why a certain faltering of the rate of growth, at the close of the frontier, may be the most likely outcome. Finally, we shall attempt a broader view of the process of growth where the frontier case can be identified as a special instance of growth based on non-normal profits.

SOME FRONTIER MOVEMENTS

The western world has seen several great expansionary waves. Even though the earlier examples are only remotely suggestive of what we

* Some of the arguments used in this paper are an extension of those presented by the author, some time ago (di Tella and Zymelman, 1960, 1967). The present

have to say later on, an overview of some of them may still throw light on our problem. The expansion of Europe from the tenth to the thirteenth century is a case in point, most clearly visible in the German eastward movement – the *Drang nacht Osten* – and in the Spanish expulsion of the Moors – the *Reconquista* – which lasted somewhat longer.

At the beginning of this process, and in relation to population, land was plentiful and easily available. A frontier movement took place, based on the existence of virgin land. Europe transformed itself from 'a vast wilderness into a well colonized region' (North and Thomas, 1973). But 'until the middle of the thirteenth century land was amply available and as development took place the frontier continually expanded' (Cipolla, 1976). While in previous centuries large tracts of land had been left unoccupied, at the end of the expansion land was virtually entirely incorporated into the economy. While land was available, development took place, but when it was fully absorbed, the process came to a halt (although strongly influenced by independent events like the great plague of the fourteenth century). In the Spanish case, the expansion of the frontier was to a great extent the consequence of demographic pressure in the north from the tenth century onwards, and the search for new, more fertile land, a set of factors which explains to a considerable degree some of the dynamism of the *Reconquista*. Except for an initial stage during the crossing of the so-called 'Duero desert', the new lands were not empty but their populations were partially evacuated, either at the time of the conquest or just after (Vicens Vives, 1957–9). The expulsion of Jews and Moors was not generally intended to achieve religious homogeneity.

The eastward expansion of Europe, which had come to a halt in the thirteenth century, was resumed later on by the Russians in Asia, assisted by the new military technology of the fifteenth century. However the European superiority on land was not as large as its superiority on the seas, a consequence of the great improvements in naval technology (cartography, astronomy, and auxiliary sciences) which made possible the Spanish and Portuguese conquest of the New World. This process had much in common with the previous expansion in the Iberian peninsula, i.e. in the allocation of land to the conquering armies, the treatment of the new subjects,

version has greatly benefitted from discussions held with J. Fogarty, E. Gallo, C. P. Kindleberger, D. C. M. Platt, and A. Petrecolla, although the responsibility for the ideas set forth remains with the author.

etc. After an initial stage in which existing gold and silver was pillaged and the native population decimated, a second and more permanent stage opened up where the incorporation of land, whether agricultural or mineral, became of central interest and where population was looked on as a source of manpower, through different systems of indentured labour – *encomiendas, mitas*. In this second stage new land and new labour were considered the basis for the creation of rents, profits and wealth. While in the Spanish *Reconquista* the demographic push was as important as the pull exercised by the possibility of appropriating new resources lying beyond the frontier, in the conquest of the New World the pull of new resources was more important (Elliot, 1963).

These frontier expansions are interesting in themselves but the expansion which has bearing on our story is that which took place in the late eighteenth and the nineteenth centuries, for the group of countries described as areas of 'recent settlement' (Nurkse, 1959).

This expansion, over the American West, Canada, Australia, New Zealand, Argentina, the South of Brazil and South Africa, was even more impressive than those of previous centuries, and if one adds the expansion of Russia over Siberia, it shaped the Western world of today. Again these processes were characterised by the initial existence of abundant land, mostly unoccupied, and by a substantial migration of capital and people. This dramatic expansion was the consequence of the ascendancy of Great Britain and of new technologies that made it possible. New armaments, coupled with better and cheaper ocean and land transportation, allowed the effective occupation of vast areas which had been known for some centuries but had barely been colonised on some of their borders. While the initial American settlements were clustered near the eastern seaboard, after Independence, in less than a century they reached the western seaboard. As Turner quoted:

> up to and including 1880 the country had a frontier of settlement, but at present the unsettled area has been so broken into by isolated bodies of settlement that there can hardly be said to be a frontier line. (Superintendent of the Census, 1890)

Turner was quite aware that this initial American expansion was a unique and unrepeatable experience. He thought, however, that the expansive character acquired by American society during its frontier days, would ensure that development would go on 'though continually demanding a wider field for its exercise'. The idea was clearly there that a qualitative change was to take place at the close of the frontier, although not necessarily that a lull would follow.

This process was repeated in the other areas of 'recent settlement'. In Canada the westward expansion was to a substantial extent the consequence of the search for these abnormally high profits to be derived from the exploitation of recently discovered natural resources (Innis, 1930).

The expansion proceeded by several expansionary waves, some of them into areas suited to the fur trade, while others – later on – were based on the incorporation of agricultural, timber and mineral land.

At times natural obstacles brought the westward expansion of the frontier to a halt, but it was not uncommon that 'relatively minor links (like bridges and canals) were essential to complete a change and were followed by extraordinarily rapid development' (Innis in Neill, 1968). Either because of the different natural resources involved in the discontinuity in the building of the 'links' to overcome physical obstacles, the westward expansion proceeded by spurts, a concept that lies behind the staple approach developed by Innis and his followers. The countries in the southern hemisphere followed a not entirely dissimilar pattern. In Argentina (di Tella and Zymmelman, 1967) the peculiarity was that the frontier movement was based exclusively on agricultural and pastoral land and ended not at any clear natural boundary but on the more imprecise limits imposed by the arid areas of the west and south and by the woodlands of the north. In the case of Australia, the expansionary waves were the consequence of bringing into the economy agricultural and pastoral areas, inter-mixed with mineral discoveries (Macarty, 1964; Fogarty, 1966).

The nineteenth century territorial expansion had come to an end by the beginning of the twentieth century when most of the better and more fertile known lands were already incorporated into the respective economies. A last territorial burst took place in the early part of the twentieth century, as a consequence of the dry farming techniques, as in the case of Australia, and somewhat later, in the middle of our century when the world witnessed the so called 'opening of the tropics', as new technologies allowed the cultivation of high temperature areas.

This is not to say that development took place only in these areas and at these junctures, but that certain common characteristics set them apart from other expansionary processes, increasingly important, which were based not on the incorporation of natural processes, but on the accumulation of capital and in particular on technological innovation. Our version of the Frontier can be considered to some extent as a model with 'limited supplies of land', akin to W. Arthur Lewis's model of growth with 'limited supplies of labour', but with a factor changed.

THE TWO DIFFERENT KINDS OF FRONTIERS

In order to understand the economies of the frontier movements which we have mentioned, it is helpful to think in terms of two different kinds of economic frontiers, one that fits easily into the neoclassical model, and the other that does not.

In the neoclassical version the frontier is the place where the marginal cost of agricultural goods is equal to its price, i.e. where rent is nil. In the areas which lie short of the frontier, differential rent is possible, the greater the further away from the frontier; expansion is assumed to proceed first into the more productive lands, leaving for later the less productive. This concept of the frontier, as a no-rent locus, is shared by neoclassical economists and by some who are not so neoclassical (Joan Robinson, 1965). If costs are reduced (C_{-1}, C_0, C_1, C_2 and C_{eq} in figure 13.1), or if prices are increased, the frontier expands.

The reduction in costs can be assumed to be a permanent trend in the long term, as technological improvements are bound to take place rather indefinitely, even if some kind of diminishing returns to innovation will eventually appear. But what has to be pointed out is that the level and rate of change of technology and the location and rate of expansion of the frontier are closely interrelated. A rise in prices can also force an expansion of the frontier but this cannot be easily assumed to be a permanent trend. On the contrary, if the developing areas are very significant, their output may depress prices and therefore have a restraining effect on the expansion of the frontier. In this description of the frontier, there is nothing that explains the abrupt nature of the expansions described initially and in particular the idea of a process that has a beginning or an end.

While at certain stages the expansion of the frontier can be of this neoclassical kind, it is claimed that the significant expansions we have mentioned, particularly the latter ones, require a different interpretation i.e. one that assumes a kinked cost curve of agricultural goods, instead of the usual smooth positively sloped curve.

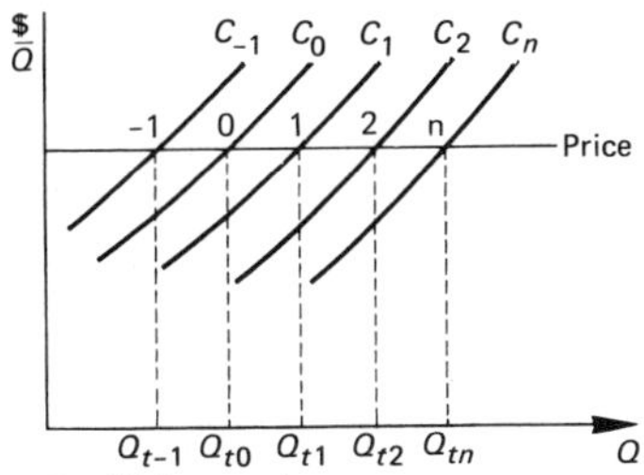

Equilibrium version

FIGURE 13.1

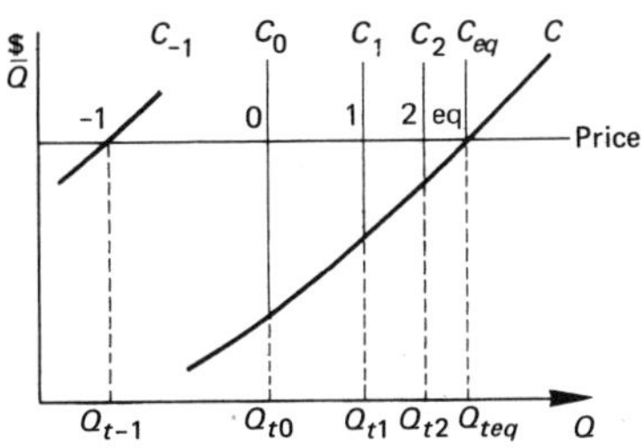

Disequilibrium version (a)

FIGURE 13.2a

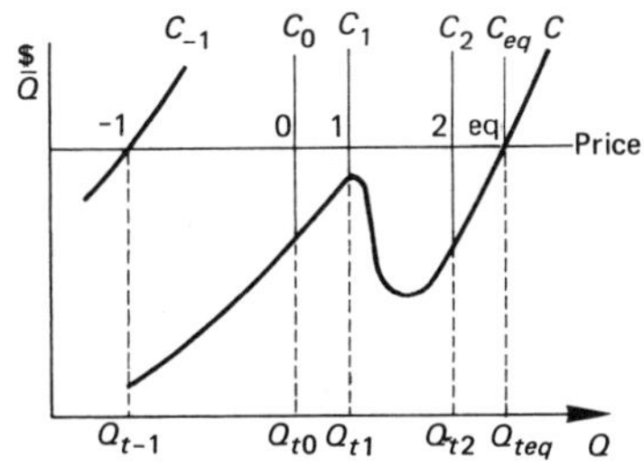

Disequilibrium version (b)

FIGURE 13.2b

If each drop in costs is marginal the expansion takes place instantaneously; only the equilibrium situations (-1, 0, etc.) are of interest. If on the other hand, the initial drop in cost is sharp, (from C_{-1} to C in Figure 13.2a) not only the initial and final equilibrium points (-1 and eq in Figure 13.2a) are of interest but also the intermediate positions depicted by the kinked cost curves (C_0, C_1, etc. in Figure 13.2b), instances of the adjustment process.

The reason for the kink is that although the conditions for the expansion of the frontier exist, there has not been enough time to move resources, people and capital to the ultimate frontier. If time is allowed, the frontier will move on. From the point of view of the known long-term costs and prices the expansion of the frontier should have taken place up to its no-rent limit. The frontier is in a state of disequilibrium, bursting with business opportunities with big profits and economic excitement, evidence of the existence of rent at the frontier. Expansion takes place so as to appropriate the potential rent which exists in the extra-marginal lands. It is a kind of ex-ante rent which requires a known but not yet made effort, so as to convert it into an ex-post rent.

In the real world the expansion of the frontier takes time. It is not that easy to move capital to the frontier, build towns, lay railroads, move people, clean land: the expansion of the frontier is part of the adjustment to the new economic conditions, a moment of intrinsic disequilibrium as indicated by the existence of rent at the frontier. The existence of disequilibrium and its intensity are what lie behind the dynamism of the expansionary process. To say that the process comes to an end is to say that the neoclassical equilibrium situation has finally been reached.

After this it is still quite possible for the frontier to move, but only in a neoclassical way: i.e. through marginal movements, gradually advancing, with none of the drama of the previous stage. As we have seen the initial non neoclassical expansion can take place only if at a certain point in time costs are drastically reduced, creating such a huge economic opportunity that it can not be grabbed instantaneously. The initial discontinuous and sharp drop in costs (or an equally sharp rise in prices) is what sets the whole process going on. We are back to the old idea that '*Natura facit saltum*', at least at certain junctures which are the ones that interest us.

We may wonder which are the actual circumstances which may cause this sharp downward shift in the cost curve. There are few clear cut instances in which such a phenomenon necessarily takes place, while in others it is just a coincidence of several circumstances. The clear cut case is the outright discovery of a new land, agricultural or mineral. One could say that before discovery, costs were infinitely high, dropping thereafter to a point where economic development becomes feasible.

Discovery, in economic terms, implies that producers become aware that unappropriated rent lies fallow, so to speak, waiting to be taken up. If one imagines the new land as being of homogeneous quality, with a sharp and clear cut delimitation, the expansion will be dramatic and the end will be sharp. As soon as the discovery takes place, people and capital will move in. This will be the period of frantic expansion which will continue until the whole of the land is incorporated into the economy. Once achieved, this kind of development comes to an end.

If we allow for differential quality of land – a rather more realistic assumption – the speed of expansion will depend on the amount of rent to be appropriated, and the end will be more or less abrupt, according to the shape of the cost curve. If costs increase gradually as the frontier expands, the tapering off of the expansionary process will be equally gradual. If on the other hand, the cost curve remains more or less constant until the very end, then the expansionary process will end abruptly.

This interpretation assumes that the greater is the rent at the frontier the more intense will be the efforts to expand it, and the quicker will be the pace of expansion. This fact is in line with the diminishing speed of incorporation of new land depicted in Figure 13.2a, or the pace of Figure 13.2b, which varies according to the variation of rent at the frontier as one can imagine situations in which the incorporation of new lands does not proceed according to their decreasing fertility, but according to their proximity. As has been said of the early European case 'paradoxically enough, the expansion . . . was probably characterised by increasing marginal returns . . . (as) some of the areas taken into cultivation were in fact better than those already cultivated' (Cipolla, 1976).

It is not because of profits derived from new investment that capital flows into new lands but because it can in some way get hold of part of the rent. It is in profits-cum-rent that capital is interested, not in profits alone. But the discovery of new lands may not be the more common case. In many instances the so-called new lands had been discovered for a long time but some of the necessary preconditions for their development had not been fulfilled. The most common of these preconditions is the military pacification of the new lands, which very seldom are really empty spaces. Again, one can translate this in terms of costs: considering those of insecure areas as prohibitively high, falling abruptly after pacification and opening the way to development. If the previous population can be enslaved, or through some other legal artifice can be made to work for a wage below its marginal productivity, another source of 'rent' may be created, actually an oligopolistic quasi-rent consequence of the imposition of a non-market price for labour. But even if the previous population was to be paid according to its marginal productivity it would be welcomed, since it avoids the need and the cost of transferring population to the new lands, eliminating one of the most common reasons for the delay in the initial expansion of the frontier. Pure discovery or military pacification are not the only two reasons behind the abrupt fall in costs that starts on frontier expansions.

Technological innovations of a cost-reducing kind are the other significant cause, although they are less prone to provoke sharp downward shifts in the cost curve. Still, in the nineteenth century, the introduction of the steamboat and the railroad revolutionised the cost of transportation, making possible the development of enormous new areas. Although of less universal significance, the development of freezing techniques allowed the export of meat and the expansion of cattle raising in Australia, New Zealand and Argentina.

Even if somewhat lagged, agricultural techniques improved drastically, mostly as a consequence of the application of mechanical power and of specific developments in harvesting and threshing (particularly in wheat, cotton and maize). The process had some parallels with the revolution in high farming that transformed English agriculture in the second half of the nineteenth century. The incorporation of new lands and the development of new technologies interacted. While the effects of innovations and cost reducing technologies on expansion are more clear, it is also true that the inverse phenomenon was in operation, i.e. the effect of the expansion of the frontier and its new needs on the innovative capacity. In the American and Australian cases, the stimulating effect on innovation of the abundance of land has been observed (Habakkuk, 1962; Blainey, 1964b.), a fact which is true for other new countries as well. The extraordinary economic opportunities opened up by the expansion of the frontier and the set of relative prices reflecting the availability of new resources stimulated the development of new technologies. But of the two influences, the effect of technological innovation on expansion was more intense and clear cut than the effect of expansion on innovation.

Up to now we have talked of new agricultural lands, leaving aside other resources such as minerals and oil. Although it is useful to avoid undue generalisations, there is no good reason not to include as part of the same phenomenon the case of mineral land, despite the fact that the social and economic consequences have been quite different. Particularly significant has been the difference between the greater diffusion of the economic benefits of agriculture compared to mining. The latter has given rise to enclave economies more linked to the country or region supplying capital and technology – or purchasing the produce – than to the rest of the domestic economy, a phenomenon which is at times observable in tropical agriculture based on the plantation system; even then, enclave development has been better than no development at all.

But the distinctive characteristic of expansion based on minerals is that the resource is depletable, so that the end of the frontier may mean not only the end of growth but a reduction in the absolute economic level previously attained. This is what has forced a greater awareness of the transitory character of the expansion of the mineral frontier compared with the case of renewable resources.

The difference between agricultural and mineral based development may not be so sharp, as the expansion of the frontier has meant at times the exhaustion of the fertility of the new land, making it somewhat similar to mining. On the other hand, while mineral exploitation clearly depletes resources, there is some kind of built-in technological progress, allowing for a rather continuous process of incorporation of new resources, making it a predictable aspect of mineral exploitation. But while these exceptions may blurr the difference, in certain instances, depletable and non-depletable resources stand as a long-term distinction.

But what is clear is that in the nineteenth century it was a combination of these factors: military pacification and technological innovations – in war, transport, agricultural and mineral extraction – which lay at the root of the sharp reduction in costs and the exceptional expansion of the frontier. The rise in prices up to the 'seventies' accelerated the expansion, while conversely, falling prices during the last decades of the century, hindered it to some extent.

While disequilibrium conditions characterised most of the expansionary processes already mentioned, most of them showed an alternation of non neoclassical, energetic frontier movements, with more tranquil neoclassical equilibrium stages, '*Natura facit saltum*', but not always.

As we have already mentioned, the disequilibrium version of the frontier is very much in line with the so called Turner thesis and with Innis's staple approach, the first emphasising the agricultural frontier, the latter emphasising the existence of several frontiers. Both are not incompatible with Adam Smith's 'vent for surplus' concept, which emphasises the crucial role of putting into economic use formerly idle resources.

As in the case of the staple approach, the interrelation with foreign trade is greatly stressed. The three are different ways of looking at the problem which we have studied here. A disequilibrium version of the frontier has some forerunners of distinction.

THE GROWTH PATH

Although we have already touched on the problem, it is time to analyse the implications of the two different kinds of frontier development on potential growth paths.

In fact the more neoclassical version of the frontier implies in the medium term a rather smooth and continuous rate of growth as a consequence of marginal additions of resources and capital and marginal improvements in the technological level. In this medium term version the idea of a starting point of the growth process, or of an end, is quite alien. In the very long run diminishing returns would eventually be felt, reducing the rate of growth to nothing.

On the other hand, the disequilibrium version of the frontier does have a distinguishable beginning as a consequence of the sharp drop in costs (and /or the rise in prices) followed by an increase in the rate of growth. This high growth stage will not last forever and will begin to taper off as soon as the neoclassical equilibrium frontier is reached. At this juncture, *if no other factors intervene*, the economy will return to a lower neoclassical rate of growth, higher however than the previous one prevailing in the neoclassical stage prior to the expansion, as the increased rent will have certainly become a new source of accumulation and investment. If, on the other hand, while the expansionary wave takes place, the economy can develop a non-resource based sector, it will find it easier to continue with a high rate of growth, even if on a completely different basis.

If it does not develop such a sector and goes back to neoclassical frontier based expansion, the rate of growth will certainly suffer. The likelihood of one thing or the other depends on several factors, derived from the circumstance that during the expansion of the frontier all the extraordinary profits are made in connection with the frontier, and that there will be few unrelated activities which will show profits as high as the profits-cum-rents that can be obtained at the frontier. But the expansion of the frontier does not mean that only those activities which are physically located there are the ones to benefit, as the newly discovered rent may just as well be transferred, through some kind of oligopolistic manipulation of prices, to the country which makes the discovery, quite independently of the normal benefits derived from the demand for their products originating in the new areas. This is also important as territorial expansion creates a demand for goods related to investment at the frontier.

In the case of early developers, like the USA, a good part of this demand was channeled to its own industrial sector in the eastern states as not all the goods required were even available from Great Britain or Europe. In the case of late developers this was not necessarily the case, and one can see the expansion of the frontier increasing the level of industrial activity of the mature countries where local industry was scarcely capable of supplying the necessary goods.

One of the most obvious factors which influence the impact of the frontier on the overall growth process, is the relative economic importance of the expansion compared with the previous size of the economy. The smaller the economic significance of the frontier expansion and the larger the previous size of the economy, the greater will be the likelihood that growth will not suffer at the end of territorial expansion.

At times the frontier expansion was huge in absolute terms, but its economic significance compared with the rest of the economy was not so great. This may have been the case even for the United States compared with the Canadian, Australian and Argentine experiences repeated in the case of the more recent tropical expansions of the 1930s and 1950s.

But the most important factor determining whether an industrial non-resource based sector can maintain the intensity of the growth process after the close of the frontier, is whether the previous expansion was just the consequence of one big single wave, or a series of different waves interrupted at times. In the latter case there will be an alternation of stages when the economy expands as a consequence of the large profits made at the frontier – where new resources are brought into the economy – and periods when the frontier stops moving, and non-resource based growth resumes its leading role, to be lost only when expansion starts again. But the repetition of these waves and stoppages will mean that at the end of the last expansionary wave, industry – the non-resource based activity – will have attained considerable dimensions being able to become its leading sector.

The whole economy will have a momentum not too dissimilar to the previous rate of growth, perhaps fulfilling Turner's hope of uninterrupted growth. In the more successful cases one can see the existence of a multiplicity of expansionary waves. In the Canadian and Australian cases the variety of different staples, some agricultural and some mineral – equally important at times – allowed an apparently smooth process of growth which in fact was the consequence of the superimposition of self extinguishing spurts. In the Argentine case there were no minerals, a basic difference with the Australian case with which it has been compared; quite peculiarly there was only one big expansionary wave with a most distinct beginning, an astonishing rate of growth, and only minor and short lived interruptions until its clear end around the First World War. The boom of the 1920s which Argentines considered a continuation of the pre-war expansion was in fact the consequence of nearly a decade of increasing prices, blurring the fact that it was an altogether different phenomenon and could not be the basis of a permanent trend. At the end of the expansion, the country's non-resource based sector was of only minor importance, so that, even despite the fact it grew at a significant rate, it was not in a position to replace the central role which the expansion of the frontier had had in the past.

Although the growth of the Argentine economy had not been particularly bad after the close of the frontier – 3.5 per cent per year since 1918 – the idea of a long-term economic failure has become deeply ingrained in Argentina, being widely shared elsewhere.

The expansionary phase created extraordinary expectations, blurring the fact that it was based on a process that was bound to come to an end. But as the expansion was believed to be of the neoclassical type, there was no reason to think that growth could not continue unabated. Expectations stemming from a linear extrapolation of the rates of growth of the years of the non neoclassical expansion of the frontier were so strong that even in the face of an acceptable economic performance, the image of failure has become prevalent while in fact most people compare actual events with a most improbable and unrealistic alternative. The oil producing countries which in the twentieth century have replaced the countries of recent settlement as the great resource based growth areas, will also have to face the enormous difficulty of changing from the relatively easier resource based growth, to a different, more difficult, more sophisticated, non-resource based process. It is even more absurd to extrapolate their past performance, as they run the risk not only of reaching a stationary situation but even of reducing their absolute level of income. The recent prosperity originating in the post-1973 price rise can with even less reason be extrapolated.

It is clear that the price of oil is the consequence of a duopolistic struggle, the final price determining not only the economic neoclassical frontier but the extent of the transfer of the rent – and quasi rent – to the more industrial economies, or quite conceivably, from them towards the resource based economies. This depends on whether the post-1973 prices are above the equilibrium competitive price or not. If they are, an oligopolistic quasi rent will accrue to the oil producing countries over and above their competitive rent. But the question of their ultimate growth path depends, as in the past, on what they do in the meantime, with their non-resource based activities, a difficult task as they have to compete with the high profitability (and rent) of their oil activities. To start and develop the non-resource based sector too soon would be unwarranted, but to do so too near the exhaustion of their oil frontier, would be an equally serious mistake.

It would mean a reduction in their rate of growth and eventually of income, as in this case, an end to oil discoveries would mean not only a stop to production increases but an actual reduction of total production.

RENTS, QUASI RENTS, NORMAL PROFITS AND THE PROCESS OF GROWTH

Before concluding I would like to make a short comment on the more general view that emerges from our story. Development seems to be intimately related to the existence of abnormally high profits. The Marshallian competitive 'normal' profits are quite alien to the entrepreneur's mentality which looks at them as uninteresting or as outright disastrous. Most of their efforts are devoted precisely to achieving extra-ordinary profits by whichever means. The opening of new lands is one of them, as it gives rise to the possibility of appropriating the new rent, adding it to the normal profits on capital, attracting people and capital to the frontier. The potential rent can be divided in very different ways. At times, entrepreneurs who are developing the frontier, whether railroad companies or land speculators, get hold of the land and make abnormally high profits from the appreciation of land values (Swierenga, 1966).

In other instances railroads may not wish to own land, being able themselves to take their share of the rent through the oligopolistic manipulation of rates, achieving 'extraordinarily high earnings the result chiefly of skimming the cream of virgin natural resources' (Innis in Neill, 1968).

But this is a situation that may not last. While during the frontier expansion rent from land and profit from capital, being the consequence of the same development, accrue to the same entrepreneur, as the frontier closes the classic difference between owners of rent-yielding assets and profit-making ones reasserts itself. The manipulation of rates tends in due time to be restricted by governments as railroads lose their association with the expanding frontier. Earnings move back to the hated 'normal' Marshallian profits, while the flow of investment towards the now occupied lands diminishes or disappears altogether. Still, at the end of the expansion, the economy is much better off, as the new rent allows a process of accumulation that was not possible before the expansion. The frontier does not expand any more, but financing for a different kind of growth process becomes available. But the development or discovery of new lands is not the only way to obtain extraordinary earnings.

Technological developments can also be seen as an attempt by entrepreneurs of the more mature economies to create oligopolistic situations which – even if transitory – allow more than normal profits by adding to them the quasi-rents brought about by the transitory oligopolistic power of the innovator. The new countries experienced their highest upsurge as a consequence of rents derived from natural resources. To move from land-based, to capital and technology-based growth, is not an easy task and it is one in which many new countries have not succeeded. In such trying circumstances it is tempting to replace technological quasi rents with easier collusive quasi rents, derived from 'scarcity' rights granted to business firms, (protective tariffs or quotas) or more generally through some kind of collusion among business firms, restricting market behaviour. In any case the search for rents and quasi rents – of whatever character – to add to normal profits is one of the basic motivations of entrepreneurs and investors, and is the basis for the process of growth. Normal profits are of little interest, compatible only with periods of modest growth. Rent-cum-profits, or quasi-rent-cum-profits, are what it is all about, at least for entrepreneurs. Discoveries of land, agricultural or mineral, discoveries of technology, and restrictions on free competition, are all aspects of the same process. The peculiar type of frontier movement which we have analysed is but a special case of a rent-based process of growth, a case that unfortunately has a transitory character and one that poses a significant problem when it comes to a close – a problem, the intensity of which will depend on the success of creating a new quasi rent-based stage of development which, if grounded on technological innovation, will allow a more permanent and dynamic growth path. If instead of just one big expansionary wave, as in the case of Argentina, there are several territorial spurts, interrupted by non-resource based growth, as in the case of the USA', the possibility of continuing growth, based on industry and technology is much greater. However, the trouble found by Argentina, after the close of the frontier, may be more characteristic than the relative success of countries like the USA, Canada, and Australia, which continued at an unabated pace even when switching their process of growth from a land-based to a capital-and technology-based process, a most remarkable achievement that has to be acknowledged as such.

One may wonder if the latter are, after all, the more 'abnormal' countries, indeed a fortunate abnormality.

REFERENCES

Baldwin, R., 'Patterns of Development in Newly Settled Regions', *The Manchester School* (May 1956).

Berttram, G., 'Economic Growth in Canadian Industry, 1870–1915: The Staple Model and the Take Off Hypothesis', *Canadian Journal of Economics and Political Science* (May 1963).

Billington, R. A., *Westward Expansion: A History of the American Frontier* (New York: Macmillan, 1974).

Blainey, G., 'A Theory of Mineral Discovery. Australia in the XIX Century', *The Economic History Review* (Aug 1970).

Blainey, G., 'Technology in Australian History', *Business Archives and History*, vol. IV (1964) no. 2.

Bogue M. B., and A. G. Bogue, '"Profits" and the Frontier Land Speculator', *Journal of Economic History* (March 1957).

Caves, R., and R. Holton, *The Canadian Economy: Prospect and Retrospect* (Cambridge: Harvard University Press, 1959).

Caves, R., '"Vent for Surplus" Models of Trade and Growth', in R. Baldwin (ed.), *Essays in Honour of G. Haberler* (Chicago: Rand McNally, 1965).

Cipolla, C. M., *Before the Industrial Revolution. European Society and Economy, 1000–1700* (London. Methuen, 1976).

Cornblit, O., E. Gallo and A. O'Connell, 'La Generación del 80 y su proyecto', *Desarrollo Económico* (Jan 1962).

Cortés Conde, R., 'Algunos rasgos de la expansión territorial en Argentina en la segunda mitad del siglo XIX', *Desarrollo Económico* (April–June 1968).

di Tella, G., and M. Zymmelman, 'Las etapas del desarrollo económico argentino', *Revista venezolana de economía* (Nov 1960) and with the same title the book published by Eudeba, Buenos Aires, 1967.

Elliott, J. H., *Imperial Spain 1469–1716* (London: Arnold, 1963).

Farnie, D. A., 'The Mineral Revolution in South Africa', *South African Journal of Economics* (June 1958).

Fogarty, J. P., 'The Staple Approach and the Role of Government in Australian Economic Development: the Wheat Industry', *Business Archives and History*, vol. VI, (1966) no. 1.

Gallo, E., 'Agrarian Expansion and Industrial Development in Argentina: 1880–1930', in R. Carr (ed.), *Latin American Affairs*, St Antony's Papers (Oxford, 1970).

Geller, L. 'El crecimiento industrial argentino hasta 1914 y la teoría del bien primario exportador', in M. Giménez Zapiola (ed.), *El régimen oligárquico. Materiales para el estudio de la realidad argentina hasta 1930* (Buenos Aires: Amorrortu, 1975).

Habakkuk, H. J., *American and British Technology in the XIX Century* (Cambridge University Press, 1962), Chap. III, pp. 36–43.

Haberler, G., *International Trade and Economic Development* (Cairo National Bank, 1954).

Hennessey, A., *The Frontier in Latin American History* (University of New Mexico, 1978).

Hicks, J., *Growth and Antigrowth*, Oxford Economic Papers (Nov 1966).

Innis, H. A., *The Fur Trade in Canada* (New Haven: Yale University Press, 1930); 'Snarkov Island' and 'A Defense of the Tariff', reprinted in R. Neill, *A New Theory of Value. The Canadian Economics of H. A. Innis* (University of Toronto Press, 1968).

Krueger, A. D., 'The Political Economy of a Rent Seeking Society', *The American Economic Review* (June 1974).

Lewis, W. A., 'Economic Development with Unlimited Supplies of Labour', *The Manchester School* (May 1954).

Mabro, M. *Aspects of Development of Iran* (London: Chatham House, 1976).

McCarty, J. W., 'The Staple Approach in Australia's Economic History', *Business Archives and History*, vol. IV, (1964) no. 1.

Myint, H., 'The Classical Theory of International Trade and the Underdeveloped Countries', *The Economic Journal* (June 1958).

North, D., *The Economic Growth of the United States 1790–1860* (New Jersey: Prentice Hall, 1961).

North, D. and R. P. Thomas, *The Rise of the Western World. A New Economic History* (Cambridge University Press, 1973).

Nurkse, R., *Patterns of Trade and Development* (Stockholm: Almqvist and Wiksell, 1959).

Potter, D. M., 'Abundance and the Turner Thesis', in *People of Plenty* (University of Chicago Press, 1954) pp. 142–169.

Robinson, J., *The Accumulation of Capital* (London: Macmillan, 1965) p. 331.

Schumpeter, J., *The Theory of Economic Development* (Cambridge: Harvard University Press, 1936) Chap. II.

Smith, A., *The Wealth of Nations*, edited by E. Cannan (London: Methuen, 1904) p. 413.

Swierenga, R. P., 'Land Speculator "Profits" Reconsidered: Central Iowa as a Test Case', *Journal of Economic History* (March 1966).

Turner, F. J., *The Frontier in American History* (New York: Holt, 1921).

Vicens Vives, J., *Historia de España y América, social y económica* (Barcelona: Vicens Vives, 1957–9).
Watkins, M., 'A Staple Theory of Economic Growth', *Canadian Journal of Economics and Political Science* (May 1963).
Williams, J., 'The Theory of International Trade Reconsidered', *The Economic Journal* (June 1929).

Index